Our
101
BEST
STORIES

Stories of Appreciation
for Mothers
and Their Wisdom

Jack Canfield
Mark Victor Hansen
Amy Newmark

CSS

Chicken Soup for the Soul Publishing, LLC
Cos Cob, CT

Chicken Soup for the Soul

Contents

❸
~Maternal Insights and Lessons Learned~

❹
~On A Mother's Support~

❽

~The Bond between Mother and Child~

❾

~Letting Go~

~Gratitude~

Chicken Soup for the Soul

A Special Foreword

by Jack & Mark

For us, 101 has always been a magical number. It was the number of stories in the first *Chicken Soup for the Soul* book, and it is the number of stories and poems we have always aimed for in our books. We love the number 101 because it signifies a beginning, not an end. After 100, we start anew with 101.

We hope that when you finish reading one of our books, it is only a beginning for you too—a new outlook on life, a renewed sense of purpose, a strengthened resolve to deal with an issue that has been bothering you. Perhaps you will pick up the phone and share one of the stories with a friend or a loved one. Perhaps you will turn to your keyboard and express yourself by writing a Chicken Soup story of your own, to share with other readers who are just like you.

This volume contains our 101 best stories and poems about mothers and their wisdom. We share this with you at a very special time for us, the fifteenth anniversary of our *Chicken Soup for the Soul* series. When we published our first book in 1993, we never dreamed that we had started what has become a publishing phenomenon, one of the best-selling book series in history.

We did not set out to sell more than one hundred million books, or to publish more than 150 titles. We set out to touch the heart of one person at a time, hoping that person would in turn touch another person, and so on down the line. Fifteen years later, we know that it has worked. Your letters and stories have poured in by the hundreds of thousands, affirming our life's work, and inspiring us to continue to make a difference in your lives.

On our fifteenth anniversary, we have new energy, new resolve, and new dreams. We have recommitted to our goal of 101 stories or poems per book, we have refreshed our cover designs and our interior layout, and we have grown the Chicken Soup for the Soul team, with new friends and partners across the country in New England.

We have selected our 101 best stories and poems on mothers and their wisdom from our rich fifteen year history to share with you in this new volume. The stories that we have chosen were written by mothers and by their children. Some of them made us laugh, some made us cry. They all made us appreciate the special bond between mothers and children, the unerring wisdom about everything from the mundane to the life-changing, and the hard work that goes into being a mother every day.

We hope that you will enjoy reading these stories as much as we enjoyed selecting them for you, and that you will share them with your families and friends. We have identified the 33 *Chicken Soup for the Soul* books in which the stories originally appeared, in case you would like to continue reading about motherhood and families among our other books. We hope you will also enjoy the additional books about families, parenting, and women in "Our 101 Best Stories" series.

With our love, our thanks, and our respect,
~*Jack Canfield and Mark Victor Hansen*

Chapter
1

Moms Know Best

The Power
of a Mother's Love

A Mother's love perceives no impossibilities.
~Paddock

Mom's Favorite Child

Each day of our lives we make deposits in the memory banks of our children.
~Charles R. Swindoll, The Strong Family

For weeks, both our mother and our brother had been near death with cancer. Mom and her dying son were inseparable, whether at home or as patients in the same hospital. None of us siblings resented that she turned to him so much during those final days. On a cold day in November, her four remaining sons carried her to his funeral, certain that they were fulfilling her last wish.

The long night that followed was both a horror and a blessing. My oldest sister, Marie, and I stayed with Mom in our childhood home. No matter what we did, Mom wept with grief and writhed with pain. Her cries mingled with the sounds of the icy rain blown against the windows of the old farmhouse, first in gusts, then in brief intermissions of heavy calm. Finally, around three o'clock in the morning, after telling us repeatedly that she would not see another dawn, she closed her eyes. An eerie silence settled over the house, as if death were very close to us again.

When Marie and I saw that she was not dead but was resting peacefully, we knew we should rest too. But we couldn't sleep and started to talk.

Marie was the second child; I was the ninth and last. The two of us had never even lived in the same house, as she already had her own home when I was born. We looked and acted like members of the same clan, but we had never talked real "soul talk." In the dim light of the room adjoining Mom's, she and I whispered stories about our family.

Seeing my mother near death, I felt like a little girl again. I told Marie how I remembered so often the special solace of Mom's lap. That was my retreat when I sought comfort for aching ears, or refuge from warring siblings, or just the closeness of her hug. To me she was always wonderfully soft and warm.

Marie knew the feeling. The shadows danced on the wall, a background to our animated whispers about childhood—the family struggles, the strict discipline and hard work, the inevitable fights with our siblings.

Then she made a shocking statement.

"It wasn't really so hard for me, though, because I was always Mom's favorite."

I was astounded that she said the word out loud! Mom didn't have favorites! Yet as I let myself think about it, I had to reply, "I can't believe you said that ... I guess I always thought I was her favorite."

Marie and I both chuckled, each believing that the other had certainly placed second. Then the truth began to unfold, as we continued to swap stories about the calm and loving woman asleep in the next room.

"I have an idea," I told her. "When the boys get here in the morning, let's ask them who was her favorite."

Two of our brothers awakened us at dawn, anxious to see if Mom had made it through the night. She had, and was still dozing. Over coffee at the big family table, I asked them the unspeakable question.

"Marie and I were talking last night, and couldn't agree on something, so we thought we'd ask you. Who do you think was Mom's favorite child?"

Coffee mugs stalled in midair. The two men's eyebrows arched, and their mouths fell open. They squirmed in their chairs and looked out the window as intently as if counting the raindrops. Marie and I waited.

Finally, one brother spoke. "Well, you know Mom never played favorites ...." Then, making uneasy eye contact again, he said, "But if I were honest about it, I guess I'd have to say I always thought I was her favorite."

The second brother, grinning with relief that he didn't have to say it out loud first, confessed that he thought he was her favorite.

For the first time in months, we all laughed, as only childhood friends can laugh when finding a hidden treasure and sharing the secret.

How did she manage to make each of us feel like the favored child? She never told us we were. She showered none of us with gifts or special privileges. She was not very physically affectionate with us, and "I love you" was not part of daily conversation. But in her quiet way, she had a gift of presence more powerful than words. My husband (knowing secretly that he was her favorite son-in-law) summed it up: "When she was with you, she was all yours, as if you were the most important person in the world. Then she would go on to the next person, all his for a while."

In those days just before her death, my brothers and sisters and I discovered together what each of us had felt all along. Mom's love had no limits—each child was her favorite.

~Sue Thomas Hegyvary
Chicken Soup for Every Mom's Soul

I Love You, Daddy

And now these three things remain: Faith, hope and love.
But the greatest of these is love.
~1 Corinthians 13:13

How could any of us possibly know what is going to happen from day to day? Certainly the entire world was unprepared for what happened on the bright, autumn day of September 11, 2001. As for my world and the world of those I love most, life was forever altered on that fateful Tuesday morning.

My wife Shelley and I took separate cars to work on September 11. We usually drove in together, the two of us and our two children, Drake and Chandler, but Shelley's office was preparing to move to the other side of the Pentagon in two days, so she would be staying late. I wasn't very pleased about this, and I told her so the night before, but she was proud of the confidence that her supervisors had placed in her and wanted to set an example—I couldn't argue with that.

She left for work before I did that morning. I had the kids in my car, and when I stopped at Burger King to get them some breakfast (a treat for being good while I was alone with them in the car), the attendant told me that Shelley had just been there. She stayed ahead of me the whole way into town, and I didn't see her again until I brought the kids into the Pentagon day care. She was standing at one of the windows looking into a classroom when I saw her. I'll never forget the moment she saw us: She was wearing navy blue chinos, a blue oxford-cloth shirt and her beautiful smile. The kids ran to her as soon as they saw her, and we took them to their respective classrooms.

After we dropped the kids off, Shelley followed me to my car where she gave me an air kiss so she wouldn't get any lipstick on my cheek. Then I drove off to my office a few miles away. I talked to her again, at about 9:30, when she called me about the World Trade Center attacks.

Ten minutes later, my beautiful, gracious, kind, passionate wife—devoted mother to our beautiful children, a woman who loved all children and life itself—was gone.

Words can't begin to describe the loss.

Shelley remains a part of my life and the kids' lives in little miraculous ways. I've struggled to find the right way to keep her memory alive daily, and I think I'm succeeding. I'm still working on me, on going on without her physical presence next to me, but I've come to the point where I know she is with me, all around me, whenever I need her. She has let me know in many ways that she is watching over us, and knowing how much she loved us, I can honestly say that I'm not surprised.

At the end of September, the kids and I left Washington and moved to my parents' house in Morgantown, West Virginia. They live in the country, their nearest neighbor about a quarter-mile away, so we had lots of sunshine and peace and quiet, just when we needed it. Chandler was twenty months old at the time, and just beginning to put two or three words together to form rudimentary sentences. One day in early October, I was standing under a tree with Chandler in my arms. Holding her, I found myself crying because the child psychologists had told me that Chandler probably was too young to retain any of her own memories of Shelley into adulthood—that Chandler's memories of her mother would be composites, pieced together from the recollections of those who knew her mother. Reflecting on how much Shelley loved her children, the unfairness of it all overwhelmed me, and I wept quietly.

The child psychologists also told me not to hide my feelings from the kids, but to explain them, so they would know it's okay to grieve. So I looked at Chandler with tears in my eyes and said, "Daddy's crying because he misses Mommy."

Chandler looked up at me with her innocent blue eyes and said: "I love you, Daddy."

Given the simple two- or three-word sentences she had put together up until that point, I was surprised that she had put these words together so cohesively. I had never heard her say the word love before. Over the next two weeks, whenever I told Chandler that I missed Mommy, Chandler would reply with: "I love you, Daddy."

One day in mid-October we were standing under the same tree. Again, I told Chandler that I missed Mommy. Again, Chandler said, "I love you, Daddy."

I was suddenly curious, so I asked her, "Who taught you to say that?"

Without a moment's hesitation, Chandler replied, "Mommy."

Several months after September 11, one night when I was feeling particularly down, I decided to do a little housecleaning to take my mind off my sadness. I came across a piece of paper on which Shelley had typed her notes for the reading that she gave at her brother's wedding in July 2001. The reading was from Corinthians, and as my eyes raced across the words, they came to rest on the last line: "Love never ends."

I stand in awe of Shelley's never-ending love for our children and for me.

~Donn Marshall
Chicken Soup for the Single Parent's Soul

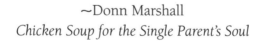

A Mother's Intuition

Trust your hunches.
They're usually based on facts filed away just below the conscious level.
~Dr. Joyce Brothers

An orange-sherbet sunrise heralded the day as I reached for my morning tea. Glancing at the clock I knew Amanda would soon be on her way home, tired from her night shift at the coffee shop in the city.

I went about my usual morning routine and thought how determined my daughter was to earn enough money to help put herself through college. It was a challenge for her to juggle two jobs but she managed. As I drifted from dishes to dusting I felt an unusual surge of concern for my now late-arriving daughter. I tried to keep busy, but I found myself watching out the window and listening for the familiar sound of Amanda's car pulling into the driveway.

A wave of nausea washed over me and my heart raced for a moment. I closed my eyes and prayed for her safety, then chastised myself for being a paranoid mother. Amanda often jokingly reminded me about my smothering-mothering tendencies. I countered with the "Wait until you have children of your own" lecture. Was this one of those moments? I called Amanda's cell phone. No answer.

Something was terribly wrong. I felt an urge to jump in my car and look for her. First, though, I called out to God for direction. I cannot say I heard an audible voice—it was more like a gentle nudge, but I truly felt God wanted me to leave the house.

My heart raced as I followed the likely route Amanda would take home. I kept pushing the redial button on my cell phone, but Amanda was not answering. I felt a sudden grip of fear and pulled over to the side of the road, wondering what to do. I remembered the countless times I had told Amanda to pray—how it was the most important step to take when fear crouched on the doorstep. So I prayed. I prayed that God would send His angels to protect my daughter.

My fear, thankfully, did not turn into panic, as I still felt compelled to drive. I drove for forty minutes but there was no sign of Amanda. Then my cell phone rang. My heart jumped to my throat. It was a female voice. The connection was so poor that I could hardly make it out: "... accident... Bethel Sideroad ...." I thought it was Amanda's voice, but I couldn't be sure. I was about fifteen minutes away from the Bethel Sideroad, so I did my best to keep my composure and drove, praying without ceasing.

A sickening sight awaited me. An ambulance and two police cars blocked the path of oncoming traffic. I saw Amanda's little grey car wrapped around a broken hydro pole. The whole car was crushed. I gasped in horror and knew Amanda had surely perished in such a wreck. Feeling faint, I jammed on my brakes. A policewoman approached me and I wailed in agony. I jumped out of my car, frantically screaming for Amanda. Just then, she stepped out of the ambulance. "Mom!" she called. I raced to her and clung to her with my arms and heart.

How had she survived? The paramedics kept saying it was nothing less than a miracle. The police officers, after they had calmed me down, told me they had expected to pull a body out of the car. In their estimation, no one should have survived such a horrendous accident.

Amanda had apparently fallen asleep at the wheel and as she hit the side of the road, her car had flipped twice and hit the hydro pole. The entire car was crushed—except for the driver's seat. She was taken to the hospital for observation, but other than a few scratches and bruises, she was fine.

I still marvel at the power of prayer and the sense of urgency that flooded my mind and heart that morning. The Almighty Protector shielded my Amanda—and sent His angels to protect her, just as I had prayed.

~Glynis M. Belec
Chicken Soup for the Christian Woman's Soul

Birthday Girl

Faith is putting all your eggs in God's basket,
then counting your blessings before they hatch.
~Ramona C. Carroll

Several years ago, while I worked for Visiting Nurses, I made an initial home visit to a family in a poor part of the city. Misty Harper (not her real name), my new patient, was five years old. She had been born with defects of the heart, liver and kidneys. The doctors predicted she wouldn't survive long enough to leave the hospital.

Anna Harper, a large, smiling woman, introduced herself as Misty's grandmother. She sat me down on the well-worn, overstuffed sofa in a living room crowded with furniture. Mrs. Harper had something she wanted to show me before Misty's assessment. She pulled out a huge scrapbook full of photos, articles and newspaper clippings. The first was a newspaper article reporting Misty's birth, the damage to her internal organs and the sad predictions for the future. Her daughter, Misty's mother, had been so stricken with grief that she was afraid to bring her baby home from the hospital. She believed that if Misty came home, her older three children would grow too attached to the baby and would be devastated by the loss.

"What happened?" I asked, suddenly understanding the closeness of this family.

"I took her home myself," Mrs. Harper said. "My instincts and my faith just told me she was not going to die."

We sat together for a while longer looking at the album. It held photographs of a sweet infant, then of a beautiful toddler growing up to be a lovely little girl.

She pointed to little newspaper clippings that filled the album. "Every year I send an announcement to the newspaper to celebrate Misty's birthday. It's just my way of telling everyone who cares that Misty is still with us."

Then she opened the door to the kitchen, and I saw a happy little girl eating breakfast with her sister and two brothers. A younger version of Mrs. Harper, Misty's mother, Coral, was spooning out more cereal. She smiled and beckoned me into the kitchen.

"My mother watches my kids every morning before school starts. In a few minutes, I go off to work."

Not wanting to disturb them I told her I didn't think I'd do an assessment that day. Next week I would come back. I closed the door quietly. Mrs. Harper walked me to the front door. As I was leaving she said, "Whenever a new doctor or nurse comes to our home to check Misty, I show them my album. Children are more than statistics. They are love and faith and what you put into them."

I felt humbled. She was right. Misty was proof of that.

"She will be six next May. Be sure to check the paper," Mrs. Harper teased.

In May I searched the announcements. There I found it.

MISTY HARPER WILL CELEBRATE HER SIXTH BIRTHDAY. THANK YOU LORD FOR ANOTHER MIRACLE YEAR.

Every May, I still look for the announcement and remember the family telling me in their own good-humored way, "Medicine doesn't know everything."

~Barbara Bloom
Chicken Soup for the Grandparent's Soul

Love Can Last Forever

I can honestly say it was the best of times and the worst of times. I was joyfully expecting my first child at the same time that my once-energetic, zestful mother was losing her battle with a brain tumor.

For ten years, my fiercely independent and courageous mother had fought, but none of the surgeries or treatments had been successful. Still, she never lost her ability to smile. But now, finally, at only fifty-five, she became totally disabled—unable to speak, walk, eat or dress on her own.

As she grew closer and closer to death, my baby grew closer and closer to life inside me. My biggest fear was that their lives would never connect. I grieved not only for the upcoming loss of my mother, but also that she and my baby would never know each other.

My fear seemed well-founded. A few weeks before my due date, Mother lapsed into a deep coma. Her doctors did not hold any hope; they told us her time was up. It was useless to put in a feeding tube, they said; she would never awaken.

We brought Mother home to her own bed in her own house, and we insisted on care to keep her comfortable. As often as I could, I sat beside her and talked to her about the baby moving inside me. I hoped that somehow deep inside, she knew.

At about the same time that my labor started, Mother opened her eyes. When they told me this at the hospital, I called her home and asked for the phone to be put to Mom's ear.

"Mom—Mom—listen. The baby is coming! You're going to have a new grandchild. Do you understand?"

"Yes!"

What a wonderful word! The first clear word she'd spoken in months!

When I called again an hour later, the nurse at her house told me the impossible: Mom was sitting up, her oxygen tubes removed. She was smiling.

"Mom, it's a boy! You have a new grandson!"

"Yes! Yes! I know!"

Four words. Four beautiful words.

By the time I brought Jacob home, Mom was sitting in her chair, dressed and ready to welcome him. Tears of joy blocked my vision as I laid my son in her arms and she clucked at him. They stared at each other.

They knew.

For two more weeks, Mother clucked, smiled and held Jacob. For two weeks she spoke to my father, her children and grandchildren in complete sentences. For two miracle weeks, she gave us joy.

Then she quietly slipped back into a coma and, after visits from all her children, was finally free of the pain and confines of a body that no longer did her will.

Memories of my son's birth will always be bittersweet for me, but it was at this time that I learned an important truth about living. For while both joy and sorrow are fleeting, and often intertwined, love has the power to overcome both. And love can last forever.

~Deb Plouse Fulton
A Second Chicken Soup for the Woman's Soul

6

The Sandals That Saved My Life

A baby is born with a need to be loved — and never outgrows it.
~Frank A. Clark

My junior high days were the darkest and the hardest time in my life. During that time, I didn't feel like I had any friends, except for this one person. This "friend" used to tell me that we would always be "friends forever." Friends are people who care for you and who are there for you whenever you need them. They nurture you when you're down. I never felt that way about her.

We only had one class together, so I didn't see her very often. She was all wrapped up in her own thing—her boyfriend, her social life, all her other friends. When I would walk the halls of junior high by myself, I would see her hand-in-hand with other people and she would just stare at me as I walked by. She never came over to talk to me except in that one class.

One rainy day, I got on the Internet and instant-messaged her. I thought it was the greatest thing in the world that we could talk on the Internet back and forth; it was so cool. We started chatting about school, boys, everything that two normal preteen girls would talk about. I brought up that I had gotten a new movie, and I wanted her to come over and watch it with me. I waited and waited for her reply, and when it came it was like daggers in my heart with unbearable pain.

She said, "Why would I want to come and watch it with you? Every time you get something new, you always have to brag about it to me and it makes me sick. You brag about everything all the time." I apologized to her up and down, that that's not what I meant, and I kept on apologizing.

Then she wrote back, "I am not going to sit here and fight with you about it, even though it is true," and she signed off.

I sat in my chair for ten minutes in a daze, wondering how a person who said she was my friend could say something like that to me. I went into the living room and sat down next to my mom, then burst out crying. She comforted me and reassured me that whatever it was, everything would be okay.

When I went to bed that night, I couldn't sleep. I felt so alone; like no one really loved me and like I was just some person that other people could just use whenever they felt like it. I felt almost invisible. I cried and cried until I finally fell asleep.

The next morning, I woke up around 8:00. My mom came into my room and said that she and my dad had doctor's appointments and that they would be back in a couple of hours. After they left, I sat on my bed and wondered what would be a good way out of this. Then, something came to my mind.

I would kill myself and put everyone out of their misery. That way, they wouldn't have to pretend that they like me, or that they are my friends. My social life wasn't the only reason that I decided to do this. Other things, too, were really bothering me—my grades, for one.

I sat and thought about how I would do it. Should I shoot myself or take pills, or should I cut my wrists? I settled on pills. I put the pills on the table next to my bed while I sat and wrote my final words to my family and friends.

I was ready to pop the pills for my final minutes on Earth.

Then the phone rang.

It was my mom calling to see what my shoe size is because she had found the cutest pair of sandals at Old Navy. I said, "Oh ... yeah, okay, I wear an eleven."

Then she went on, "What's wrong? Are you feeling okay?"

I was like, "Yeah, Mom, I'm fine."

Then the words that I had longed to hear from anyone came out, "I LOVE YOU, and I'll be home in an hour." I hung up the phone. I sat in a daze, with the pills in my hand, thinking, How could I have forgotten that someone actually does love me?

When my mom came home, she hugged me and kissed me and said that she loved me a lot. I never told her what I had been thinking about doing.

The next day my "friend" called and said, "I was only kidding about the whole thing." I never told her about it, either. I kept it to myself. To this day, I still haven't told anyone about what I almost did. I have never actually blamed anyone but myself.

I am so blessed that my mom's phone call got through to me. Not only did it make me realize that I really am loved and cared about, but that suicide is never the answer. Maybe I just needed to hear the words "I love you" more often. Maybe we all do. Even when I have problems at school, my family is always there for me and I needed to remember to value that support. I know that I have to be there for them, too.

According to my definition of friendship, my mom's the best friend I'll ever have. My mom doesn't know how really special she is and how much of a hero she is. Thank you, Mom, for loving me so much—and saving me—without even knowing it. You're my forever friend.

~Mallorie Cuevas
Chicken Soup for the Preteen Soul 2

7

The Mailbox

Kids spell love T-I-M-E.
~John Crudele

"You're a wonderful mother," I wrote on the Mother's Day card with the picture of sunflowers, garden gloves and watering can. "You were always home for me after school, with warm cookies and milk. You led our 4-H club and worked in PTA. Best of all, now you're my friend, sharing with me a love of beauty, puzzlement at the mysteries of men and respect for children."

I walked out the gravel driveway to the mailbox, opened the metal door and slid in the card. As I shut the door and pulled up the red flag, I remembered another mailbox from long ago....

As a child I spent hours in a small playhouse in the back yard. I decked it out with curtains strung on twine, a window box planted with marigolds, and a mailbox made from a coffee can.

The can was nailed to the outside wall of the playhouse, next to the window. It was painted with green house paint and fitted with a small board inside to create a flat horizontal surface.

One languid summer day I ran into the house and found my mother mopping the kitchen floor.

"Mama," I asked, "could you bring me some mail?"

She straightened up and held the mop in one hand, massaging the small of her back with the other. She smiled, and her eyes softened as she looked at me, her suntanned, pigtailed sprite.

"Well, yes, I think I can, after I finish this floor," she said. "You go back to the playhouse and wait awhile. I'll be there."

So I ran outside, letting the screen door slam behind me. I skipped down the narrow brick path to the clothesline and under it to the playhouse beside the dwarf apple tree. I busied myself with little-girl housekeeping: washing my doll dishes, tidying the bed, sweeping the floor with the toy cornstraw broom.

Then I heard steps on the brick path.

"Mail time," Mama called in a high voice. Then I heard the thunk of envelopes firmly striking the inside of the coffee can.

I waited to give her time to walk back to the house, then rushed out of the playhouse and reached into the can to grab my treasure. Shuffling through it, I found three envelopes, a catalog and a small package. What a haul!

I sat on the grass that sloped down to the garden to open it.

Naturally, I went for the package first. Tearing away the brown grocery sack paper, I lifted the lid from a tiny box. Wow! Two sticks of Juicy Fruit gum, a square of waxed paper wrapped around a handful of chocolate chips, raisins and miniature marshmallows, and a new Pink Pearl eraser. I munched on the snack mixture while I explored the rest of my mail.

Thumbing through the seed catalog, I enjoyed the brightly colored flower pictures. Then I spread the envelopes out in my hand. Each was addressed to "Patty, Playhouse, Back Yard, Oregon" and posted with an S & H Green Stamp. I slipped my finger under the flap of one and ripped it open. It held a flyer from a car insurance company. In the next I found an advertisement for magazine subscriptions with a hundred tiny stamps to stick onto the order form. From the last envelope I pulled a page of notepaper.

"How are you doing?" I read in my mother's perfect printing. "It's been beautiful weather here, though a little hot for me. I've been canning beans. We have a lovely, large garden, as usual. Do come visit us. You know you are always welcome. Love, Mama."

She signed it in "writing" with swirls at the beginning of the "M" and at the end of the "a."

That was probably forty years ago.

I thought Mama and I had become close friends only recently. But remembering the mailbox, I realized I was wrong. The mother who took the time from her mopping and canning to gather up some junk mail and trinkets to put into a package, write a personal note and deliver it all in true play-acting style was my special companion even back then. Mama was always my friend.

~Patty Duncan
Chicken Soup for the Mother's Soul 2

A Loving Mother

We don't see things as they are, we see them as we are.
~Anaïs Nin

I'm a girl with bipolar disorder. That's when your moods go up or down way too far. Sometimes with bipolar, you feel so happy that you get kind of hyperactive, bouncing off the walls and jumping for joy. Then, within minutes, bipolar can make you feel really sad or so mad that you start throwing stuff around, screaming and stomping.

With bipolar, when a person gets either really, really happy or really, really sad or mad, they have no idea why they feel that way. They can think of nothing that caused their mood to be so extreme one way or the other.

When I was seven years old, I got mad at my mom for no reason. We got into a fight over nothing, and I got so mad that I threw my glass piggy bank at her. Pretty bad, huh?

Maybe some of my anger was due to the fact that my parents had recently divorced and my mom and dad were not getting along well. My dad had been following my mom around. Then one night, he came into our house and attempted to hurt her, and she ran outside to call the police. At that point, he started to go up the stairs to find me. I was asleep and my stepdad kept him from getting to me. He ran away before the police got there, but the next day, the police arrested him for harassing our family.

That next day, I was supposed be with my dad but, of course, he didn't show up. That's when I knew something was wrong. My mom tried to protect me from finding out why he didn't come. She just told me that he had done something wrong and couldn't be with me. I cried every night because I missed him, and I became really depressed. Finally, I bugged my mom enough that she told me what had happened that night. In a way, it just made me more upset because everyone had kept the truth from me.

Around that time, I also began experiencing these extreme mood shifts. First I'd be really, really happy and then the next minute I'd be really, really mad. Then I couldn't stop myself from crying. It was very confusing, and I felt like I had no control over my emotions anymore. When I would get into trouble, I couldn't understand why I was behaving so badly. I would later come back to my mom and apologize to her for being so out of control, and she would always say, "It's okay, Holly. You're forgiven. Tomorrow will be a better day." It was hard on her, I'm sure, but she tried to deal with it by giving me love and understanding. She somehow knew that I couldn't help myself and suspected something more was wrong with me when one day I got so depressed that I asked her, "Why don't you just get rid of me?" I had been so down that I didn't even want to live anymore.

She didn't think that my behavior was all because of what was happening between her and my dad. So, she took me to see a doctor who helps kids that have the same kind of issues that I was dealing with. It helped to know that there was someone out there who could understand me. It didn't seem like my family was able to do that at that time.

The day I threw the piggy bank my mom realized that I had gotten so out of control of my emotions that I could be a danger to myself and others. So, she and the doctor agreed that putting me in the hospital would help keep me safe while they ran some tests. It was there that I was diagnosed with bipolar disorder. The good news was, once they knew what I had, they could find the right medication to help me balance out. While in the hospital, I also learned about bipolar and the challenges of living with this illness.

I felt so much better after I got out of the hospital. I stopped feeling so sad and then suddenly totally happy. Finally, I felt normal for the first time in a long time.

Still, when I had some bad mood swings after I got out of the hospital, I thought that Mom would want to send me back there as punishment for my actions. But my mom never wanted to punish me for doing something that I couldn't control. She explained to me that she never wanted to be away from me, she only wanted to find the help that I needed to get better and stay better.

Sometimes I would think about how my mother could have given me away because it was so hard to deal with me when my bipolar was going on, but she is too much of a loving mother to ever do that. Instead, she was always behind me, supporting me with tons of love and patience.

When I begin to get a little out of hand, my mom watches to see if I continue the behavior. If I do, it usually means that I need to change medications because the one I'm on has stopped working. That's part of the challenge of living with bipolar. Sometimes, body chemistry can change, causing the medications to act differently or the body just simply stops working with the medication and you have to change it.

Not long ago, I began hearing voices telling me to do stuff. I had to go into the hospital again to get off of the medication that I was on and start a new one. It was hard to face going into the hospital and going through another adjustment, but after being there for a few days and getting a new medication, the voices went away and I felt more like myself again—more balanced.

It's been five years now since I was diagnosed with bipolar. For the most part, I am doing well, and my emotions are more in the middle now and less "way too up" or "way too down." I can thank my mom for helping me make sure that I don't get sick and out of control. No matter what, she's there for me. Knowing that, I can cope with having an illness that I'll always have to work at managing.

With her there, I can get through another day.

~Holly Howard
Chicken Soup for the Preteen Soul 2

Mother's Goblets

can't remember the last time I saw my mother. Actually, I don't remember her at all. She died shortly before I turned three. The stories I've heard about her are other people's memories, not mine. Life cheated me out of hearing her voice and feeling her touch. She remained out of focus, a shadowy figure, until the day I found her glasses. Suddenly, thirty-three years after her death, she was real as if she reached out to help me when I needed her most.

Don't get me wrong. My life was good. My wayward father wisely left me with his in-laws who gave me pretty much everything—especially a home filled with love. Growing up, I was vaguely aware of several mysterious boxes that had something to do with my elusive mother. Since I was too young for the contents to mean anything to me, my aunt faithfully guarded her sister's belongings for over twenty years.

Eventually, I got married and moved into my own house. My aunt, feeling her tour of duty was over, gave me the boxes. Like treasure hunters, we eagerly opened each carton. A teacup collection. Fine china. Tarnished silver. Exquisite crystal. The most beautiful glasses I'd ever seen—clear and delicate and etched with roses. We handwashed and arranged them in the china cabinet. They came out only on holidays or special occasions along with the china and silver. I proudly used them until the day the water goblets broke.

I can't remember how it happened. An accident, I'm sure. No one's fault really. Two water goblets simply broke. Carefully picking up the pieces, I set them way back inside the china cabinet with a promise that one day I'd have them repaired. From then on, no one could touch my mother's glasses. Forbidden. I couldn't risk losing any more.

Some time later, at an antique show, I found a man who repaired crystal. I took the broken pieces to him hoping he'd make them whole again. To my bitter disappointment, he couldn't repair them without destroying the rose etchings.

"Are you sure there's nothing you can do?" I asked with the slightest hope.

"Let me show them to my wife," he offered, noting my distress. "Maybe she'll have an idea."

He carried the pieces to a woman seated on the other side of the booth and asked her if they had any similar glasses back in their shop. She only laughed, "Where in the world would I get expensive glasses like these? They're Heisey Roses!"

"What are Heisey Roses?" I wanted to know, my curiosity aroused.

Pulling out a magnifying glass, the man pointed out a tiny diamond with an "H" inside it, engraved on the stem of each glass. "These glasses are worth about forty dollars each. They were made by the Heisey Company of Ohio. I really am sorry that I can't fix them."

If he was sorry, I was sorrier. "Do you think I could buy two water goblets to replace these?"

"Chances are a million to one you'll ever find these glasses anywhere."

Feeling bad, but determined to find replacements, my search began. Antique shops. Antique shows. Yard sales. Garage sales. Rummage sales. Flea markets. Michigan. Ohio. Florida. Massachusetts. California. Pennsylvania. Anywhere. Everywhere. Years went by and still no glasses, but something inside me wouldn't give up.

As time passed, I developed severe back pain that only grew worse. The diagnosis? Scoliosis, curvature of the spine. The solution? Surgery. Possibly two surgeries and no guarantee that things would improve. With two small children depending on me, it wasn't an easy decision to make. I prayed for a sign—something to let me know whether I was on the right track. No sign came.

My doctor scheduled surgery for early January. Mid-December, he changed his mind. Instead, he wanted me to consult with a doctor in Minnesota—one of the finest spinal surgeons in the country. It was winter, and Minnesota seemed so far away, but my husband insisted we go. More discouraged than ever, I continued to pray for that sign, but still none came.

The Minnesota doctor described a relatively new surgical procedure that would accomplish everything I needed in one grueling twelve-hour session. The good part? I wouldn't need a second operation just when I started recovering from the first one. The bad part? The surgery had to be done in Minnesota, a very long way from home. I made no commitments that morning. No final decisions. I needed time to think. Besides, I still hadn't gotten that sign I'd been waiting for.

We left Minnesota right after the consultation. It was a long drive, and we were anxious to get home before any bad weather hit. From habit, we watched for antique shops and malls along the way. If we could find one right off the highway, it would be a nice way to stretch our legs. We passed up a few shops: one was closed, the other out of the way, and one we just couldn't find. We hit the jackpot at an exit in Tomah, Wisconsin. Not only was there an antique mall, but a cheese shop, a gas station and a pay phone so we could call the kids. What more could we ask for? Only that darn sign I hadn't stopped praying for.

We filled the gas tank, made our call and bought some cheese. Our last stop was the antique mall. Once inside, the number of dealers selling hundreds and hundreds of items overwhelmed us. As we passed the first couple of booths, something caught my eye. I held my breath as I peered closer into the locked display case. My mother's glasses! Not just water goblets, but salad dishes, cordial glasses, an ashtray and more! A Heisey Rose dream!

I couldn't take my eyes off them. Refusing to move from the spot, I sent my husband to find someone who could unlock the cabinet. Once the glass case was opened, I picked up one goblet at a time studying every inch, making sure there were no mars or chips. The glasses were perfect and the forty-dollar price tag just didn't matter. After all these years, I'd finally found my mother's glasses!

As the saleslady wrapped the goblets, my thoughts ran back to the man who repaired crystal. He had told me so long ago that my chances of finding these glasses were a million to one. A million to one! So how did I end up here? What brought me to this place? I suddenly realized that I hadn't just found my mother's goblets, but the sign I'd been so desperately praying for. My mother came through loud and clear. Words couldn't have been more to the point. Now, there were no more doubts. I had to return to Minnesota for the twelve-hour surgery we discussed with the doctor just hours earlier! And I learned something else. My mother has always been with me. I just never knew it, until the day I found her goblets.

~Debra Ann Pawlak
Chicken Soup for the Mother & Daughter Soul

A Mother Sings

ill paused halfway down our front steps. She turned and said, "Mom, will you sing to me? Will you hold me and sing like you used to when I was a little girl?" Her husband and her two little stepdaughters stopped and looked back.

I always sang to my kids when they were young. Jill and her older brother shared a bedroom, and I knelt between them, holding one's hand and stroking the blond head of the other. I sang and crooned through "Dona, Dona" and "Kumbaya." I swayed in rhythm to "Swing Low, Sweet Chariot." I never missed a verse of "Hush, Little Baby." I made up songs too, a habit that drove my husband crazy. On nights when I was out, the kids begged, "Sing 'The Horse Broke the Fence,' Daddy," or "No, we want 'The Big Wheel' song." And they didn't mean "Proud Mary," which he might have managed, although he really couldn't carry a tune even when he knew the words.

But the kids and I always finished with "All Things Bright and Beautiful," as I watched their active bodies quiet and their eyes grow dreamy as they imagined the purple-headed mountains and ripe fruit in the garden of the old hymn. By the time I warbled my way through the refrain for the last time, one of them had usually twitched and fallen asleep.

As Jill grew from child to adult, it became apparent that she had inherited her father's trouble carrying a melody. She cuddles with her girls every night and she reads to them, but she just can't sing to them.

Recently, I babysat for our granddaughters. After I tucked them into our king-size bed, I sang "Dona, Dona," "Kumbaya," and all the others. Hannah, the six-year-old, lay still as a stone, gazing at the ceiling. Four-year-old Brianna came forward onto her hands and knees, staring into my eyes from so close that her features blurred. In the dim light coming through the open door, I saw her lips parted, glistening. Trance-like, she held perfectly still, listening as if she wanted to inhale the songs directly from my mouth.

It was a few days later that Jill asked me to once again sing to her. She said, "The girls talked about your singing, Mom, and it brought back all the wonderful memories. I remember my cool pillow and your hand on my hair. I remember my nightgown with the sunbonnet dolls on it and the pink ice cream cone quilt you made. Sometimes I would wake up when you kissed me one last time."

That's when she turned and asked, "Mom, will you sing to me again?"

Her husband stood beneath the street lamp with a child balanced on each hip. Her father and brothers stood behind me, illuminated by the porch light. She's very tall, this girl of mine. Standing on the step below me, she still had to stoop to put her head against my chest. I wrapped my fingers in her long hair, and she wound her arms around my waist.

"What shall I sing, Jill?" I asked.

"You know, Mom," she said, looking up and smiling.

"'All Things Bright and Beautiful'?"

"Of course." She snuggled closer. "All the verses."

I kissed the top of her head and began to sing.

Swallowing a lump in my throat and stroking her back, I continued through the verses. Off-key, she joined in.

She began to cry, and so did I, but the words still flowed from my mouth as my mind drifted back over the years. I remembered her birth, how ecstatic I was to have a daughter—what an easy child she was. I remembered how she loved to please others—and still does. This girl who married young and took on the daunting task of raising another woman's children is no longer under my wing. She's a young woman now, and I can't tuck the ice cream cone quilt around her shoulders each night. I can't protect her from pain, from hurt and from mature responsibility. I can't make growing up any easier for her.

Jill's tears soaked through my T-shirt that night and mine dropped onto her bowed head. She clung tightly and then looked up into my face.

"The purple-headed mountains. Don't forget the purple-headed mountains," she whispered, staring at me through the dim light, just as Brianna had a few nights earlier, drinking in the words, the memories, the song. Drinking in my love.

My voice cracked, and I could sing no more. We stood locked together on the stairs. I know the enormity of the task she's taken on is sometimes almost more than she can handle. I know how hard she's working to create a home.

Cradling her in maternal love, allowing her to remember falling asleep to a mother's singing, was the best I could offer my daughter this night. Jill squeezed me tightly and then turned toward her husband and her stepdaughters. Her dad hugged me as we watched her settle the girls into the back seat of their car—and then I heard the hymn again. I strained my ears, listening. Jill was still humming the refrain. Then Brianna's thin, little child's voice burbled from the open car window as they pulled away from the curb: "All things wise and wonderful, the Lord God made them all."

~Peggy Vincent
Chicken Soup to Inspire a Woman's Soul

Moms Know Best

Great Times with Mom

*I am convinced that the greatest legacy we can
leave our children is happy memories.*
~Og Mandino

Salsa Lessons

Growing up, Saturday was cleaning day. Protest did no good, so, reluctantly, my brother and I would drag our feet into the kitchen where my mother would tell us what we had to do.

My mother did all the heavy cleaning, and we usually had something simple to do. I would dust all the furniture and make the beds. My brother would vacuum and throw out the trash.

Just before we got started, Mother, who has always had a knack for making even the most mundane chore fun, would turn on the record player. No matter how tired we were, once the music came on, we came alive. With salsa blaring from the record player, cleaning somehow became easier.

My mother would dance with the broom, the mop, or a pillow; anything could be a dancing partner. My brother and I would laugh, and eventually we would all end up dancing. The beat of the bongo drums in salsa music has a way of crawling into your soul, and once you're hooked, there's no turning back.

I have always loved music and was eager to learn to dance. Mami began teaching me steps. She instructed me how to keep my upper body steady while swaying my hips and moving my feet to the beat. My mother knew most of the words to the songs, and she would sing while twirling me around the room. We would do conga lines, and dance in and out of all the rooms in our little house. Every time a good song came on, we would drop what we were doing and begin dancing. It wasn't uncommon for my dad to come home for lunch and find his wife and children dancing, and the housecleaning still not done.

At first, my brother wasn't too enthusiastic about learning to dance. He would roll his eyes, pretending he wasn't interested, but my mom never got discouraged. She would ignore his sulking and entice him to join us. As he got a little older and realized that girls like boys who can dance, his interest grew. Although salsa is very different from other forms of dancing, learning to dance gave us the ability to pick up steps to the music of our generation.

The habit of putting on music whenever I have to do chores at home has never left me. Any time I have to get busy, you'll hear salsa blaring from the speakers installed all over my house. I also dance with sofa cushions and imaginary partners while my children laugh at their nutty mom. I taught my sons how to dance this way, and now my five-year-old daughter and I share in weekly dance sessions.

Thinking back on those Saturday mornings, I realize that we were learning more than just how to dance. We learned that while life isn't always easy or fun, we have the ability to make the most out of every situation. The important thing is the attitude we choose to have when dealing with the circumstances we find ourselves in.

Music kept my mother sane those first few years in the United States. It helped her deal with her sadness. It helped her forget how broke we were and how uncertain the future was. I'm sure the music took her back home to Guantánamo, to the carnavales and a carefree time in her life.

Salsa takes me straight to my Caribbean roots. The words to the songs talk of the island where I was born. Salsa helps me stay connected to a place and a way of life I have always been curious to know more about. When I'm dancing salsa, the drums beat steadily with my heart, and for a moment this Cuban girl is back in Guantánamo.

~María Luisa Salcines
Chicken Soup for the Latino Soul

A Bus Trip for Mom on Mother's Day

You don't choose your family.
They are God's gift to you, as you are to them.
~Desmond Tutu

One early May, I had to attend a convention in New Orleans. It was just what my eighty-six-year-old mom wanted to hear.

"Why can't I go, too? I'd love to see New Orleans again!"

I had misgivings about Mom traveling, especially since an old hip injury was acting up. But she was so enthusiastic I figured a nice, quick plane trip would be just fine. That was not what Mom had in mind, however.

"Remember when you were a kid and we traveled all over on the bus? Wasn't that fun?" Mom asked with a grin.

Memories of harrowing hours in bus stations and rushed sandwiches in roadside diners made words other than "fun" leap to my mind. But then Mom brought out the big guns: "It is almost Mother's Day. That can be your gift to me. A bus ride to New Orleans."

So much for my protests.

So off we went, leaving San Diego one chilly morning and heading east. Mom quickly made friends with the Hispanic men going home to the Imperial Valley after working all week in San Diego.

Before I could hoist her bag up and down from the overhead rack, two darker-skinned young men were beating me to it. And Mom was raving over the sights of the mountains and the desert.

"Look at all the vegetables growing," she cried, "even more than when we went through the Imperial Valley before."

The giant sahuatob of Arizona delighted her, and Texas was everything she dreamed it would be: the wildflowers, the hills, the bubbling little rivers and the goats grazing in the brushy fields. Mom had raised goats when I was small. Most of the bus passengers in Texas were African-American, and Mom reminisced with them about the time our family first moved to California in the late 1940s. I could always tell which row of the bus Mom was in when I would return with snacks. She was where the laughter was.

The chili in the San Antonio bus station was so good that Mom insisted on congratulating the girl dishing it up. From then on long after we got home, Mom wanted chili, though it never tasted quite as good as it had in San Antonio.

By the time we reached New Orleans, I was worried that Mom was getting tired. I kept remembering the dim view friends took of an eighty-six-year-old lady spending so long on a bus.

"We'll get a hotel room in New Orleans and rest for a couple of days before heading home," I told Mom.

"No," she laughed, "I want to get back on the bus and see everything from the other direction!"

And so after a day of watching Mississippi river boats, being serenaded by jazzmen and strolling through the French Quarter, we were heading west.

Mom remembered all the landmarks and looked forward to the lights over Sierra Blanca and the goats again.

Seeing Mom enjoy herself turned out to be the highlight of the trip. My convention appearance sank into insignificance.

When we got back to San Diego, Mom regaled everyone with our adventures. She had friends and family in stitches over the snafu of "losing" our bus in Phoenix. Somehow we got off without boarding passes and then couldn't find our bus. I told someone that all we remembered was that our driver was about fifty with glasses. When we relayed that description to an annoyed agent, he growled that, "All the drivers are about fifty with glasses."

Our family had taken many trips by bus, train and finally our family car with Mom at the wheel pulling a travel trailer. But this was the first trip for just Mom and me. It frightened me when I realized how close I had come to not going on a trip with my mom, an experience that proved to be one of our sweetest memories.

Mom remained with us for another seven years and almost to the last she mentioned the trip to New Orleans at least once a day. Her eyes would light up, and she'd say, "Do you remember all those goats?" and "I still can't believe we had to ride the escalator up to see the Mississippi River!"

Three years ago, Mom left us for the shores of a better world, but I still savor the memory of the best Mother's Day gift I ever gave her, and what a gift it was to me. I had feared eighty-six was too old for such an adventure, but it turned out to be just right. Mom was usually the oldest passenger on the bus, and always the one having the most fun.

~Anne Schraff
Chicken Soup for the Mother & Daughter Soul

Too Late

My ninety-year-old mom, Bert, is in the late stages of Alzheimer's and has been in a nursing home for twelve years.

I am her only family and love being with her as much as I can. We find meaningful, loving times together. I sing to her. We hug. We speak primarily through touch. Once a fun, witty woman, now she rarely has lucid moments where we can communicate. I am simply that "nice lady." She cannot move herself at all. Her hands are atrophied and the only movement of her body is when the nurses turn her in bed every two hours.

One day an aide went to check on my mother, who had been sleeping. She was shocked to find Mom on the floor, with no apparent injury, still asleep and snoring. The aide called to the nurse, "Bert has fallen out of bed!" The nurse immediately headed to her room saying, "Bert doesn't move. She doesn't roll. This can't be." Even when in the room, looking at my mother on the floor, she was amazed and repeated, "This can't be! Bert doesn't move or roll."

The aide wondered out loud, "Maybe we should pull up the bed rails."

From my mother, came, "Don't you think it's a little late for that now?"

Mom grinned. The staff burst into laughter.

~Esther Copeland
Chicken Soup for the Caregiver's Soul

Picture-Perfect Bologna

My mother-in-law's reputation as a cook extraordinaire is without blemish. Rumor has it if she swished her hand in a pan of dishwater, her guests would rave it was the best soup they ever tasted.

Her culinary skills were tested daily as she prepared three meals for fifty or more guests at the ranch-resort where she was employed as a cook. She didn't own a measuring cup or spoons. Her knack for blending just the right amount of ingredients made every meal she prepared a mouthwatering masterpiece.

Hers was the generation before fast-food restaurants, drive-throughs and cafeteria lunches for kids. She didn't know the luxury of grabbing a quick meal on the way home when her last ounce of energy was spent on the evening shift. Her kitchen chores extended into the wee hours after returning home to her family of eight children.

And so it was, late one night, when she began making sandwiches for the family's next-day lunches. She reached into the refrigerator for a jar of mayonnaise and the almost-empty package of bologna. She had packed so many lunches, she could make bologna sandwiches with her eyes closed. And a good thing it was, because most nights it was difficult to stay awake as she spread mayonnaise on the row of white bread slices. She tucked the last pieces of bologna into two sandwiches for her youngest son.

The following evening, during the sandwich-making ritual, her youngest son came into the kitchen.

"Mom, I want to talk to you about my lunch."

"You want something different than bologna?"

"No. Bologna's fine," he said. "It's about today's lunch."

"Oh?"

"Well, Mom... the first sandwich was good. It was the second one that was hard to chew."

"Why is that?"

"The first sandwich was real bologna. The second sandwich was the cardboard picture of bologna from the top of the package."

A picture-perfect bologna sandwich. Her reputation remains untarnished.

~Diane M. Vanover
Chicken Soup for the Working Woman's Soul

15

The Nightgown

In the bottom drawer of my mother's walnut veneer dresser lay a Joan Crawford-style nylon and lace nightgown. It was blue and wrapped carefully in white tissue with a tiny flowered lavender sachet tucked into its folds.

I was ten or eleven when Mother first showed me the nightgown. I thought it was the most beautiful, most elegant thing I'd ever seen. "Your father gave this to me; I'm saving it for when I go to the hospital some day," she would say quietly, as if to herself. Every now and then if I happened to be around when the dresser drawer was open, she'd let me look at the gown. I would run my fingers over it lightly, and we would joke about the slim chances of its ever being worn.

"You're never sick, Mom. You'll never wear this nightgown if you wait for the hospital," I would scold gently.

She would smile and say firmly, "It's too good for every day."

In truth, there was no occasion special enough—in or out of a hospital—for her to have worn such a nightgown. I eventually learned that it was not because the gown was too good but rather that my mother did not feel entitled to wear it. That kept her from ever knowing its elegance next to her skin.

I think there must have been a time, before I was born, when she might have believed otherwise, when she was a "heartbreaker," according to her high school yearbook. I imagine that in 1936 she might have danced and swirled in a filmy, blue nightgown to seduce my handsome teenage father, as she flirted with her wide brown eyes and sweet smile. I imagine she might have sung him a love song in her rich alto voice or sat quietly holding his hand and sharing dreams. She was young and seemingly invulnerable, even to her alcoholic father's rages and her mother's sudden death in that same year. And she had my father, who was suffering his own pain, his parents' divorce and the humiliating poverty that followed. They had each other back then, and I doubt that entitlement entered her mind.

The nightgown remained in the bottom drawer for the next thirty-some years, disturbed only when it was packed up and moved a few times. Finally, it was moved to a small apartment and into the bottom drawer of an early-American dresser, taken from my parents' bedroom. By now, my mother had long since stopped dancing and flirting. Years of betrayal and conflict had dimmed the light in those brown eyes, and divorce had left her alone, depressed and bitter. She functioned well enough—found a job, developed a small circle of women friends, traveled occasionally to visit my sisters, even remarried briefly. She loved her grandchildren and the Pittsburgh Steelers and her devoted cat Poppy. But she had clearly given up caring deeply about her life and her dreams. It was in this resignation and unresolved grief that my mother's cancer was born.

I want to write about the times my mother did go to the hospital and wore only regulation gowns, about the horror of watching the IVs of crippling medicine flow into her veins, medicine that would prolong her deteriorating life by only six months. I want to write complaint after complaint about how indifferent and incompetent her doctor and the nursing staff seemed, how insensitive I believed the entire world was being to my dying mother. But that would take me away from the story that matters more, the one about my mother's lost and then found sense of entitlement.

It happened one night early on in the series of chemotherapy treatments, which were fairly routine but required an overnight hospital stay for observation. By now my mother's body had become weakened by days and nights of severe nausea and vomiting. When we got to her room, we found a team of doctors and nurses tending to her roommate, who was in apparent cardiac arrest. While the medical staff ran back and forth past Mother's bed, I helped her settle in to wait for the chemo IV. Occasionally, a nurse would stop by to verify why Mother was there; occasionally, still another nurse would stop by to see if someone had stopped by yet, presumably to set up the IV. Three hours passed. Our shared abilities to find humor in bad situations were tapped. Although the woman in the next bed was now stable, this good news had no positive effect whatsoever on the level of care Mother was getting. Then a nurse came into the room to say that Mother's chart had been lost and they were waiting for her doctor to call back. Again, we waited. At last, a different nurse came into the room. She said to Mother, "We still haven't heard from the doctor. Do you happen to remember what color the medicine is that goes into your IV?"

The question hung in the room for a moment. Mother stammered, "Well, I think it was blue ...."

I jumped from my chair.

"What color is it?" I said, "What color is it?"

Mother patted my hand, a clenched fist. She looked so tiny and frail in that oversized bed. It broke my heart. I turned to the phone and started dialing the doctor's answering service. I handed the phone to mother to wait for a connection and left the room, furious, looking for anyone who resembled a doctor on duty. I approached two residents in the hallway and launched into my problem. Before I could finish, one of the residents put his hand on my shoulder and said, "Look, dear, I'm not your mother's physician; you'll just have to wait ...."

I jerked away from him as if touched by a hot wire.

"Don't you dare call me dear!" I said, feeling faint with outrage.

I returned to the room, shaking. Mother was talking to the doctor on the phone. She said, "What do you mean, my values are misplaced?"

I watched her brown eyes flicker with anger. She sat up on the edge of the bed. In that moment, something in each of us seemed to click. I went to the closet and got Mother's clothes and began dressing her, first the socks, then slacks, then the blouse. She moved her legs and arms cooperatively and shifted her butt when needed, still holding the phone to her ear. The flicker in her eyes began twinkling, the hint of a smile forming. I packed up her few toiletries and got her coat, as she slammed down the phone.

"He told me my values are misplaced," she said. "He said I should be willing to go through a little inconvenience to prolong my life. He told me I'm being childish. Can you believe that?"

"Easily," I said.

It was well past midnight and we had been in the hospital for hours. "Mom," I said, "let's get the hell out of here."

I held her coat as she put her arms through the sleeves.

"I'm ready," she said.

I found a wheelchair in the hallway and helped Mother into the seat. I tucked my coat around her legs and piled the overnight bag and our purses on her lap. She gripped the handles of all three bags until her thin knuckles turned white. She looked up at me, her face illuminated by a full smile. "Let's go," she said.

Halfway down the hall, the nursing supervisor stepped in front of the wheelchair. "Where do you think you're going?" she demanded of us both.

"I'm going home," my mother said quietly and firmly.

"You're going home? And just why are you going home in the middle of the night like this?" the supervisor demanded even more loudly.

Mother locked glares with the nurse for a moment. Then she said, just as quietly and firmly as before, "Because I've had enough of this crap."

For the second time that night, a sentence hung in the air. The nurse stepped aside. I patted Mother's shoulder approvingly, and we flew to the elevator door and into the chilly April night.

Following my mother's death a year later, I found the blue nightgown in her bottom drawer. The lace felt stiffer than I had remembered, and the tissue had yellowed some, but the lavender scent was still strong as I held the gown to my face for a long time. Then I placed it into a plastic trash bag designated for Goodwill. I did not want a keepsake that my mother had seen as too good for her. I thought back to those wonderful moments after we left the hospital that April night.

When we had gotten a safe distance away, I pulled into the parking lot of a fast food restaurant, and we collapsed into tearful, hysterical laughter. While I stuffed myself excitedly with french fries and Mother tried to swallow a milkshake, we relived the night, minute by bizarre minute, and savored our triumph—over the system maybe, maybe even over death and, although neither of us spoke it, I think we knew we were also savoring, for this brief, shining hour, my mother's triumph over resignation and depression and bitterness, and over all of the unresolved pain of generations before her.

~Alicia Nordan
Chicken Soup for the Mother & Daughter Soul

Trouble Brewing

fter an exhausting weekend, I woke up Monday morning and sleepily packed lunch for my eight-year-old. When I got home from work late that day, she handed me a note from her teacher, requesting I see her. "What's this all about?" I asked sternly.

Opening her lunch box, my daughter showed me the drink I had given her that morning. It was a can of beer.

~Cynthia Briche
Chicken Soup for the Working Woman's Soul

Making Memories

fter eating breakfast, my little girl says, "Mommy, will you watch this show with me?" I look at the breakfast dishes in the sink and then at her big brown eyes.

"Okay," I say, and we snuggle together on the couch and watch her favorite show.

After the show, we put together a puzzle and I head for the kitchen to wash those dirty dishes when the phone rings. "Hi," my friend says, "What have you been doing?"

"Well," I say, "watching my little one's favorite show with her and putting together a puzzle."

"Oh," she says, "so you're not busy today."

No, I think to myself, just busy making memories.

After lunch, Erica says, "Mommy, please play a game with me." Now I am looking at not only the breakfast dishes but also the lunch dishes piled in the sink. But again, I look at those big brown eyes and I remember how special it felt when my mom played games with me when I was a little girl.

"Sounds like fun," I answer, "but just one game." We play her favorite game, and I can tell she is delighting in every moment.

When the game ends, she says, "Please read me a story."

"Okay," I say, "but just one."

After reading her favorite story, I head for the kitchen to tackle those dishes. With the dishes now done, I start to fix supper. My willing little helper comes eagerly to the kitchen to help me with my task.

I'm running behind and thinking about how much faster I could do this if my sweet little one would just go play or watch a video, but her willingness to help and her eagerness to learn how to do what her mommy is doing melts my heart, and I say, "Okay, you can help," knowing it will probably take twice as long.

As supper is about ready, my husband comes home from work and asks, "What did you do today?"

I answer, "Let's see, we watched her favorite show and we played a game and read a book. I did the dishes and vacuumed; then with my little helper, I fixed supper."

"Great," he says, "I'm glad you didn't have a busy day today."

But I was busy, I think to myself, busy making memories.

After supper, Erica says, "Let's bake cookies."

"Okay," I say, "let's bake cookies."

After baking cookies, once again I am staring at a mountain of dishes from supper and cookie baking, but with the smell of warm cookies consuming the house, I pour us a glass of cold milk and fill a plate with warm cookies and take them to the table. We gather around the table eating cookies, drinking milk, talking and making memories.

No sooner have I tackled those dishes than my little sweetie comes tugging at my shirt, saying, "Could we take a walk?"

"Okay," I say, "let's take a walk." The second time around the block I'm thinking about the mountain of laundry that I need to get started on and the dust encompassing our home; but I feel the warmth of her hand in mine and the sweetness of our conversation as she enjoys my undivided attention, and I decide at least once more around the block sounds like a good idea.

When we get home, my husband asks, "Where have you been?"

"We've been making memories," I say.

A load in the wash and, my little girl all bathed and in her gown, the tiredness begins to creep in as she says, "Let's fix each other's hair."

I'm so tired! my mind is saying, but I hear my mouth saying, "Okay, let's brush each other's hair." With that task complete, she jumps up excitedly, "Let's paint each other's nails! Please!" So she paints my toenails, and I paint her fingernails, and we read a book while waiting for our nails to dry. I have to turn the pages, of course, because her fingernails are still drying.

We put away the book and say our prayers. My husband peeks his head in the door, "What are my girls doing?" he asks.

"Making memories," I answer.

"Mommy," she says, "will you lay with me until I fall asleep?"

"Yes," I say, but inside I'm thinking, I hope she falls asleep quickly so I can get up; I have so much to do.

About that time, two precious little arms encircle my neck as she whispers, "Mommy, nobody but God loves you as much as I do." I feel the tears roll down my cheeks as I thank God for the day we spent making memories.

~Tonna Canfield
Chicken Soup for the Mother & Daughter Soul

A Time for Memories

One balmy summer afternoon, I sat on an old blanket under a pine tree chatting with my mother. For years, we had been coming to this park for family picnics and gatherings, and my mother and I often sat in this same spot.

In recent years, we usually just talked about life, but sometimes we recalled events from my childhood. Like the time I was thirteen and had my first date, when Mother brought me to this spot under the tree and told me about the facts of life. Or the time a few years later, when my hair turned out pink for my senior prom and she'd held me while I cried. But the most special event that occurred next to this tree was when I told Mother I was getting married. Tears filled her eyes and this time I held her while she cried. She told me she was sad to lose her little girl but happy to see that I had turned into a beautiful young woman.

Over the years, we'd watched the pine trees in this park grow tall and straight until their needles seemed to touch the clouds. Each year of their growth seemed to match our increasingly close relationship and the deepening love we had for each other.

On this particular sunny afternoon, Mother and I sat quietly breathing in the scent of freshly mown grass. She was unusually solemn and took me by surprise when she asked me, "Who will you bring here after I'm gone?"

I gave her one of my arched-eyebrow inquiries, then smiled. After a few moments, when she didn't return my smile, I began to wonder what made her ask such a disturbing question. Mother picked up a blade of grass and began to shred it with her fingernail. I'd become well acquainted with my mother's habits, and this particular one indicated she had something serious on her mind.

For several minutes, we sat in silence gathering our thoughts. A couple of blue jays squawked nearby and an airplane flew overhead, but they didn't ease the awkward moment between us. Finally, I reached over and took my mother's hand in mine. "There's nothing you can't tell me, Mother," I said. "We will handle this together, like we always have."

She looked into my face, and her eyes filled with tears that spilled down her cheeks—cheeks that were alarmingly pale. Even before she said it, I knew what was coming. Mother was dying.

I held her tightly while she told me that her heart condition was worsening and couldn't be repaired. I think I had known for quite a while but had not been willing to admit it to myself. She'd had several heart attacks and, a few years ago, even open heart surgery. What I didn't know, and what she had kept from me, was that her condition wasn't improving. We talked about her options, which were few; we cried, held each other and wished for more time together.

That was many years ago. Mother died soon after that day, before my sons had a chance to know her. I still come to the park, but now I bring my boys. I still sit under that same sturdy pine tree on an old blanket and talk to my sons of family picnics, gatherings and the grandmother they never knew. Just as my mother did with me, I tell my children about their youthful antics and praise them for their accomplishments as young adults. We come to this special place to create our own memories—memories that I know would make my mother smile with pride.

Not long ago my oldest son wanted to come to the park and talk, so we came and sat under our tree. He hemmed and hawed for a few minutes, then he finally told me he was getting married. I cried tears of joy as my son hugged me—his hug a rare and special treat. I told him how proud I was of the man he had become.

As I sat there that cool April afternoon soaking up the sun and the smell of freshly mown grass, I felt I had come full circle under this giant pine tree. Holding my son in my arms, I was happy for him, just the way I knew my mother had been happy for me all those years ago when I told her I was getting married.

Looking over my son's shoulder, I saw that several young pine saplings had been planted recently. As these trees grow straight and tall, I thought, will the lives of my family continue to grow with them? I wanted to share this spot with my grandchildren, too.

The branches above were swaying in the breeze and in them I heard a whispering voice: Who will you bring here when I'm gone? It was my mother's voice, and I tightened my arms around my son.

~Sharon Wright
Chicken Soup for the Mother's Soul 2

Picking Marshmallows

Sweet, wild berries plucked from roadside patches are a delightful side benefit of camping. Each summer, my husband Bob and I would send the kids off with their little metal buckets, and the next day we would all enjoy the fruits of their labor: raspberry pancakes turned on the grill, or firm blackberries to dot a hot cooked-on-the-campfire, peanut-butter sandwich.

The children looked forward to picking. We could usually find just about anything, from blueberries in early summer to raspberries and blackberries in August. Every year—except one.

"There's nothing around here to pick!" five-year-old Julie complained, poking a stick into the dying fire one late summer evening.

The season had been too dry; what few blackberries were left on the bushes were hard as marbles.

"Yeah, I looked all over," added four-year-old Brian. "Wish there was something."

That night, after the kids were zipped into their sleeping sacks and I was sure they weren't awake, I handed Bob a bag of large marshmallows and I grabbed a bag of the miniatures.

"Get the lantern and follow me," I said. "We're going to make a memory."

"What?" He looked puzzled.

I told him about the kids' campfire conversation and Bob grinned, "Let's go!"

The next morning over pancakes, I said, "Kids, I think you're going to have something to pick today."

"Really!" Julie's eyes shone. "What?"

"What?" echoed Brian.

"Marshmallows," I said, as though I'd said it every summer. "Last night Daddy and I walked down toward the lake, and it looks as though they're just about ready to pick. It's a good thing we're here now. They only come out one day a year."

Julie looked skeptical, and Brian giggled. "You're silly, Mom! Marshmallows come in bags from the store."

I shrugged. "So do blackberries, but you've picked those, haven't you? Somebody just puts them in bags."

"Daddy, is that true?" he demanded.

Bob was very busy turning pancakes. "Guess you'll just have to go find out for yourself," he answered.

"Okay!"

They were off in a flurry, little metal buckets reflecting the morning sun.

"You nut," Bob said to me, laughing. "It won't work."

"Be a believer," I answered.

Minutes later, our two excited children rushed into the clearing.

"Look! I got some that were just babies!" Julie held up a miniature.

"I picked the big ones!" said Brian. "Boy, I want to cook one! Light the fire, Daddy, quick!"

"All right, all right, settle down." Bob winked at me. "They won't spoil." He lit some small sticks while the kids ran for their hot dog forks.

"Mine will be better because they're so little," predicted Julie. Brian shrugged, mashing two large ones on his fork.

We waited for the culinary verdict.

"Wow!" Brian's eyes rounded with surprise. "These sure are better than those old ones in the bags!" He reached for another. "These are so good!"

"Of course," I said. "These are really fresh!"

Julie looked puzzled. "How come all those marshmallow bushes don't have the same kinds of leaves?"

"Just different kinds, that's all," I replied quickly. "Like flowers."

"Oh." She licked her fingers, seemingly satisfied with my answer. Then, studying the next marshmallow before she popped it into her mouth, she looked up with the sweetest smile and said softly, "We're so lucky that they bloomed today!"

~Nancy Sweetland
Chicken Soup for the Nature Lover's Soul

20

Oh, to Be Rich!

Not what we have, but what we use,
not what we see, but what we choose—
these are the things that mar or bless human happiness.
~Joseph Fort Newton

I lay on my bed, legs propped up against the white cinder block wall, desperately wishing my mother would call. But I remembered the last time I'd seen her, right before the train for Providence pulled out of the station, "You know how expensive it is to call," she said, then squeezed me tight and said goodbye.

This was my first birthday away from home, and I missed my mom, missed my sister, and most certainly missed the special pound cake my mother always made for my birthday. Since getting to college that year, I would watch jealously as the other freshmen received care packages from their parents on their birthdays—and even on ordinary days. Big boxes containing summer slacks and blouses, brownies and packages of M&M's and Snickers, things they needed and things they didn't. Instead of feeling thrilled about my upcoming eighteenth birthday, I felt empty. I wished my mom would send me something, too, but I knew that she couldn't afford presents or the postage. She had done her best with my sister and me—raising us by herself. The simple truth was, there just was never enough money.

But that didn't stop her from filling us with dreams. "You can be anything you want to be," she would tell us. "Politicians, dancers, writers—you just have to work for it, you have to get an education."

For a long time, because of my mother's resourcefulness, I didn't realize that we were poor. She did so much with so little. She owned and took care of our house, practically nursing the forty-year-old pipes and oil furnace to keep us warm throughout the cold winters. She clothed and fed us. She found ways to get us scholarships so that we could take violin, piano and viola lessons from some of the best teachers in Philadelphia. She never missed an opportunity to have a tête-à-tête with our schoolteachers, and she attended all our plays and musical performances. My mother had high hopes for my sister and me. She saw the way out of poverty for us was education. We didn't play with the other children on the street, didn't jump double-dutch or stay out late on the porch laughing and talking with our neighbors. We were inside doing our homework and reading books. She sat with us while we did our work and taught us how to learn what she didn't know by plowing through the World Book Encyclopedia or visiting the library. And she did it all on eight hundred dollars a month.

I have vivid memories of Mom sitting with us on the concrete steps out back, under the far-reaching branches of the sycamore tree. Her voice would float up as she recited, "I think that I shall never see, a poem as lovely as a tree," or "We are climbing Jacob's ladder." Then she would hug us. I can still feel the sense of safety that washed over me like warm water. I felt my chest expand with joy as I listened to her voice close to my ear saying how she yearned us into being: "I told your dad, 'I've already got sons, now I need girls.' And within five years, he gave me not one, but both of you."

But what a struggle it was for her.

"Please, Mom, can we go to the movies?" we'd beg.

"No, we can watch a movie at home," she'd say, turning to channel 10.

"Can't we get nicer pants than these ugly green things?" we'd say as we went through the black plastic bag filled with hand-me-downs from our cousins.

"These will do you fine for now," Mom would say.

"Why can't I have money to buy french fries after school?" I would plead, my nostrils full with the remembered smell of sizzling grease and freshly salted potatoes.

"No, you don't need that mess. Besides, I've made split-pea soup with carrots and potatoes."

She never bought anything that she could make herself, and only for emergencies did she tap the spotless credit she maintained at Sears and at Strawbridge & Clothier, a Philadelphia, family-run business based in Center City.

I felt our lack most deeply after Christmas, when the other kids talked about the new games and expensive outfits they had found tucked under their live Christmas trees. I didn't mention our silver tree that we unpacked and repacked every year, or that there were only a couple of items for me under the tree: some books, socks, maybe a pair of shoes that I needed. And because my dad wasn't around, Mom pressed me into service—I would wrap my younger sister's gifts so that she could wake up excited, believing that Santa had left goodies for her on the floor beneath the tree.

Thanks to my mom's sacrifices and big dreams, I'd made it to the Ivy League: Brown University in Providence, Rhode Island. Yet I was afraid that I wouldn't measure up to the other students. They seemed to exude confidence and the smell of money. I felt so lost, so far away, as if my mom had said, "Well, if you're old enough to go six hours away, you're old enough to take care of yourself."

My roommate joined me on the bed. "Hey. After we study, we'll go to Campus Center and get ice cream and cake." I nodded, closed my eyes and imagined the cake my mom would have made. She would take out her stand-up mixer and the chrome bowl, then add the butter that she'd let sit out until it was soft. She would pour in the sharp sugar grains in a narrow stream. Mmm. I could see the golden yellow of each of the twelve eggs, swallowed under the rapid blur of the spinning beaters, and I could almost smell the vanilla and nutmeg filling the house while the cake baked.

As I daydreamed, there was a knock on the door. My roommate opened it to find a deliveryman asking for me. He handed her a large rectangular box, which she carefully placed on the desk near my bed. "Open it." I did, and inside was a vanilla cake with chocolate frosting. In icing were the words: Happy Birthday, Sande! Love, Mom and Rosalind. My skin tingled with excitement, as if my mom were right there hugging me close. How had she managed to afford it? I felt as if I were back on the steps with her, safe and secure while she sang and told me how much she loved having me in her life. I ran out to the hall and knocked on my dormmates' doors. "Birthday cake," I called. As I cut cake for the ten students gathered in my room, then watched their faces as they ate, I didn't need to eat to feel both full and rich inside.

~Sande Smith
Chicken Soup for the Single Parent's Soul

21

Whittled Away

Could we change our attitude, we should not only see life differently,
but life itself would come to be different.
~Katherine Mansfield

"Connie Ann!" Mom caught the piece of tinfoil in midair. "We might need this next time we bake potatoes. You know better than that."

Ashamed, Connie Ann gave a gusty, seven-year-old sigh and retreated from the kitchen. Yes, she knew better. The Whittle family creed demanded that everything, even a piece of foil, be used again... and again. Especially now, with the divorce and all.

And she knew about other things, too. Like salvaging buttons and zippers from old clothes to use on the new ones her mom sewed. Like gagging on dust clouds each time someone emptied the vacuum bag instead of throwing it away. Like walking everywhere when most of her friends rode in cars. Of course, the Whittles didn't own a car; Dad had left them the Pumpkin.

The bronze-colored, short-bed pickup couldn't hold all ten children at once, so the Whittle children walked. To school. To church. To get a gallon of milk. Mom said it was simpler than buying a car. Besides, they got exercise and saved on gas at the same time.

Mom said she liked doing things the simple way. In fact, that's how she got rid of the Christmas tree, too.

Without Dad there to haul it out that year, she puzzled over the problem. "How will we get rid of this monstrosity?"

She circled the tree.

"It seems like a waste to just throw it away. It should be good for something, shouldn't it?"

Connie Ann nodded in agreement, knowing Whittles never wasted anything.

"It still smells good." Mom poked both arms through the brittle needles to heft its weight. "Hmmm." Her brow furrowed a bit, and she glanced over her shoulder where coals still glowed in the fireplace.

"Our gas bill has been sky high." She scooted the tree from its nook in front of the window. "If I just push it in ... a bit at a time ... as it burns ...." She wrestled the tree to the floor.

"Connie Ann, you grab that end while I drag the bottom."

Wincing from the pain and prickles of the browning evergreen, they struggled to get their handholds.

"What could be simpler?" Mom half-shoved it across the floor with a grunt. "A fragrant room freshener," she tugged at the trunk, "and free heat," she gave one final push, "and we get rid of this thing."

With a precise aim, she poked the tippy-top of the tree right into the middle of the glowing embers.

KA-VOOOOM!

In a roar as loud as a sonic boom, the entire tree—from its bushy head to its board-shod feet—burst into one giant flame. Screaming, Mom dropped the trunk, and they both jumped across the room.

WHOOOOSH!

All the branches disappeared. In one big breath. Just like magic. Nothing was left of the Christmas tree except a charred trunk, some scraggly Charlie Brown twigs—and a trailing, tree-shaped shadow of white ashes.

For one long, bug-eyed moment, Mom caught her breath. Then she pulled Connie Ann close to search for burns and swept a glance over herself for singes. And she examined the carpet for damage. Finding none, she slowly shook her head in wonder.

After a stunned silence, Mom brushed her hands together effi-ciently. "Well! I guess that takes care of that."

Then she picked from among the newly formed crowd of wide-eyed, jabbering children.

"You and you and you," Mom pointed at the oldest, "help me haul this tree outside. At least now it's manageable."

Connie Ann nodded in agreement. She knew how much Mom liked things kept simple. It was, after all, the Whittle way.

~Carol McAdoo Rehme
Chicken Soup for the Soul: The Book of Christmas Virtues

A Second Chance

grew up as a foster child from the age of eight. Unlike most children I knew, I never really had a biological mother. I never got to experience the unconditional love and wonderment a mother gives her child. So growing up was a bit harder on me than on most other children. A drastic change came suddenly when I was in the eleventh grade. I was now in my second foster home and had been there for the past five years. I was surrounded by a warm and caring family. But still something pained me deeply. I felt "out of place." I wasn't her birth child, so I remained distant, not allowing myself to love her as much as I could.

In one night, things changed for the better and forever. I was doing homework while waiting for the rest of the family to return home from their events. It was a daily routine. I spent most of my nights by myself finding things to keep me busy. As I was reading a paragraph for English I heard the closing of the back door and my foster mom calling for me. I walked into the kitchen where she was holding a hardcover children's book that she had borrowed from work. "I want you to read this," she said excitedly. "It's absolutely wonderful." She handed me the book, and I glanced at it with curiosity: *The Kissing Hand* by Audrey Penn. I was just about to question her when she smiled at me. "Trust me. You'll love it!"

Reluctantly I grabbed a stool and made myself comfortable at the counter and began to read the book. I thoroughly enjoyed it. It was a touching story of a raccoon mom who places a kiss in the palm of her child's hand to remind him that if ever he should get scared he just has to press his Kissing Hand to his cheek. That way he can always remember that his mommy loves him. I wondered why my foster mom asked me to read it. But I shrugged off the unknown answer and headed back to my room to complete my unfinished homework.

Later that night, I was sitting at the same spot where I had read the book and talking with Mom when suddenly she did something totally unexpected. She ever so gently took my hand and put a warm loving kiss in the center of my palm. She then quietly closed my hand and held it between hers and spoke words that I had dreamt of hearing for so long. "Whenever you get scared or sad, remember that your mommy loves you."

As the tears began to form in my eyes, I began to understand, and so I smiled a smile that touched the very depth of my once-wounded heart. I truly do have a mother. No, she wasn't biological, but she was mine just the same.

~Cynthia Blatchford
Chicken Soup for the Mother & Daughter Soul

23

Buried Treasure

No act of kindness, no matter how small, is ever wasted.

~Aesop

My mother, Eloisa Ferrer y Uria, was born in Trinidad, Cuba, during the Depression. It was a place and time where nothing was wasted. During her childhood, containers of all sorts were hoarded and reused. Broken clothespins and scraps of cloth were made into toys. The silk threads used to tie cement sacks were crocheted into beautiful bedspreads and shawls. And any bare patch of soil could be a garden. In the central courtyard of her family's old Spanish-style home, her father planted mangoes, orchids and chili peppers, filling every nook with beautiful and useful plants.

On Valentine's Day 1947, my mother met Martin Mondrus, a visiting artist from Los Angeles who had seen photographs of picturesque Trinidad and had decided to paint its colonial architecture. They fell in love and were married.

When my mother moved to California with my father, her thrifty habits persisted. She scrubbed out empty bleach bottles and cut holes in them to make birdhouses and planters. Balls of string became embroidered ornaments. Bits of cloth turned into elegant patchwork quilts and garments.

Outdoors, abalone shells and river rocks were set into home-made stepping stones. The decorative pathways wound through a tangled mass of wild castor beans. There, my mother put to work the gardening lessons she had learned from her father in Cuba. Gradually, she transformed the wilderness, tackling the dense clay soil of Los Angeles with shovels and hoes. The steep hillside that served as our backyard was transformed into a beautifully terraced garden filled with avocado, almond and guava trees, roses, nasturtiums, amaryllis and cymbidium orchids.

For years, as she worked in the garden, my mother would unearth abandoned toys. There were tiny plastic soldiers holding broken weapons, miniature cowboys mounted on horses with smashed legs and glossy, rainbow-hued marbles streaked with hairline cracks.

Most people would have tossed these damaged playthings into the trash; my mother saw them as precious. When my sister and I teased her about saving someone else's trash, she shook her head gently and smiled.

"Just think," she marveled, "this house has a history. Somebody's children grew up here." It was easy for her to imagine adventurous little boys building cardboard forts in their castor bean wilderness.

With the mud lovingly wiped off, the salvaged toys went into a shoe box on a shelf above the washing machine. Year after year, they took up space and gathered dust, but my mother just couldn't get rid of them. She knew that a child had once treasured the shabby soldiers, cowboys and marbles. That made them important enough to save.

One day, long after my sister and I had grown up and left home, a middle-aged stranger knocked on my parents' door. My mother greeted him. He introduced himself with some embarrassment.

"I grew up in this house," he explained apologetically. "I'm in town for my father's funeral, and I've been feeling nostalgic. Would you mind if I looked around outside?"

My mother sighed with sympathy and relief.

"I believe I have something that belongs to you," she said. She went to the back of the house, unearthed the box and handed it to the stranger. Puzzled, he lifted the lid—and then gasped in surprise at the bits and pieces of his boyhood so lovingly preserved.

Overwhelmed by the rush of memories, his eyes misted over. He could barely stammer his thanks.

Mother just smiled. She had always known that, sooner or later, her garden's buried treasures would be needed again. Like dormant seeds, the memories held in those tiny fragments of plastic and glass were just waiting for the right time to sprout.

~Margarita Engle
Chicken Soup for the Gardener's Soul

24

The Gypsy Angel

Let us not be too particular.
It is better to have old second-hand diamonds than none at all.
~Mark Twain

It was 1993, the beginning of another great summer at the lake. My fifty-five-year-old mother, Helen, who had just recovered from a partial mastectomy and many months of chemotherapy and radiation, announced that she was now the proud owner of a boat.

I smiled and shook my head because I never knew what my adventurous and free-spirited mother would be up to next. I remember one Christmas she told her family and friends that all she wanted was power tools so she could learn how to build things. When she initially told us she wanted a boat and a friend had one for sale that needed a little bit of work, I was worried. I had seen my mother drive our wave runners at a very fast speed. When she announced that it was a slow-moving pontoon boat, I was relieved—until I saw it. The conglomeration of metal made her idea of "a little bit of work" a huge understatement. I did not see how this thing was going to float, much less run. Momma insisted that with a good cleaning and a few repairs, the boat would look brand new. I, on the other hand, didn't think it would make much difference, but I didn't have the heart to tell her.

After taking the boat to a local car wash and hosing it down, we took it to a neighbor who serviced boats. With the repairs completed and the addition of a new canopy, I must admit it looked pretty good.

But looking at my mother's face, you would have thought she was the owner of a millionaire's yacht.

The next step was taking it out on the lake and seeing how it would run. I was still apprehensive as we backed it down the ramp and put it in the water for the first time. We held our breath as Momma put the key into the ignition and turned it. The first three tries, nothing, but on the fourth try, it came alive with a low humming of the motor. We started venturing out of the cove and onto the open lake. Before long, we were soaring across the water with the wind softly blowing on our faces. The sound of the water slapping against the boat was like music in the air.

I was in awe of my mother, and in my eyes there wasn't anything she couldn't do. As I looked at her behind the wheel of her new boat, her hair finally growing back, I saw she was absolutely glowing, and I knew she was in her element. Later that evening, we sat under the stars, trying to pick the perfect name for her new treasure. We tossed around a few and finally decided on the Gypsy Angel. Momma had collected angels for many years, and we all knew that she was part gypsy, because at the drop of a hat she would be off to a new place to add another experience to her life.

Many mornings at the break of dawn, Momma would wake me and her small grandbabies and we would head out to check the limb lines that she had baited the night before. We were still in our pajamas, mind you, and were assured we would come right back before it got too light outside, which was never the case. We did eventually come back to the house, but only to eat lunch, change into our bathing suits, and of course grab more bait, and then we would head right back out on the Gypsy. It took us to places on the lake that we hadn't before discovered, and we would get ourselves so deep in some of the coves that we didn't know how we were going to get out. Somehow the Gypsy Angel never failed us.

During one incident, Momma had set out some new limb lines, and we went to check them the following morning after it had stormed all night. As we were nearing one of the limb lines, Momma noticed that the line was frantically moving. She maneuvered the Gypsy

Angel over as close as she could, but the branches on the trees were very low, and with the water being up so high from all the rain, she couldn't quite reach the line. Momma knew she had a big one, and she wasn't about to leave it behind. I heard a big splash and looked to find Momma out in the water swimming with a knife in her teeth, which she used to cut the line. What a sight: her swimming back to the Gypsy Angel with a huge catfish by her side. I hurriedly grabbed the camera and took a picture of her holding that eighteen-pounder over her head, her eyes gleaming with excitement. Her grandchildren must have thought they had the craziest grandmother in the world.

As I recollect all the times we stayed overnight on the Gypsy Angel and shared so many magical moments among a grandmother, her children and grandchildren, it came as a shock when Momma decided she should sell it. She couldn't afford to keep up with the repairs that the old boat needed. She promised us that when the time was right, she would buy a newer one.

As that glorious summer ended, the Gypsy Angel was sold. When the new buyer came to get her, we told him all the wonderful memories that had been made because of her. With our voices cracking we pleaded, "Please take good care of her." I know he must have felt somewhat guilty for having to take her away from us. As we watched from our front porch, Gypsy rolled down the country dirt road, out of our sight and out of our lives forever, leaving us all with broken hearts. We mourned for days. The vacant spot by the dock was too painful to look at. Little did I realize how much Gypsy Angel would come to mean to us. She nourished our souls and helped us establish a lifetime bond with each other.

When I look back, I am so thankful that my courageous mother had the desire to become the owner of a pontoon boat. The following year Momma started feeling pain again. After many tests and a bone scan, the doctors confirmed our worst fear: the cancer was back. It had metastasized and was spreading fast. In the short months I was able to take care of her, we talked endlessly about our escapades on the Gypsy Angel. Her eyes would light up with each memory. On June 4, 1999, I said goodbye to the most adventurous and free-spirited soul I had ever known, my best friend, my mentor, my mother—my Gypsy Angel.

~Lucinda Shouse
Chicken Soup for the Fisherman's Soul

Moms Know Best

Maternal Insights and Lessons

Life is a succession of lessons which must be lived to be understood.
~Helen Keller

25

A New Home

Happiness is a warm puppy.
~Charles M. Schulz

"Mom, watch out!" my daughter Melissa screamed as a drenched brown pooch charged under our van. Slamming my foot on the brakes, we jerked to a stop. Stepping out into the freezing rain, we hunched down on opposite sides of the van, making kissing noises to coax the little dog—who, miraculously, I hadn't hit—to us. The shivering pup jumped into Melissa's arms and then onto her lap once she sat down again in the heated van.

We were on our way home from Melissa's sixth-grade basketball game. Her once-white shirt with the red number 7 was now covered in dirty black paw prints. I stared at the mess as she wrapped her shirt around the small dog.

"That shirt will never come clean!"

"Well, at least we saved his life," she frowned as she cuddled him. "Running through all those cars he could have been killed."

She continued petting him. "He's so cute. And he doesn't have a collar. Can we keep him?"

I knew how she felt. I loved animals myself—especially dogs. But I also knew the mess they made. Dogs dig through the garbage. They chew up paper, shoes and anything else they can fit in their mouths. Not to mention the little piles and puddles they make when you're trying to housebreak them. I didn't need a dog. I loved the clean, bright house we had recently moved into, and I wanted to keep my new house looking just that—new.

I glanced at the ball of brown fur and the black mask outlining his wide, wondering eyes. She's right. He is cute.

The smell of wet dog escalated with the burst of heat coming from the vents, bringing me to my senses. I turned the heat down and shook my head. "Melissa, we've been through this before. I told all four of you kids when we moved into the new house: absolutely no pets."

As we pulled into the drive, she said, "But Mom, it's the middle of February. He'll freeze out here."

I glanced at the pup licking Melissa's fingers. "Okay," I decided. "We'll give him a bath, keep him for the night and call the animal shelter tomorrow."

Still frowning, Melissa nodded and slid out of the van. Carrying the dog in her arms, she entered the house. By the time I reached the door, the news was already out.

"We've got a new puppy!" Robert, Brian and Jeremiah chorused.

"I'm afraid not," I said, as I took off my shoes. "We're only keeping him overnight."

Wiggling out of Melissa's arms, the pup scampered across the room and jumped up on my couch.

"Get down!" I shouted, pointing my finger at him and toward the floor.

He licked his nose remorsefully and sat there shaking.

"Mom, you're scaring him." Melissa scooped him into her arms. "C'mon, boy, I'll take you to my room."

"Ah-ah," I corrected, "bath first."

All four kids crowded around the puppy in the bathroom. I listened over the running water as each became excited over every splash the dog made. Their giggles brought a smile to my face. Maybe it wouldn't be such a bad idea to have a dog.

I glanced around the kitchen with its shiny black and white tile floor. Picturing a dog dish, with food and water heaping into a sloshing puddle of goo, I turned toward the living room. With this messy weather, I envisioned my pale-blue carpeting "decorated" with tiny black paw prints. Not to mention the shedding, fleas and all the other things a dog can bring. I shook my head. A dog will ruin this place.

After his bath, Melissa brought him out wrapped in one of our good white towels. He looked like a drowned rat, except for his big, brown puppy-dog eyes. The boys raced around the kitchen getting food and water.

The water sloshed back and forth in the bowl. "Be careful, Jeremiah," I warned. "You're gonna spill—" When Jeremiah heard my voice he stopped with a sudden jerk. Water splashed onto his face and down the front of shirt and blue jeans, soaking the floor.

I ran to get towels. When I returned, I watched in horror as the pup tramped through the water. Even after his bath, his feet were still dirty and left muddy little prints all over my kitchen floor. "Wipe his feet and put him in your room, Melissa. Now!"

Melissa snatched the dog up, with the boys traipsing at her heels. I sighed as I wiped up the mud and water. After a few minutes, the floor shined like new, and laughter erupted from Melissa's bedroom.

My husband, John, came in from work moments later. "What's so funny?" he asked after he kissed me on the cheek.

"A dog."

"A dog?" he asked, surprised. "We have a dog?"

"Not by choice," I explained. "It ran under the van. And of course I couldn't just leave him in the middle of the street."

John smiled. "What happened to no pets?"

"I told them he's going tomorrow."

After John joined the kids he came back out. "You know, he is really cute."

"Yeah, I know." He didn't have to convince me; my resolve was already slipping.

The next morning, the kids mauled the dog with hugs and tears. "Can't we keep him?" they sobbed. I watched how he gently and tenderly licked each one as if to comfort them.

"I promise we'll take care of him," Melissa said.

"Yeah, and I'll water him," Jeremiah added. I smiled, remembering the incident the night before. "But I won't fill his dish so full next time."

How could I say no? He's housebroken. He's cute. And he's great with the kids.

"We'll see," I said, as they scooted out the door for school. "But first, I'll have to call the dog pound to make sure no one is looking for him."

Their faces lit up as they trotted down the drive. With John already at work, the pup and I watched from the door as the four kids skipped down the street. Once they turned the corner, I grabbed the phone book and found the number for the animal shelter.

The lady at the shelter informed me that no one had reported a brown dog missing. However, she instructed me to put an ad in the local paper about him for three days, and if no one responded, we could legally keep him for our own. I called the newspaper and placed the ad. Although I had mixed feelings, mostly I hoped his owners would claim him.

Each day, the kids would ask the same question, "Did anyone call?" And each day it was always the same answer: "Nope."

By the third day, the dog and I had spent so much time together that he followed me around the house. If I sat on the couch, he'd jump in my lap. If I folded clothes, he'd lie by the dryer. If I made dinner, he'd sit by the refrigerator. Even when I went to bed, he'd follow, wanting to cuddle up with me.

"Looks like we have to come up with a name," I said Sunday morning at breakfast.

The kids cheered and threw out some names. When we returned from church, I played the messages on our answering machine, my heart sinking when I heard: "I think you may have my dog."

After speaking with the lady, I realized that Snickers was indeed her dog. She explained she'd be over to get him within the hour. As we sat around the table, picking at the pot roast, tears flooded our plates like a river. Even I had grown attached to this sweet little dog.

When the lady arrived, I met her at the door. I clenched a wet tissue in my hands and invited her in. She took in the scene: four mournful children sitting in a huddle around the little dog and petting him, while Snickers, perched on Melissa's lap, licked her tears away.

After a long moment, she said, "I want you to have him. I can see you love him and we already have another dog."

I gave her a hug while the kids cheered in the background.

Snickers has definitely left his mark on our house. Still, I wouldn't trade his muddy paw prints for anything—not even the nicest-looking house in the world! For, although he makes little messes sometimes, he has filled our hearts with love. Before Snickers came into our lives, we had a new house. Now we have a new home.

~Elisabeth A. Freeman
Chicken Soup for the Dog Lover's Soul

26

Only Love Lasts Forever

esterday, after telling my brother, Rhys, and me to stop play-ing like wild animals in the house for what she said was the thousandth time, Mom went to take a bath. That's when it happened. We were playing around, bopping each other with pil-lows, when one slipped from my brother's grasp and smashed the glass dome on the coffee table, shattering it into a zillion pieces!

With her supersonic hearing, my mom heard the tremendous crash and then the sound of glass hitting the tile. Wasting no time, she came flying into the room to find out what had happened. I was sure my brother and I were dead meat and she was going to start yell-ing at us, but instead she just knelt by the pieces and began to cry.

This made Rhys and me feel pretty awful. We went over and put our arms around her, and she explained to us why she was so upset. Under the shattered glass dome was a white porcelain rose. Dad had given it to her on their first wedding anniversary. He had said that if he ever forgot to bring flowers for an anniversary in the future, Mom was to look at that one. It was like their love—it would last a lifetime.

Now it lay chipped on the floor, one petal gone. We began cry-ing, too, and offered to glue it for her. She said that wouldn't really fix it. Now that it had been broken, the value of the "limited edition" had lessened. We got our piggy banks out to pay for it, but Mom replied that to her the rose represented Dad's love and could never truly be restored.

As Mom slowly began to pick up the mess, we tried everything we could think of to cheer her up, but even our best funny faces didn't work. Mom just looked away. Rhys and I were even really nice to each other, which always makes her eyes twinkle, but she didn't seem to notice. The tears kept coming down her cheeks as she cleaned up the mess.

After everything was picked up and Mom was on her way back to the bath, I stopped her in the hall and said I had something important to tell her. She tried to go around me, replying "Not now," but I wouldn't let her by. I told her, "I want to say something very important; it's a rule of God."

I put both hands on her shoulders and told her, "All things can be broken, Mom; everything breaks sometime. The only thing that isn't like that is love. It's the only thing that can never be broken."

Mom hugged me very tightly then and finally smiled. She said that I was pretty wise and understood some things that even much older people didn't!

After dinner that night, we had a family meeting. We discussed mistakes and the importance of learning from them. Mom glued the petal back onto the rose. The tiny petal now had a thin, almost invisible line of glue. Then Mom softly said, "Even though other people have 'limited edition' roses, mine is truly unique. Its tiny flaw reminds me of something more important: the realization that only love lasts forever."

~Denise and Rett Ackart
Chicken Soup for the Preteen Soul

27

Lessons
My Mother Taught Me

Each day of our lives we make deposits in the memory banks of our children.
~Charles R. Swindoll, *The Strong Family*

It was Christmas time in Puerto Rico. A lady, a friend of the lady and a little girl were among the many people with a long list of gifts to buy for Three Kings Day.

They were shopping in an elegant, large mall. With life's great irony, this luxurious building was located next to one of the island's poorest government housing projects.

After a long, exhausting morning of gift buying, the three of them decided to get a bite to eat. They went to a small cafeteria on the first floor of the fancy mall. The very small eating place was packed with people carrying bags with assorted gifts. The lady, the friend of the lady and the little girl were standing in line choosing between empanadillas, alcapurrias, rellenos de papas and more, when they heard a sweet and shy voice. It was coming from a skinny, dirty, dark-skinned boy wearing a ragged blue shirt. He was extending his small, empty hand toward the lady. He said:

"Señora, I am hungry. Could you spare some coins so I can buy some food?"

Without a moment of hesitation, the lady looked inside her huge black purse and grabbed as many coins as she could fit in both hands.

Without counting, she placed the coins in the boy's outstretched hand. The lady always gave, so this action did not take the little girl by surprise. She was used to the lady's acts of kindness. As the coins were being passed from the lady's hand to the boy's hand, the little girl continued debating to herself between having a bocadillo or a pizza empanadilla. The friend of the lady did not find the lady's behavior as common as the little girl did. The friend of the lady called the lady foolish and naive.

"Do you really believe that the boy was hungry?" she said. "Do you really believe that right now he is spending that money on food? How can you be so trusting?"

By this time, with orange trays full of food in their hands, the lady, the friend of the lady and the little girl were trying to get through all the hungry Christmas shoppers toward the only empty table in the small cafeteria. Once they were seated, the lady turned to her friend:

"So what if he does not spend the money on food?" she said. "It's Christmastime. Let him get a brand new toy or a comic book if that's what he wants."

The friend of the lady continued telling the lady how she still considered her foolish and naive.

Her reprimands were interrupted by the skinny, dirty, dark-skinned boy wearing a ragged blue shirt. In one hand, he was carrying an orange tray with a white paper plate on it. On the plate were a small chicken leg and a buttered biscuit. He was extending his other hand for them to see a dime, one nickel and two pennies. Then he said with his sweet, shy voice:

"Señora, I did not have enough money for a soda, see? Can you spare just a little more?"

With a wonderful, bright smile on her face, the lady got out of her seat and walked with the boy to the food counter. There she bought him a large soda, French fries and a piece of chocolate cake for dessert.

Years later, this episode is still fresh on the little girl's mind.

I am that little girl. I do not give skinny, dirty, dark-skinned boys money when they ask for some. I walk to the closest food place and buy them the whole meal, French fries and all. You see, I am afraid that I will not give these boys enough money for a soda and they might not have the courage to come back for more.

These boys owe those meals to a lady once called foolish and naive.

I am proud to call that lady "Mom."

~Marta A. Oppenheimer
Chicken Soup for the Latino Soul

28

A Forgiving Heart

*The heart of a mother is a deep abyss at the bottom of which
you will always find forgiveness.*
~Honoré de Balzac

This morning, I was in a hurry to get home after running some errands. As I made the right turn into my neighborhood, which is slightly obscured by shrubs, a small boy in a bright yellow T-shirt flashed across the street in front of my car. He stood on the pedals of his red bike, legs pumping, oblivious to me—or any other danger—secure in a boy's invincible immortality.

He passed inches, literally, from my front bumper. I slammed on my brakes, a meaningless physical reflex since he was already long gone. I was shaking, and it took a minute to catch my breath. In one terrible instant, that boy's life surely could have ended. His parents would have been in pain forever, and my own life would have been a nightmare.

I continued down the street, recalling the image of the boy's face. Magnified by my fright, I could clearly picture his eyes wide with a dazzling mix of bravado and fear, a bright haughty smile lit by yet another triumph over the dull world of adult concern. He was so startlingly energetic, so fearless that my shock at very nearly killing him was almost immediately replaced by anger bordering on fury.

Churning with rage—at his carelessness, not mine—I went home. The agitation my near-miss brought upon me troubled me most of the day. Then, at twilight, I remembered Mikey.

Growing up, Mike Roberts was my best buddy. My father was a doctor in a small Ohio River town, and my parents and Mike's parents were close friends. In fact, his house was one vacant lot away from my father's clinic.

Mikey, as we all called him, was adventurous and daring. His mother, Judy, was easy on us kids and made the best peanut butter cookies in the universe. They never locked their doors, and I had the run of their house.

One Friday, my mother planned to go to Cincinnati to shop and told me I should spend the day at the Roberts's house. Judy was expecting me. I was not to eat too many cookies or ride my bike in the road.

When my mother left that morning, I set off on my bike to the Roberts' house. I was about fifty yards from the turn that led to Mikey's street when I heard a sound that I can still hear sometimes in dreams. It was the fierce squeal of tires when you put on the brakes really hard. It seemed to last for a very long time, although I am sure, in retrospect, that the noise died quickly. And then there was the harsh sound of metal crushing. In a flash, I took off on my bike and rounded the corner at full speed.

There was a truck in the road, turned almost sideways. Beyond the front fender was Mikey's red Schwinn, folded so that it seemed to be just half a bike, two tires now flattened against each other.

Mikey was lying on the grass, a great hulk of a man bent over him. I got off my bike, dropped it, and ran to where my friend lay, silent and still on a carpet of leaves. At that instant, the front door of his house opened and his mother came out. I don't think I have ever seen anyone run so fast. At the same time, a gurney appeared from my father's clinic followed by my dad and an orderly.

Instantly, there was quite a crowd. Judy knelt at Mikey's head and passed her hand gently over his forehead. My father told Judy not to move her son and bent to examine him. The truck driver sat down heavily a few feet away. He must have weighed over two hundred pounds. He had great round shoulders and a thick neck that had deep circles of wrinkles that shone with sweat. He had on blue coveralls and a red plaid shirt.

Now he sat on the grass like some stunned bull. His head rested on his drawn-up knees and his shoulders shook, but I don't think he was crying.

I stared at the man, trying to make him feel how mad I was. He had probably not been paying attention, I thought. Not an unfamiliar failing among the adults I knew. They often seemed careless to me, and this one had hurt my friend. I wanted to hurt him back in some terrible way.

In a few minutes, Mikey was awake and crying. My father had him immobilized on a stretcher board and loaded onto the gurney. Judy held Mikey's hand, and they all moved away into the clinic's emergency entrance. I was left alone with the trucker who was now sitting with his head bowed on his crossed arms. His body was still shaking like he had a chill.

We sat in silence for what seemed a long time. Then Judy came out of the clinic's front entrance and walked over to us. She said that Mikey would be fine. It was only his arm. It could have been much worse.

I thought she surely would slap the driver or at least give him a severe talking to. But what she actually did astonished me. She told him to come with her into her house. "And you, too," she said to me.

She asked the driver his name and told him to sit by the fireplace and she would get some coffee. He raised his hand to wave her off but she brought coffee anyway, and milk and cookies for me. Stan, the driver, couldn't eat or drink. He sat in the blue armchair, filling it completely. From time to time, he would shake and Judy would put her arm around his shoulder and talk to him in her wonderful gentle voice, "It's not your fault. You weren't speeding. Mikey takes stupid risks, and I am so sorry about that. I'm just grateful he wasn't hurt badly. And I don't blame you. You shouldn't blame yourself, either."

I listened to her incredulously. How could she say such things to the man who'd nearly killed her son, my friend? What was the matter with her? Before long, she got the driver sort of put back together—at least that's how it looked to me—and he got up to leave.

As he reached the door he turned to her and said, "I have a boy, too. I know what it took for you to help me."

A Forgiving Heart: Maternal Insights and Lessons 87

Then, to add one more astonishment to the day, Judy stood on tiptoe and kissed him on the cheek.

I had never been able to understand how Judy could offer ease and comfort to a man who had very nearly killed her child... until today, when I turned the corner into my familiar neighborhood and came within inches of what surely would have been a terrible and irreversible act.

Still trying to shake the dread that had occupied my mind all day, I thought of Mikey's mother and that day in a long-ago autumn. And although there was no one there to comfort me, to tell me that I had not been at fault, that bad things do happen no matter how careful you are, the memory of that day reached across time to help me.

That one mother's empathy, like all other gifts of goodness, had never left the world, and it could be called upon to console and heal. And would continue to do so... perhaps forever.

~W. W. Meade
Chicken Soup for the Mother's Soul 2

29

Pink and Blue Makes... Green?

Children are the living messages we send to a time we will not see.
John W. Whitehead, The Stealing of America, 1983

It's come to my attention that there are two types of pregnant people in this world: those who find out the gender of their child as soon as they can and go around calling their stomach "Tommy" or "Jennifer" for the next nine months, and those who refuse to find out the gender of their child one nanosecond before the actual birth, no matter what.

Let me just stop right here a minute and say that I, in no way, advocate one choice over the other. I firmly believe it's a personal choice that should be left to the parents.

But, that said, what I don't understand is why the very same people who refuse to look at the sonogram screen in the doctor's office, are perfectly fine with relying on old wives' tales to predict their baby's gender.

Take, for instance, my friend Linda, who tried to find out what she was having by twirling a needle on a string over her stomach. "It's a girl," she announced gleefully over the phone. "The needle spun in circles."

She was so sure, in fact, that she painted the nursery pink and stenciled ballerina bunnies on the walls. But, as luck would have it, when she tried it again two months later, the needle moved in a straight line, mostly between the refrigerator and television set. And everyone knows what that means.

But that's not all. Once, when my friend Julie was pregnant with her second child, she heard she could tell what she was having if there was a white line above her top lip. "Can you come over," she said frantically over the phone, "I think I have a lip line. But I can't tell if it's really a line-line or a pale wrinkle or a milk mustache left over from the bowl of cereal I ate for breakfast."

The big drawback to this method was that, once we determined that it was, indeed, a bona fide line-line, we had absolutely no idea if that meant she was having a girl or a boy.

And, oh all right, then there was the time I tried the Chinese lunar calendar method. But just for the record I want you to know it's a highly respected system based on a complicated numerical combination of the father's birth year, lucky elements, planetary rotation and the number of his favorite local take-out place. (But I could be wrong about this last one.)

But what I didn't see coming was that to get an accurate result you need to be fairly good at math. So, after spending hours adding and subtracting cycle scores and percentages and all that, I came out with a bizarre triple negative number that's only been seen on university entrance exams and certain Wall Street corporate earning reports.

But, that's just the kind of answer I usually get whenever I try to walk on the mystical side of life.

The other day, my friend Linda, who's now six months pregnant, said to me over coffee, "I've tried everything. According to the needle test I'm having a boy, the lunar calendar says I'm having a girl, the heartbeat test falls somewhere between a boy and a girl, and the Drano test doesn't say anything at all, but it smells really, really bad," she sighed. "I don't know what to believe anymore."

"Then why don't you save yourself the trouble and just ask the doctor?" I asked.

"What?" she said. "And spoil the mystery? Every parent knows that the gender of your child is the one greatest mystery in the world. Why would I want to go and ruin it?"

Granted I could've mentioned that she was a person who had just mixed urine with Drano to see if it would make green.

But instead, I said simply, "You're right."

With pregnant women, sometimes that's the best way.

~Debbie Farmer
Chicken Soup for Every Mom's Soul

30

In Her Golden Eyes

One reason a dog can be such a comfort when you're feeling blue is that he doesn't try to find out why.
~Author Unknown

My six-year-old daughter, Mariah, held on to my hand as we walked through the animal shelter. We wanted to pick just the right puppy for her sister Vanessa's twelfth birthday. I scanned each cage, noticing all the pairs of needy brown eyes staring back at us. It was neediness for love and a happy home—things the girls and I also hungered for since their father and I had divorced.

"Here are our newest arrivals," the volunteer said. He led us to a cage where three puppies were sleeping. They were the size of small bear cubs with beautiful fur.

"What kind are they?" I asked, stooping down to take a closer look.

"They're chow mixes," the boy said. "I've never seen such awe-some-looking dogs."

My heart quickened as the pup in the middle suddenly yawned and looked up at us. She was breathtaking, with oversized paws and silvery-black wolf markings on her face. Most of all, it was her eyes that struck me. They were so gentle and sweet. As golden as her fur. Something told me that she was the one.

As long as I live, I'll never forget Vanessa's face when we surprised her with her new companion. It almost made the pain of the last several months disappear.

"I'm going to name her Cheyenne," Vanessa beamed.

In the coming days, Cheyenne accomplished exactly what I was hoping for. Instead of the children feeling homesick for the life we'd lost, they spent time playing with their new puppy. Instead of feeling depressed over missing their daddy, they romped and laughed for hours. It gave me hope that they would make this very difficult transition a bit better—if only something would help me do the same.

It was on a late April afternoon that things took a horrible turn. The girls were in the backyard playing with Cheyenne while I went to the store. When I got back home and pulled into the driveway, a pickup truck came speeding down our street. I got out of my car, keys in hand, and saw that Cheyenne had gotten loose. She ran past me in a blur.

"Cheyenne!" I called out. "No! Get back here!" But it was too late. She chased after the truck, caught up to the front tires, and was flipped in the air before landing with a thud on the side of the road.

Luckily, the vet was still open and they took her right in. I kept watching Cheyenne's side, willing her to keep breathing as the vet put her on the examining table.

"The front leg appears to be the worst of her injuries," he said, pinching between her toes with a silver clamp. "The nerves have been damaged and she doesn't have any feeling. I'm afraid we'll have to amputate."

The day of Cheyenne's surgery was the longest day of my life. Nothing prepared us for what we would see once we went to pick her up. In the bottom cage, Cheyenne lay panting and blinking sleepy eyes, the entire right side of her body shaved clean from her stomach to her neck. A huge white bandage was wrapped around the shoulder area where her leg used to be. A plastic tube was also taped to the area to help the surgical site drain. She looked totally miserable. Tears slid from my eyes as I saw Cheyenne's tail give a faint wag.

That night we all camped on the floor to sleep next to Cheyenne. As she moaned in agony and lay on her side unable to move, I kept trying to picture her as she used to be: running, playing, jumping up on the bed to snuggle down next to me. I felt frightened and uncertain, wondering how she would ever be that same carefree pup again. In a way, I understood the kind of trauma she was going through. One day you were happy, then life just shattered, inexplicably, leaving you in a world of pain.

Vanessa and I took shifts for the first few nights. We'd keep watch, try to comfort her, give her pain pills and feed her vanilla ice cream from a spoon. She'd doze, but usually she was too uncomfortable to sleep. Every few hours, we'd carry her outside and help her stand so she could go to the bathroom. We were exhausted, but nothing was more important than Cheyenne coming back to us—even if she would never be the same again.

On Monday, I had to take care of her myself when Vanessa went to school. Mariah kept busy with her coloring books while I constantly hovered over Cheyenne. I changed her bandages and made sure she wasn't trying to bite at them. I stroked her head and kept telling her how strong she was. Seeing her so miserable and watching the blood ooze from her drainage tube broke my heart over and over again. I missed her sweet eyes looking at me with love instead of so much suffering.

"You're a survivor," I whispered in her ear. "We need you, so you have to get better. Those children are depending on you, so please ... don't give up. Fight and get through this."

As I said these things to her, something struck me deep inside. The same words applied to me. It had been a nightmare since the divorce, the pain so deep that I wanted to curl up and die; I didn't see myself able to stand on my own. But weren't the children depending on me, too? Didn't I have to fight and get through this? Tears ran down my cheeks as I lay my face against Cheyenne's muzzle. It was so soft and her breath fanned my skin. Breath that reminded me how precious life was.

"I'll make a deal with you, girl," I said. "If you fight and get through this, I'll fight my way back, too. We'll learn how to walk on our own together."

From that day on, things steadily improved. Cheyenne looked more alert and comfortable, daring to take her first steps, while I started crying less and smiling more. A healing was beginning to take place and it felt so very good. One day at a time, one step at a time, Cheyenne and I were making it together.

"Look, Mom! She's doing it! Cheyenne's walking on her own!" Vanessa pointed as Cheyenne wandered about the yard one week later. She managed just fine with the front leg missing. In fact, it seemed as if she didn't miss it much at all.

Mariah clapped happily. "Just like her old self!"

I thought about that a moment and had to disagree. "Actually, sweetheart, I think Cheyenne's going to be better than she used to be. She'll be stronger because she's a survivor now. Just like us... better than ever."

In that instant, Cheyenne stopped and looked at me. The gleam was back in those golden eyes. We both had a new life to look forward to, one precious step at a time.

~Diane Nichols
Chicken Soup for the Dog Lover's Soul

Always a Nurse

$\mathcal{S}$ome people credit their decision to become a nurse to a life-changing event. Not me. I just always knew I wanted to become a nurse. From my early years, I used my (sometimes willing, sometimes unwilling) sisters as patients. My dolls were constantly bandaged and dotted with marks from ballpoint pen "shots."

I loved nursing school and was filled with pride the first time I put on my uniform. I even liked the cap! Graduating from nursing school ranks as one of the happiest days of my life, as does the day I opened the letter announcing I had passed State Boards. At long last, my dream had come true. I was a nurse!

After graduation I worked in a psychiatric hospital, a nursing home, a telemetry unit and doing private duty with sick children. My satisfaction and confidence in doing assessments, starting IVs, learning medications, and relating to patients and their families confirmed my career choice.

When our first child was born, I quit working outside the home. I loved being with my new baby. Then several months ago, I realized it had been almost three years since I had worked as a "real" nurse. Sure, I continued to read nursing journals and attend a nursing workshop occasionally, but the advances and changes in technology, medications and procedures were overwhelming. Could I ever find my place in nursing again?

I began to doubt my career choice. Had it been a mistake to spend so much time, not to mention money, on a career I was going to practice for only a few years? Did what I learned in school so long ago really matter? Could I ever be a "real" nurse again?

A few days later, our three-year-old took a fall down the front steps. With my heart pounding, I assessed him for a potential head injury. His pupils were equal in size, he was alert and annoyed at my assessment, and his motor abilities appeared normal as he chased his little sister across the yard.

I breathed a sigh of relief, and several other events from the last few days popped into my mind. I remembered the phone call from my mom, and my explanation to her of what a stroke was and how it might affect her friend.

I thought of the evening before, when I reassured our neighbor, whose husband had just returned home from the hospital after having a serious heart attack. I told her she could call me anytime, and I'd be right over. We hugged, and through her tears she said, "I'm so glad to have a nurse next door!"

And I recalled another day when I counseled my father-in-law on the importance of taking the whole course of antibiotics he'd been prescribed, and not stopping the medication when he felt better.

As I looked back, I realized I don't have to work in a big hospital or know all the details of the latest high-tech procedure to be a nurse. I use my education every day, and will continue to use it every day of my life. My career choice was the right one.

I am, and always will be, a nurse.

~Shelly Burke
Chicken Soup for the Nurse's Soul

Don't Close the Door

When I was a freshman in college I received in the mail a bulging envelope from my mom. It was a card of encouragement—with a brown, plastic doorstop in it. "Don't 'close the door' yet," she wrote.

I hated college when I first got there... and not the way many freshmen hate it for the first half hour. They all got over it at the first frat party. I didn't get over it for a year. I wanted to go home, sleep in my own room, go to a state school I could drive to, and only endure minimal amounts of change. The doorstop stayed with me throughout that year, a constant reminder to persevere. I made it through, with the support and encouragement provided from home. I embraced school after that.

During my junior year, Mom asked me to block off a chunk of time during a visit home over a college break. A family meeting. They were common for some families, but not in my house. I don't think we were ever called for a family meeting. I was excited and thought it was good news to be shared with all three kids all at once. Remarried, perhaps?

But when I went home I learned that not only was Mom not getting remarried, but the news wasn't good at all, and my brother and sister already knew. My mom was sitting in front of the fireplace, John next to her, my sister on the couch, and my brother on the love seat. I was in a chair.

Cancer.

I was at her side, crying. It had returned after five years of hiding, just when she was about to throw her arms up in triumph. The magical five year mark dangled just out of reach as doctors told her of a recurrence.

It was Thanksgiving and her birthday, and I was bound and determined not to go back to school. When we found out five years earlier, my aunt picked me up from school, and I spent the ensuing days taking Mom water and soup and clearing away tissues and stroking her hair back as I had done as a child to coerce her into falling asleep so I could stay up past bedtime.

This time, I wanted to go with her to Boston as she gathered second and third opinions. She wouldn't let me, though, telling me not to throw away a semester of work; she'd be fine, she'd call me with any news... but there wouldn't be much news to report anyway, and I'd be home for Christmas in no time at all.

I went back to school, as detached as I'd been that first year, halfheartedly going through the motions and longing to be home by her side—as I'd been through the first attack on my mother's body from the inside out. But I knew I had to stay, if not for myself, then for her. I knew the last thing she needed was the added worry of me wasting an academic year.

That year I had also been trying to define a senior honor's thesis and was discouraged at my lack of inspiration. I was jealous that students with other majors had noble purposes to explore: a public relations campaign to increase organ donation; a scientist working on a cancer-related treatment. What in the world could a photographer do that would make a difference? My world was defined by art, not finding cures.

Finally it came to me one day. My two problems shared a common thread.

I embarked on a project for my mom. It was a photographic tribute to cancer survivors. Through words and pictures, I journeyed through the struggle of cancer survivors—anyone courageous enough to fight that fight is a survivor in my mind—and the inspiration they focused on to endure the debilitating and excruciating treatments. I went to support groups and asked for volunteers. Most everyone was willing.

Mom visited while I was studying in London, and I took her to the Vidal Sassoon school for her "first" haircut after radiation and chemotherapy. I photographed her soon after that in the new daring cut she had wanted for years but was afraid to get. She was the centerpiece of my thesis. At graduation she came up and saw her photograph hanging in an exhibit. It was called "Survivor's Instinct," and she embodied it. She, along with the others pictured, define perseverance. The lesson she gave me years earlier had come full circle.

We recently had a surprise party for my mom's fiftieth birthday. I found out afterwards that she didn't think she'd make it to fifty. She's healthy now, and younger than ever. She just might make it to 100.

As for the doorstop, the funny thing is that I don't know where it is anymore, but I can picture it: brown, plastic and triangular, with scratches and scuffs. The object is missing, but the memory of that envelope and everything it meant is forever a lesson to persevere and to keep my heart open. It is the greatest lesson I learned from my mom.

~Christie Kelley Montone
Chicken Soup for the Mother & Daughter Soul

Wishing Away

There are two lasting bequests we can give our children.
One is roots.
The other is wings.
~Hodding Carter, Jr.

D o you believe that some people are sent into your life to teach you an important lesson? I do! One such special person in my life was Katherine.

At the time I met Katherine, I was an extremely busy single mother, raising three rambunctious children. Life seemed to be a continual merry-go-round of work, home, schedules and activities. My fondest wish involved a deserted island, warm sunny days, an inexhaustible supply of romance novels, and absolute peace and quiet.

I became aware that Katherine had moved into my apartment complex when my seven-year-old daughter, Amber, asked if her new friend could spend the night. "Please? Her name is Joy, and she just moved into number 18 with her mommy."

I stopped making hamburger patties long enough to gaze at my child. Standing next to her was a blue-eyed, blond-haired, gap-toothed little girl, waiting anxiously for my response. Issuing a resigned sigh, I agreed. "Go get Joy's things. We'll be eating in a half hour." With big grins, the two pint-sized whirlwinds were gone. I continued dinner preparations, wishing that I could be ordering steak in a fine restaurant.

Within minutes the phone rang. Katherine was calling to introduce herself and to confirm the invitation to spend the night. As we chatted, I noted that her words slurred occasionally and wondered if she had a speech impediment. I had little time to ponder Katherine's speech, however. I had children to feed, laundry to do and evening rituals to perform. With a hurried goodbye, I began peeling potatoes as I wished for the late-evening hours when I could retreat to the personal oasis I called "my time."

From that beginning, Joy and Amber were inseparable. I spoke to Katherine on the phone occasionally, but never found the time to meet her. I would glimpse her sitting on a bench by the apartment playground, talking to the children, and wonder how she managed to find the time to spend on such a frivolous activity. Didn't she have a job to go to? Housework to do? Schedules to keep? How I wished I knew the secret of finding time to play. What fun it would be to toss a ball and laugh in the summer sun.

As time passed, I began to notice that Katherine had problems. At times, her speech was difficult to understand. She seemed to stagger and lose her balance. She dropped things. I wondered if she had an alcohol problem and if the girls were safe with her. I decided the time had come to get to know this woman better and invited her to a family dinner.

The evening that Katherine and Joy came to dinner proved to be a pivotal point in my life. I watched her closely as she sat at the table surrounded by children.

Her speech was muffled in spots; her movements measured and slow. But I could not detect alcohol on her breath, and she declined the glass of wine I offered.

She seemed happy to focus on the children, listening intently to their stories. She asked them questions and considered their answers seriously. She flittered from topic to topic, keeping pace with their rapid thoughts. She entertained them with amusing stories of her own childhood.

After our meal, the children raced outside to play in what was left of the summer sunshine. Katherine and I followed at a more sedate pace. She walked slowly and carefully while she revealed her past life as a budding executive married to an active, high-profile man. She told me of a lifestyle filled with social activity, vacations, and diverse people and settings. She had lived the life I'd always wished for but never achieved.

We settled on a bench beside the playground and quietly watched the children at their games. I thought of how predictable and unexciting my life was compared to the picture Katherine had painted. With a sigh, I told her how I wished the children were older. Then, I would have more time to do some things for myself.

A small smile crossed her face as Katherine replied, "My only wish is to be able to stay out of a nursing home until Joy is grown. You see, I have multiple sclerosis. It's slowly taking over my body. It's changed my entire life. My husband couldn't deal with being married to an invalid, and I couldn't keep up with my career. Now, all I want is to be able to raise my daughter. I want to share as much of her world as I can for as long as I can. I've learned to treasure every minute of every day with her, because I don't know how many more of those there are left."

Katherine turned to me, and with another smile she continued, "Don't spend your life wishing away what you have. You never know when it will be gone."

Approaching darkness ended our conversation, as we became involved with herding our children to their baths and beds. But later that evening, in that quiet time between wakefulness and sleep, I could hear her words floating through my head and heart, and resolved to appreciate my world instead of wishing for something different.

Time passed quickly, as it always does. Joy and Amber progressed through childhood and adolescence. I spent as much time as I could with them and Katherine. Life was a kaleidoscope of excitement and joy, pain and sorrow. For each stage of development the girls experienced, it seemed Katherine's body paid a price as she slowly deteriorated physically and mentally.

Katherine's wish was granted. She was able to watch Joy receive her high school diploma, go on to further her education and start a rewarding career.

Some of my many wishes were also granted. The children are now raised and on their own, and I have time to pursue my interests. I have precious grandchildren to keep me focused on the wonders of the world, and friends and family to love and enjoy. And I carry with me the knowledge that I was granted something for which I never wished... the rewards of knowing Katherine and learning from her wisdom.

~Lana Brookman
Chicken Soup for the Girlfriend's Soul

Pictures of the Heart

The past is our definition. We may strive, with good reason,
to escape it, or to escape what is bad in it,
but we will escape it only by adding something better to it.
~Wendell Berry

They were the worst two weeks of my life. My husband and I had just separated, in one of the most contentious and horrible ways possible. Everyone had been involved: neighbors, police, and hospital and social workers. I was a wreck; I could barely eat, think or even walk. Our two-year-old daughter was shuffled between us like a Ping Pong ball, and I felt like there was nothing I could do. I had no idea what the future held, or whether there even was a future for any of us.

Somehow, I survived. I am sure now that it was only because of the help of family and close friends who chose to be near me and chose to give me hope. At the end of those two weeks, the phone rang.

"They're ready," a lady said when I picked up the phone. What? The words jumbled in my brain. The photos. The family photos my husband, daughter and I had sat for only days before our cataclysmic separation. I remember having picked out the pretty blue dress our little girl would wear and the smart houndstooth one I chose for myself. My husband had grudgingly agreed to have the photos taken. It wouldn't cost anything, I told him. The first small set was free, and payment was only required if we ordered more. I was determined to have a portrait of our "perfect" family in our tiny house—if only to remind us that we did have a family to hold on to.

Through the events of the past weeks, I had completely forgotten about the photo shoot. Tempted to tell the lady on the other line, "Throw them out; I'm not buying any," I hesitated. Those photos would be the only portraits my daughter would have of herself and her two parents, together. I thought of her future. Deep inside, I knew my marriage was over. But she still had two parents, and this was a picture from the past, a part of her life—then and always.

Picking up those pictures wasn't easy. The salesgirl, too, had recently become a single mother. When I told her my story and why I wasn't going to order any additional photos, she understood, so much so that she cried with me. I got home and hid the photos in the corner of my closet.

Years later, I took them out and showed my daughter. The excitement glowed on her face and I felt a tiny, bittersweet taste in my mouth, but nothing I couldn't swallow. Time had soothed the pain. I placed the photos in her hands. My daughter smiled and commented on how young I looked back then. Then I smiled.

~Joanna Emery
Chicken Soup for the Single Parent's Soul

Mom's Know Best

On a Mother's Support

The manner of giving shows the character of the giver.
~John Casper

35

Two Pairs of Eyes

When I returned home that day, the babysitter was waiting for me with an alarming message: "Call Linda right away. Something terrible has happened."

When I called, I couldn't quite understand Linda's tear-garbled words: "They found Don's truck on Bundy Road. There was a fire. There was a body in the truck."

"I'll come over right away," I said.

I drove off, realizing I hadn't learned whose body was in the truck. I knew it was Don's weekend to have their eleven-year-old son, Jason. Whose body was in the truck? I worried ever more urgently as I approached their house. Jason was the first person I saw as I knocked on their kitchen door, a momentary relief, short-lived as the enormity of the truth dawned: Don had died. Jason was fatherless.

I sat next to Jason, patting his back as he sobbed uncontrollably. What the loss would mean dawned on him bit by bit: "My dad won't ever see me get straight As again. He won't see me graduate from high school." While his shoulders shook with grief, my heart broke for him.

Sitting with him at their kitchen table, I relived sitting next to my own son four years earlier when the meaning of a parallel loss dawned on us: "We've been to the hospital this morning. The cancer grew too fast. Daddy didn't make it. He died." Jason's sobs were my son's. Jason's terrible new reality had been ours for four years: Daddy had died. Life would never be the same.

"I wish Daddy hadn't died," my son said later on the day of his dad's death.

"Oh honey," I replied. "That will always be our wish. That wish will never go away."

My son, then seven, was too young to infer the meanings that eleven-year-old Jason now saw immediately: It means my dad won't be here for this... and for this .... All the future lost moments telescoped into the present moment of grief.

Two days after my husband died, I had one of those moments that proves that, even in the midst of tragedy, life goes on. My son, struggling to let go of his training wheels, finally took off and rode his bike up the street for the first time on two wheels. He pedaled fast, thrilled with his newfound skill, full of the exhilaration the new freedom of movement gave him. I stood in our yard and watched, excited for his achievement and for the symbol of his growing independence and freedom.

But overshadowing that excitement was my longing ache for the pair of eyes that was absent—his father's. In that moment, I realized all the achievements my husband would miss, all the firsts, all the proud moments we would not share as parents. The enormity of being alone, a single mother, crashed down on me with overwhelming weight. But in that moment I also resolved to be enough. I resolved to be sufficient. If I am the only pair of eyes my son has, so be it. I would just have to look at him doubly hard. I would have to see all his life enough for both my husband and me. I would have to see this and all the future moments through two pairs of eyes.

Later in the evening at Jason's house, we went back to the things his dad would miss seeing. "But remember, Jason," I said. "Your mom is like a mother tiger who will never let anything happen to her cub." Jason smiled and nodded his blond head. "The remarkable thing about your mom is that she will now be able to see your life enough for both your dad and for her. Moms can do that," I continued. "They can see for the one who isn't there. They can see through two pairs of eyes." I knew because I'd been doing it for four years.

If in marriage two can become one, so after death, by God's grace, one can become two. We find we can see through two pairs of eyes.

~Barbara E. Stephens-Rich
Chicken Soup for the Single Parent's Soul

36

The Call at Midnight

We all know what it's like to get that phone call in the middle of the night. This night's call was no different. Jerking up to the ringing summons, I focused on the red illuminated numbers of my clock. Midnight. Panicky thoughts filled my sleep-dazed mind as I grabbed the receiver.

"Hello?"

My heart pounded, I gripped the phone tighter and eyed my husband, who was now turning to face my side of the bed.

"Mama?" I could hardly hear the whisper over the static. But my thoughts immediately went to my daughter. When the desperate sound of a young crying voice became clearer on the line, I grabbed for my husband and squeezed his wrist.

"Mama, I know it's late. But don't... don't say anything, until I finish. And before you ask, yes, I've been drinking. I nearly ran off the road a few miles back and..."

I drew in a sharp shallow breath, released my husband and pressed my hand against my forehead. Sleep still fogged my mind, and I attempted to fight back the panic. Something wasn't right.

"And I got so scared. All I could think about was how it would hurt you if a policeman came to your door and said I'd been killed. I want... to come home. I know running away was wrong. I know you've been worried sick. I should have called you days ago, but I was afraid... afraid...."

Sobs of deep-felt emotion flowed from the receiver and poured into my heart. Immediately I pictured my daughter's face in my mind and my fogged senses seemed to clear. "I think—"

"No! Please let me finish! Please!" She pleaded, not so much in anger, but in desperation.

I paused and tried to think what to say. Before I could go on, she continued. "I'm pregnant, Mama. I know I shouldn't be drinking now ... especially now, but I'm scared, Mama. So scared!"

The voice broke again, and I bit my lip, feeling my own eyes fill with moisture. I looked at my husband who sat silently mouthing, "Who is it?"

I shook my head and when I didn't answer, he jumped up and left the room, returning seconds later with the portable phone held to his ear.

She must have heard the click in the line because she continued, "Are you still there? Please don't hang up on me! I need you. I feel so alone."

I clutched the phone and stared at my husband, seeking guidance. "I'm here, I wouldn't hang up," I said.

"I should have told you, Mama. I know I should have told you. But when we talk, you just keep telling me what I should do. You read all those pamphlets on how to talk about sex and all, but all you do is talk. You don't listen to me. You never let me tell you how I feel. It is as if my feelings aren't important. Because you're my mother you think you have all the answers. But sometimes I don't need answers. I just want someone to listen."

I swallowed the lump in my throat and stared at the how-to-talk-to-your-kids pamphlets scattered on my nightstand. "I'm listening," I whispered.

"You know, back there on the road, after I got the car under control, I started thinking about the baby and taking care of it. Then I saw this phone booth, and it was as if I could hear you preaching about how people shouldn't drink and drive. So I called a taxi. I want to come home."

"That's good, Honey," I said, relief filling my chest. My husband came closer, sat down beside me and laced his fingers through mine.

I knew from his touch that he thought I was doing and saying the right thing.

"But you know, I think I can drive now."

"No!" I snapped. My muscles stiffened, and I tightened the clasp on my husband's hand. "Please, wait for the taxi. Don't hang up on me until the taxi gets there."

"I just want to come home, Mama."

"I know. But do this for your mama. Wait for the taxi, please."

I listened to the silence in fear. When I didn't hear her answer, I bit my lip again and closed my eyes. Somehow I had to stop her from driving.

"There's the taxi, now."

Only when I heard someone in the background asking about a Yellow Cab did I feel my tension easing.

"I'm coming home, Mama." There was a click, and the phone went silent.

Moving from the bed, tears forming in my eyes, I walked out into the hall and went to stand in my sixteen-year-old daughter's room. The dark silence hung thick. My husband came from behind, wrapped his arms around me and rested his chin on the top of my head.

I wiped the tears from my cheeks. "We have to learn to listen," I said to him.

He pulled me around to face him. "We'll learn. You'll see." Then he took me into his arms, and I buried my head in his shoulder.

I let him hold me for several moments, then I pulled back and stared back at the bed. He studied me for a second, then asked, "Do you think she'll ever know she dialed the wrong number?"

I looked at our sleeping daughter, then back at him. "Maybe it wasn't such a wrong number."

"Mom, Dad, what are you doing?" The muffled young voice came from under the covers.

I walked over to my daughter, who now sat up staring into the darkness. "We're practicing," I answered.

"Practicing what?" she mumbled and laid back on the mattress, her eyes already closed in slumber.

"Listening," I whispered and brushed a hand over her cheek.

~Christie Craig
Chicken Soup for the Mother's Soul 2

37

Keywords to Survival

As a young mother, I thought having four children under the age of four was a challenge. That challenge pales, however, when compared with having two weddings, a mastectomy, and serving as hostess for my husband's business conference—all in two weeks.

Survival became the keyword, followed in swift order by hurry and secrecy, along with support and humor.

In February 1980, two of our sons announced that they each wanted to be married in early June. They agreed on the first and third Saturdays. One wedding would be in Michigan, the other in Colorado.

Delighted that they had made happy commitments, we chorused, "Wonderful! It's fine with us."

"It even works well for the conference," added my husband. "We can stay in Colorado after the second wedding."

As president of the American Bankers' Association, he had major responsibilities in Colorado the third week of June. "I'll just take two suitcases," I added, thinking about my responsibilities as his hostess.

All went well until I discovered a small lump in my left breast three days before the first wedding. I hurried to my doctor who hurried me to X ray. From the moment he saw the X ray, hurry became a keyword.

The doctors rushed me into surgery for a biopsy. As I came out from the anesthesia, the wavering lines of a shape formed into the young surgeon who had done the biopsy. Groggy, I barely comprehended his words. "Remove the breast tomorrow." I tried to shout, but it was just a whisper. "No! Not now! The weddings!"

The older doctor, a friend, explained the percentages of survival based on treatment, and how long it took to recover. Everyone hastened to tell me what I must do immediately.

Finally, I announced in what I hoped was a normal voice, "This is Thursday. I will not ruin the wedding. I will come home Sunday and you can operate on Monday."

Secrecy was added to the keyword list. Had I known my daughter-in-law as well then as I do now, I might have told her. But at the time, I would not announce such frightening news to her in the midst of such joy.

Although our son, the groom-to-be, was very worried, my husband and I swore him to secrecy. "Let's wait until after the celebration," we said. Then we drove to Michigan, held the rehearsal dinner, cried and smiled during the wedding and danced at the reception. Our insistence on leaving at dawn the next day, missing the special breakfast, caused some raised eyebrows, but it could not be helped.

I went to the hospital that evening, had surgery the following morning and awoke minus a breast—but free from cancer. No chemotherapy or radiation required.

Prayers and thanksgiving were very important to us at this time, but hurry became vital again. Rapid recovery was essential. The next wedding was in twelve days, and we had to drive to Colorado.

Support joined the keyword list. Friends and family supported me vigorously. They brought food and sent get well cards. The just-married couple called from their honeymoon in Florida to thank us for not spoiling their wedding. The about-to-be-married couple in Colorado offered to change the date. But the conference could not be canceled. All had to proceed as planned.

With more prayers, thanks and all the fine support, I did begin the recovery process quickly. But other worries arose that, in retrospect, now seem trivial. How would I look? Unable to wear a prosthesis immediately, I worried about my appearance at this next wedding.

How could I look like a mother of the groom? My dress would not fit properly.

Again, support. A friend who'd had a mastectomy the year before showed me how she'd used cotton and Kleenex to fill out and look balanced during the time before she could start wearing her prosthesis.

It is easy now to look back and laugh at this and the other little strategies we devised, but at the time, conquering each problem caused pain and seemed traumatic. I had not had time to grieve about my loss in private before events pressed me into the public eye at a major occasion of my life: our second son's marriage.

However, slowly, humor began to help us cope. My left arm could not reach my back. The first time my husband awkwardly worked at the fastener of my brassiere, we exploded with laughter as he commented, "Somehow, this isn't the same as it used to be." Pulling up my panty hose initially caused frustration then giggles then snorts of laughter as I squirmed and he tugged.

In Colorado, the keyword from my family continued to be support, shown by their encouragement. While no one expressed pity, all of them built up my confidence. I could handle this happy occasion. A hug here, a pat and a smile, a chair conveniently placed nearby relieved fatigue and let me know how much someone cared. Later, I learned they'd promised each other not to pity me.

"We promised to be strong, so you would have to be," one of them told me years later.

The bride glowed with joy and gratitude at not having to change plans. The second son and his friends took over the rehearsal dinner, a relaxed picnic at which I could be a happy guest. I marched up the church aisle proudly, knowing that my dress hung appropriately. My husband and I shared the joy of this second wedding. Our dancing at the reception was limited, but I managed a dance with the groom and another with my husband. No one paid attention to my left arm hanging limply at my side. We all had more fun than I had thought possible.

Despite friends urging me to skip the conference, where my

hostess duties might be very tiring, I was determined to go. By then, my husband had become an expert at brassiere fastening and helping with panty hose. I was adept at padding appropriately. And humor had become a habitual keyword. To this day, I giggle when I squirm my way into a pair of panty hose. A banker's wife with whom I had become acquainted over the years offered to come to our hotel room any time I needed assistance with my hair. When conference duties kept my husband too busy to help me, she arrived energetically to fasten a pearl necklace, put in my pierced earrings or wash my hair. We became close friends, sharing stories of our children and of our fears and dreams. She taught me to relax with breathing techniques and to gain strength through visualization exercises. Our times together helped me survive and enjoy the conference. Most important, she helped me start the necessary grieving process so that I would eventually feel whole again. By the end of the conference, despite the hurry and emotion, I was beginning to put my mastectomy into perspective.

The words, from survival to hurry, from secrecy to support, stand out in my memory of those demanding weeks. Family and friends, prayers and thanksgiving, along with a growing sense of humor helped me resolve fears and grief. Recognizing and using keywords made survival a reality.

~Peg Sherry
Chicken Soup to Inspire a Woman's Soul

The Pink High-Tops

Man is harder than iron, stronger than stone and more fragile than a rose.
~Turkish Proverb

It was late November. We wandered the mall, shopping with the multitudes during the pre-Christmas rush. My two little ones and my mum moseyed along, taking in the holiday gala.

Then I spotted them, a pair of pink high-top sneakers.

I delighted in their pastel cockiness, gentle pale pink on aggressive high-tops. I had found my Christmas present. "That's what I want Mum, those sneakers," I said.

She looked at me as if I had lost my mind. I am sure she had expected me to suggest a cashmere sweater for Christmas, but instead I had found an inexpensive but delightful bit of fun.

A week later, when I returned from a conference in Washington, D.C., the pain in my lower back was unbearable. I went to the hospital, underwent some tests and was admitted. Surgery was scheduled for the next day. No big deal, I thought. Take out three discs, be home in four days, a few weeks off. We'll manage.

Something went wrong.

I vaguely remember waking in the recovery room screaming in pain. I remember my mother sitting beside my bed and saying her rosary. In a stupor, I could only begin to imagine what character-building events lay ahead.

While I lay in the hospital, my husband, Tom, had to shop and wrap. My father visited faithfully every day and watered my minia-ture Christmas tree. Two days before Christmas, with much pleading, I was released from the hospital and taken home heavily sedated, bent at forty-five degrees on a walker.

The words from the day before kept ringing through my head. My husband was sitting nearby, incredulous. The surgeon, my nem-esis, chart in hand, spoke. His words were crisp, clear and deliv-ered unemotionally: "You will never walk unassisted again. But with therapy, we can help straighten you some, and with time the pain will gradually subside until it can be managed."

Who is he talking to? He can't mean me. All I kept thinking was, I have two young children. I'm only thirty-one years old. Of course I'll walk upright again.

At home, I felt as if I were in a fog shrouded in pain. The tree was up. Presents were piled beneath it. I was laid in a recliner on an egg crate mattress. The recliner accommodated the bend in my body. The codeine and other drugs helped block the overwhelming pain and fear.

On Christmas morning, Mum and Dad came for breakfast. As the gifts were being opened, Mum said, "Tom, you did a fine job. Everything looks lovely." I noticed the sparkle of the paper. Look-ing closer, I saw that everything was wrapped in "Happy Hanukkah" paper. I couldn't laugh. It hurt to just turn my head. Poor Tom, he'd tried. But the paper—what a kick. Our Hanukkah Christmas is still a wonderful memory.

The little ones helped me open my gifts. And there they were, a pair of pink high-tops; I'd forgotten all about them.

I started to weep, loving them yet wondering whether I would ever be able to wear them. I wept uncontrollably. The kids didn't have a clue what was wrong. Tom rushed them to the kitchen for blueberry pancakes, the annual Christmas fare. My mother, unflap-pable as always, just looked at me without as much as a question and said, "You'll wear them."

Three weeks later, my beloved dad died unexpectedly—another bad dream—and I was back in the hospital for the first of the many tests and hospitalizations to follow. I was put into traction and finally a full-body cast, and slowly I worked my way back to some semblance of an upright position.

At first, I was bent at the waist, face to the floor. I wore weights on my ankles and a body cast. I moved on a walker. There were no high heels, no fancy dresses. There were only sweat clothes to fit over the body hardware, but my feet were dressed in pretty pink. Everywhere I went I wore my pink high-tops. For the first year, they were truly all I saw when attempting to learn to walk again.

It took three full years of pain, perseverance, faith in God and a deliberate belief in myself. It took family support, but I learned to walk and endure and to stand tall. I finally had to part with the worn and cracked pink high-tops. They were tossed reluctantly. Oddly enough, they had been a part of a time in my life I didn't want to forget.

Time went full circle, and I moved into my mother's home to tend to her during her last few years. On the eve of my mother's death, before she slipped into a morphine-induced sleep, she said to me, "How lucky I was to have had my family and to have shared yours." She dozed momentarily. When she woke, while stroking my hand, she quietly said, "We had a special relationship. You are not average, Dotty. Don't ever forget. You are extraordinary. Always stand tall, just as if you're wearing your pink feet." She said little else that night as I sat by her side and remembered every nuance of our lives together.

Now when I put the pink angel on the top of the tree, I always stretch tall and straight and remember that terrifying Christmas and the faith and love evident in my mother's gift to me. It was a basic message, one of courage and strength, emblazoned in a simple pair of pink high-tops.

~Dorothy Raymond Gilchrest
Chicken Soup for Every Mom's Soul

Rhythms of Grace

I ask not for a lighter burden, but for broader shoulders.
~Jewish Proverb

My deacon-husband left for church early, leaving me to follow with our three children. My incessant nausea, sprints to the bathroom and overwhelming urge to sleep threatened that plan. I changed the baby's diapers, mopped up spilled cereal and finally got everyone strapped into the van and on the way to church.

After a scramble in the nursery, I filed into the sanctuary. There was one seat left. I slid into the row and smiled at the stunning woman beside me. She didn't change any diapers this morning, I thought. A young girl beside the woman flashed an awkward smile.

The music ended and we all turned to greet our neighbors. The stunning woman was named Gail. I chatted with her, then extended a hand past my bulging belly to her daughter.

"I'm Kelly," she said, exposing her own curved stomach. Kelly lifted her eyes, pleading for acceptance.

"I'm Mary. It's so nice to have you," I said with a reassuring smile. Gail squeezed my elbow as we reclaimed our seats.

The pastor's words sounded distant as I remembered my own confusion and fear as a young girl—and my own growing belly then. Shame from my teenage pregnancy resurged, raw and fresh. Realization swept over me. Through Kelly, my own wounds, long crusted over, would receive God's healing love.

"And so I challenge you," the pastor's voice echoed, "to give God's comfort to someone else. Stop watching people bleed to death because you are ashamed."

My heart melted, but my muscles tightened. Tell her? I asked, already knowing the answer. Yes. Tell her, my heart replied.

We were dismissed and I stepped back to let Kelly pass. As she did, I took her hand.

"Can I tell you something?" I said, hoping no one would hear.

"Sure. Go ahead."

"When I was about your age, I had a baby. A girl. I gave her up for adoption. God reminded me today how hard it was. How mean people were. If you ever need to talk, here's my number." Half blinded by tears, I scribbled the numerals on a bulletin and shoved it toward her.

Gail, now at my side, stroked my back. She was crying too. "Thank you," she said. "This is the hardest thing we've ever been through."

Kelly was nearer to delivery than I was. Each week at church, stares focused on her belly as if it were a scarlet letter. She looked at me for anchoring. I sent tired smiles back to her, hoping to be a beacon in a forest of darkness.

Kelly came and went to church, cold and distant. I left goofy phone messages for her out of concern. She never called back.

One Wednesday, while I assembled "church night" sandwiches, the phone rang. It was Gail. She gave a breathless account of Kelly's active labor. Her voice held a hint of fear. "I'm sorry for calling you, but Kelly insisted. Can you come? It would mean a lot to her."

Gail gave me the room number and I started to hang up. "Wait," I said, a question on my mind. "Did she have my number with her?"

There was a pause. "No. She knew it by heart."

I gave the details to my husband, who nodded and threw me the keys.

I was at the hospital all night. When the midwife was called away, Gail and I coached Kelly through her contractions. Her sixteen-year-old boyfriend looked on, torn with emotions. A tear traced my face as the baby, Emily Grace, was placed in my arms, wrapped in her father's flannel shirt. "Best baby blanket in the world," the midwife said. "She'll always know her dad was here." I smiled. My Father, my God, was there too.

I gave Kelly a devotional book for new mothers and Gail compliments for her courage and faith.

They gave me the joy of giving the love and support that I had needed so long ago.

~Marilynn Griffith
Chicken Soup for the Christian Woman's Soul

40

A Canine Nanny

Dogs are not our whole life, but they make our lives whole.
~Roger Caras

was physically and emotionally exhausted. At night, I was awake more than I slept, caring for our three-week-old daughter, Abigail. By day, I chased our older daughter, Bridget, an active two-year-old. My already taut nerves began to fray when Abigail developed a mild case of colic. Bridget demanded attention each time her sister fussed. Our dog, a purebred Brittany named Two, was constantly underfoot, and stumbling over her repeatedly did not help my state of mind.

I also felt isolated. We were new to the area, and I didn't know anyone in town. My parents, our nearest relatives, lived 150 miles away. Phoning my mother on the spur of the moment to ask if she'd drop by and watch the kids for an hour while I got some much-needed sleep wasn't realistic. My husband helped as much as he could but needed to focus on his job.

One day Abigail woke from a nap. As babies sometimes do, she had soiled her clothing and crib bedding. I tried to clean her up as fast as possible, but her cries developed into ear-shattering wails before I was through. I wanted to comfort her, but I was at a loss. I had to wash my hands, I couldn't put her back into the crib and the floor hadn't been vacuumed for days. Strapping her on the changing table, I wedged a receiving blanket between her and the railing.

I promised I'd be right back. As her screams followed me into the bathroom, I neared complete meltdown. Women had handled this for generations—why couldn't I cope?

I had just lathered up with soap when Two trotted purposefully past the bathroom door. A moment later the crying ceased. Hurriedly, I dried my hands and entered the nursery to find the Brittany standing on her hind legs, tenderly licking Abigail's ear. The baby's eyes were opened wide in wonder. Two dropped down and wagged her stubby tail in apology. With a canine grin and her ears pushed back as far as they could go, she seemed to say, "I know babies are off limits, but I couldn't help myself."

At that moment, I realized why I had been tripping over Two all the time: she wanted to help! When Bridget was born, Two had enthusiastically welcomed the newest member of her family. But because she had difficulty curbing her energy, we had watched her closely. Now, at six years of age, with a more sedate disposition, Two understood she had to be gentle.

That day marked a turning point for me. During Abigail's fussy moments, I laid her blanket on the floor and placed her next to Two. Often Abigail quieted as she buried her hands and feet in the dog's warm soft fur. Although Two relished her role as babysitter, objecting only when Abigail grabbed a fistful of sensitive flank hair, I still kept a vigilant eye on them, or Abigail would likely have suffered a constant barrage of doggy kisses.

When Abigail turned four, we enrolled her in preschool. Her teacher as well as several of the other parents commented on how she was always the child who reached out to those who were alone. Extending an invitation to join in play, Abigail often stayed by someone's side if she didn't get an answer, talking quietly and reassuringly. I like to think that Two's willingness to remain lying next to a screaming infant somehow contributed to our daughter's sensitivity.

I admit I've spoiled Two since that first day when she comforted Abigail. If I leave the table and a half-eaten meal disappears, I know who the culprit is. But I don't have the heart to punish her for being an opportunist. I'm indebted to her, and losing out on several bites of cold food is a small price to pay.

Two is still part of our family, and although we all dote on her, there is an unmistakable connection between her and Abigail. Now nearly twelve years old, Two has more than her share of aches and pains. During winter, she often rests in front of the heat register. When Abigail wakes in the morning, she covers her dog with her old baby blanket and fusses over her. And when Abigail wanders away, Two trails after her, the tattered blanket dragging along on the floor. Two still considers Abigail her special charge, and I'm happy to have her help. I hope they have many more days together, looking after each other with such loving care.

~Christine Henderson
Chicken Soup for the Dog Lover's Soul

41

Mountains of Laundry

After we had been married a couple of years, my husband and I became foster parents. Our first placement was two little boys, brothers, who we were thrilled to adopt a year and a half later. When our sons were two and three, we agreed to take one and three-year-old sisters into our home. For the following two years we had our own little in-house, full-time daycare.

After the girls had been with us awhile, I attempted to get involved in a Bible study group at our church, but one thing or another always seemed to prevent me from attending. I was feeling a little discouraged, but I purchased devotional tapes and a study guide and thought I could keep up with the Bible study by myself at home.

One afternoon, after I'd put the children down for their naps, I tackled a mountain of laundry that had piled up on the sofa and needed folding. As I was folding, I began discussing my plight with God. "You know, Lord, I've started attending this Bible study and I'm trying to find time for You and everything I need to do, but I just can't seem to find enough time. I've tried getting up before daylight, but one of the kids always hears me and gets up wanting my attention, and by bedtime I'm exhausted. I guess I could do them during naptime, but that's the only time I have to get caught up with the housework and laundry. I seem to be able to keep up with most everything but this laundry! Well, I guess You know all about it. You gave me four little kids under three years old to care for, and You know they need clean clothes to wear and You know how much work this takes. I know You understand."

The following Sunday my husband and I were sitting in Sunday school class waiting for the teacher to begin, when our family's "adopted grandmother," Betty, came and sat down beside me. Betty was a widow who had raised five children. She was a wonderful woman who was always helping someone, and had personally blessed our family on many occasions.

She leaned toward me and said, "I have a proposition for you."

My curiosity was aroused. "Okay. What is it?"

She sweetly and softly replied, "I really think this is the Lord, but would you let me do your laundry?"

As I sat gaping at her with my mouth hanging open, my mind raced trying to think who I could have told about my laundry situation. I knew I hadn't mentioned it to anyone, not even my husband, Rodney. "Do you know how much laundry I have?" I whispered back as my eyes started to fill.

"Honey, I've raised five kids. Believe me, I know how much laundry you have." She continued, "You know, what you and your husband are doing raising these little children is wonderful, but I know it's hard work. I'm an old woman and I can't watch other people's children anymore, but I can do your laundry. You just have Rodney drop it off on his way to work and pick it up on his way home. I'll wash it, dry it, iron it, fold it; whatever is needed."

Shame on me, because the whole time she was talking, I was thinking, "Oh, Lord, not the underwear! I can't send our underwear to someone else to do!"

Betty was still talking. "Last week I noticed you up on the platform during praise and worship and you looked very tired. I was thinking about you all week and then I felt the Lord telling me, 'Ask Ronni if she'll let you do her laundry.'" She finished with, "Now, don't you rob me of this blessing."

I didn't know how to respond. Not wanting to hurt Betty's feelings, I said, "I'll think about it."

Even though I had poured out my heart about how difficult it was to keep up and how I missed my devotional time with Him, I was unprepared for God to actually do something about it. He had given me the task of caring for these little ones and I was a little put out that He'd taken me seriously when I said I was having trouble keeping up. So I thought, *If I just get a little more organized, I can take care of this myself.*

A couple weeks later, as I walked in and surveyed the laundry room, I sagged against the washer. The mountain of laundry hadn't diminished a bit with my efforts to get better organized. As a matter of fact, it was now bigger than ever. "Well, Lord," I said, "I guess I could send everything but the underwear."

Very clearly, I heard that still small voice say, "When I ask you for your dirty laundry, I want all of it, even the underwear."

That's when I broke. That mountain of laundry now represented the mountain of pride in my life. Who was I to look disdainfully on a gift offered in love?

As I picked up the phone, my eyes filled with tears and when I heard sweet little Betty's voice on the other end, my own voice shook as I said, "Betty, do you still want to help me with my laundry?"

My tears quickly turned to laughter at her joyful response. "Bring it on over, Honey, bring it on over!"

Our clothes were never cleaner, brighter, or less wrinkled than during the two years Betty faithfully and lovingly did our laundry. Then when our little foster daughters were placed in their "forever home" through adoption, we both knew it was time for me to resume the task.

Although she no longer does our laundry, our friendship remains strong. Betty laughed one day when I told her, " I want to be just like you when I grow up."

"You'll make a great adopted grandmother one day—and will have mountains of blessings to show for it."

~Veronica Wintermote
Chicken Soup for the Christian Soul 2

42

Locked In

Dogs are miracles with paws.
~Attributed to Susan Ariel Rainbow Kennedy

pril afternoons are warm in suburban Philadelphia, and the temperature inside a parked car rises quickly. Ila, my two-year-old daughter, was strapped into her car seat, pink-cheeked and sweaty. D'Argo, my ten-month-old chocolate Lab, was bounding from the front seat to the back, barking and panting. Helpless, I could only stand and wait.

They had been locked in the rented truck for fifteen minutes when the police car finally pulled into my driveway.

"No spare key, ma'am?" the young officer asked. The only key I had was attached to the remote door lock control, which was lying on the driver's seat, along with my purse, the after-school snack for the older kids, my book, the mail and the dirty dry cleaning. I had tossed everything onto the seat, buckled Ila into her car seat and shooed D'Argo into the passenger side, closing doors as I went. Just as I reached the driver's side door, I heard the clunk of the door locks. D'Argo was standing on the driver's seat, tail wagging and his over-sized puppy paws on the remote.

"It's a rental," I explained. "The agency doesn't keep spares, but the agent is trying to get a new key cut. He said he'd send it right over."

One hand on the nightstick in his tool belt, the officer circled the truck, trying all the doors, tugging at the lift gate. D'Argo trailed him from window to window inside. They came face-to-face at the front passenger window. D'Argo, his nose pressed against the window, wagged his tail and drooled, leaving large globs of spit and nose prints on the glass.

Two more officers arrived. After a quick briefing, the older, heavier officer took a long metal tool with a flat hooked end from the trunk of his squad car. He wedged it into the gap between the driver's side window and door and slid it slowly in and out, trying, unsuccessfully, to jimmy the lock. Then he attacked the keyhole with a screwdriver, succeeded only in making a few gouges in the metal and gave up. "These new cars, like Fort Knox," he muttered. "Sorry, ma'am."

I called the car rental company again. They were "still working on it," my friendly rental agent said. I pressed my face against the window, shading my eyes to see through the tinted glass. D'Argo had flopped down next to Ila's car seat, his long body stretched out across the seat and his big brown head resting in her lap. Ila's face was flushed and shiny. Drops of sweat rolled down her cheeks and her blond curls were dark and matted against her forehead. Ila looked up into my face.

"Mommy! Uppie!" she said, holding up her arms. Her wide blue eyes leaked tears.

"Mommy will get you out as soon as she can," I said, straining to sound calm and cheerful. Her face crumpled.

"Mommy! Mommy! I wan' you!" she wailed. She twisted and strained against the car seat, crying harder, legs pumping, arms reaching. D'Argo jumped into the front seat and joined in, baying with a low, guttural moan.

Fidgeting with his nightstick, one of the officers turned to me.

"We could break a window," he said, giving the front driver's window an experimental tap. D'Argo flinched, hair rising across his back, but didn't back away.

"The baby'll be okay in the backseat, but I'm afraid I'll hurt your dog, ma'am."

"We can't wait for the key anymore," I said, "we need to get them out." The men looked at each other.

"Like I said, ma'am, we might hurt your dog."

"I don't want you to hurt him either, but they've been in there too long."

The younger officer pulled his nightstick out of his tool belt and walked around to the passenger door. D'Argo met him at the window, barking and howling.

"Can you call him? Get him away?" he called.

"D'Argo! D'Argo! Come!" I yelled, banging frantically on the driver's side window. D'Argo stopped barking and looked back, but stayed where he was. The policeman raised the baton, then hesitated, looking through the window at D'Argo and then at me.

"Do it!" I yelled.

He swung down hard, smacking the glass with the nightstick. D'Argo leaped back. The nightstick thudded against the window again. D'Argo vaulted into the backseat.

"D'Argo, off! Getta offa me, D'Argo!" Ila screamed, but her voice was muffled in D'Argo's chest. The dog was standing over her car seat, covering her with his body. She beat her fists against his side and kicked her feet at his legs, but he would not move.

Suddenly, there was a loud crack as the nightstick splintered. The three officers stood together, staring at the pieces of the broken baton, then looked up at me as I came around the truck. I ran for the toolbox in the basement and grabbed the sledgehammer, the heaviest tool I could find. I handed it to the younger officer, who started pounding on the window. The sound was deafening. Ila was still screaming, punching and kicking frantically at D'Argo, who stood squarely over her, his back to the action at the window. His large body covered her small one almost completely.

The glass fractured suddenly with a crackling sound. One more blow from the sledgehammer and the window shattered. The officer reached in and unlocked the doors. I wrenched open Ila's door and D'Argo flew past me. There were shards of glass everywhere on the backseat and floor, but none in the car seat. I fumbled with the buckle, unlatched it and pulled Ila out. She was flushed, warm and sweaty, her T-shirt soaked through and her hair plastered to her head in ringlets, but she was not hurt. I squeezed her tight and sank onto the ground, both of us sobbing. I sat there for a minute, hugging her. Then I looked for D'Argo. He was twisting and lunging, trying to get away from the older officer, who was holding him by the collar.

"He's not hurt," he said, struggling to hold on, "but I'm afraid he'll run away."

But I knew he wouldn't.

"It's all right," I said, "you can let him go." D'Argo flew straight for us, wormed his big head between Ila and me and licked both our faces until we were laughing instead of crying.

~M. L. Charendoff
Chicken Soup for the Dog Lover's Soul

43

Knowing When

After moving to a new state, I looked for ways to meet new people. Then, to my delight, the neighbor living in the duplex behind mine waved in my direction. She shared a friendly smile, offered a warm hello, told me her name was Evelyn, and engaged me in casual conversation. Without pomp and circumstance or either of us being aware of it, we each invited the other into our lives and became friends.

Evelyn's knack for perfect timing never failed to amaze me.

She always knew when…. In happy times, she knew when to laugh with me and share my joy. If I was upset, she knew when to bring chocolates and listen while I vented. During sad moments, she knew when to offer me a tissue so we could cry together. If I became unsure about something, she knew when to encourage me not to give up.

Her support, whether by phone, visit or note in the mail, always arrived exactly when needed.

One time in particular her knowing when saved me….

Our fifth child's delivery date was to be later than expected. Family members, who awaited the SOS call, would be notified quickly so they could come take care of our four children. As time and schedule permitted, my husband, Eddie, would care for our three school-aged boys, but because of his irregular work schedule, he couldn't manage our one-year-old daughter.

My friend Evelyn didn't hesitate. "I'll keep her for as long as you'd like."

It put my mind at rest to know everyone would be taken care of. All I had to do was deliver the baby and return home to the rest of the family as soon as possible.

I went into labor and our plan went into effect.

But, tragically, our baby boy died from complications.

There was nothing anyone could do to ease my pain, heartache and loss.

Four days later, when I returned home from the hospital, I had no idea how to explain to our three sons what had happened. I didn't know how to comfort them in their grief, or me in mine. To my surprise, they offered more comfort than I could give. They stayed at my side and showered me with talk of their school activities. How I appreciated every thoughtful moment. Still, I knew I had to come to grips with my own grief, shock and sorrow.

As the day progressed, to my further horror, my husband became seriously ill and was rushed to the intensive care unit at the local hospital. The threat of a second loss became more than I could bear. What would I do if Eddie died, too?

My mother, already en route, arrived that very day and took over the care of the boys.

I didn't call anyone about Eddie, not even Evelyn, who still had our daughter at her house. I could only retreat to my bedroom—to be alone, to think, to brace myself for the worst, to grapple with answers to threatening questions: How will I ever recover from losing my baby boy? Will I be a single parent of four? How will I make ends meet? Will I have to get a job? Who will take care of the children, a day care service? I collapsed on the bed and sobbed, unable to leave my cocoon of grief.

Early the next morning before Eddie's parents arrived, one of the boys came into my bedroom where I remained, wallowing in self-pity and depression. "Mom, Evelyn's here. She's in her car. She said she wasn't sure just when to come in. But she told me she had something she thought would help you feel better."

Somehow I managed to drag myself to the door.

There, parked at the end of the driveway, was Evelyn with my one-year-old daughter who I hadn't seen in over a week. Walking to meet with them, I saw my little girl's face glowing with excitement. She stretched her arms up to me. I started to cry, wondering if she'd thought she'd lost me.

Evelyn opened the door, handed me our baby girl and said, "I think this is the best medicine for you now."

I embraced my daughter, held her close and looked into the eyes of my best friend. "How did you know?"

"The boys called and told me about Eddie. I knew this was when you needed all your family here."

Knowing when is an art my friend Evelyn has perfected.

But being this kind of friend is an art perfected only by God.

~Helen Colella
Chicken Soup for the Girlfriend's Soul

44

Come Back Home

All of us, at certain moments of our lives,
need to take advice and receive help from other people.
~Alexis Carrel

Finally, I had to admit to myself that I wasn't making it on my own as a single parent with a four-year-old son and a thirteen-month-old daughter. Reluctantly, I had written my parents asking if I could move in with them until I could find a teaching position and manage on my own. I knew it would not be an easy decision for them to make. Living in a small town, my mother had always worried about "what people would think."

Her response came more quickly than I had expected. As I held her unopened letter, I wondered if the rapid reply was good news or bad. With careful concern, I tore open the end of the envelope. Her typewritten letter was folded in the formal standard she had learned as a secretary after graduating from high school. It read:

Dear Linda,

You must quit beating up on yourself and feeling so ashamed over needing to move back home with the children because of your divorce. I want you to know that you are not the first woman in our family to be a single parent and fall on hard times. I hope you will find courage and take pride in the woman I am going to tell you about.

Your great-great-grandmother, Hannah Lappin, headed west in a prairie schooner with her farmer husband and three small children: a boy, six; a girl, two, and an infant son. They settled in a secluded section of Missouri. After five years of her husband's tremendous effort clearing timber, rumors circulated that land, including their claim, was in litigation. Days of anxiety followed, and her husband's health began to fail. He was diagnosed with tuberculosis, and his strength diminished steadily. They lost their farm. They made the difficult decision to make the four-hundred-mile trip back to southern Illinois to her family. There was nothing about this trip that held any attraction for a woman with three children and an invalid husband in the early spring of 1876. On many days, he was too sick to travel. At night, he would sleep outside under the wagon. Inevitably he died, and left his family among strangers in the hill country of Missouri.

He was buried along the trail under a pile of stones. Their eleven-year-old son took the reins of the wagon and skillfully drove the team through the ten-mile-wide city of St. Louis and across the big river, still a hundred miles from their family.

Hannah's problems were further complicated by her failing eyesight and the awareness that she was several months pregnant. Shortly after arriving at her Uncle David's home, she gave birth to twin boys. Refusing charity from the state, she took in washing. Making light of her blindness, she promised people, "The stains may still be in the clothes, but I will get the stink out." Her great poverty and lack of comfort was felt by her orphaned children, but it was no match for her unwavering faith in God and her ability to give thanks in all things. The three youngest sons became ministers. The oldest son returned to the West to build railroads across Kansas to Denver. Ida, her daughter, after ten years of wedded life, was left a widow with four small children. The example of her mother's faith and determination inspired her, knowing her mother's burden had been a hundred times heavier.

Linda, did you not realize that World War II made me a single parent while Daddy was overseas for two years? I had to go back to live with my parents on their farm, miles from town and friends. But it was such a blessing in disguise because Grandma was willing to rock you when you had constant earaches, and I was able to help her with her household chores. Your daddy sent us ration books, so I could get sugar and shoes and gasoline to supplement my folks' needs.

Now that you understand that you were not the first woman in our family to be a single parent, please come back home knowing that your parents, grandparents, aunts, uncles, sisters and cousins are here to be family for you. With the rich heritage of women who have found a way to give their children a wonderful future, in spite of hardships, you will be in very good company.

Come back home as soon as possible.

Love always,

~Mother

~Linda H. Puckett
Chicken Soup for the Single Parent's Soul

Close Your Mouth, Open Your Arms

We have two ears and one mouth so that we can
listen twice as much as we speak.
~Epictetus

My friend called with disturbing news: Her unmarried daughter was pregnant.

My friend recounted the terrible scene when her daughter finally told her and her husband. There had been accusations and recriminations, variations on the theme of "How could you do this to us?" My heart ached for them all: the parents who felt betrayed and the daughter who had gotten in over her head. Could I be of any help to bridge the gap?

I was so upset about the situation that I did what I often do when I can't think straight: I called my mother. She reminded me of something I heard her say often through the years. I immediately wrote a note to my friend, sharing Mom's advice: When a kid's in trouble, close your mouth and open your arms.

I tried to follow that advice while my own were growing up. With five children in six years, I didn't always succeed, of course. I have a big mouth and little patience.

I remember when Kim, my oldest, was four and knocked over a lamp in her bedroom. Once I saw that she wasn't cut, I launched into a tirade about how this lamp was an antique, that it had been in our family for three generations, that she should be more careful, and how did this happen—then I saw the fear on her face. Her eyes were wide, her lips trembling. She was backing away from me. I remembered Mom's words. I stopped in mid-sentence and held out my arms.

Kim flew into them, saying "Sorry... Sorry," between sobs. We sat on her bed, hugging and rocking, for a long time. I felt awful for scaring her and for letting her think even for a nanosecond that that lamp was more valuable to me than she was.

"I'm sorry, too, Kim," I said when she calmed enough to hear me. "People are more important than lamps. I'm glad you weren't cut."

Fortunately, she forgave me. There are no lifelong scars from the lamp incident. But it taught me that it's better to hold my tongue than try to retract words spoken in anger, fear, disappointment or frustration.

When my children were teens—all five at the same time—they gave me many more opportunities to practice Mom's wisdom: trouble with friends, being "in," not having a date for the prom, traffic tickets, science experiments that bombed, and getting bombed. I'll freely confess that my mother's advice wasn't the first thing that came to mind when a teacher or principal called. After fetching the offender from school, the conversation in the car was sometimes loud and one-sided.

Yet on the occasions when I remembered Mom's technique, I didn't have to retract biting sarcasm or apologize for false assumptions or rescind unrealistic punishments. It's amazing how much more of the story, and the motivation, you get when you're hugging a child, even a child in an adult body. When I held my tongue, I also heard about their fears, anger, guilt and repentance. They didn't get defensive because I wasn't accusing. They could admit they were wrong, knowing they were loved anyway. We could work on "what do you think we should do now" instead of getting stuck in "how did we get here."

My children are grown now, most with families of their own. One came to me a few months back. "Mom, I did a stupid thing ...."

After a hug, we sat at my kitchen table. I listened and nodded for nearly an hour, while this wonderful child sifted though the dilemma. When we stood up, I got a bear hug that nearly collapsed my lungs.

"Thanks, Mom. I knew you'd help me solve this."

It's amazing how smart I sound when I close my mouth and open my arms.

~Diane C. Perrone
Chicken Soup for the Mother's Soul 2

Moms Know Best

Moms Overcoming Obstacles and Solving Problems

*People become really quite remarkable when they
start thinking that they can do things.
When they believe in themselves they have the first secret of success.*
~Norman Vincent Peale

46

Chasing a Rainbow

People only see what they are prepared to see.
~Ralph Waldo Emerson

The year I got divorced was one of the hardest I've ever faced. An accident, just two weeks after my initial separation from my husband, kept me hospitalized for more than two months, and recuperation lasted another two months. Finally on my feet and back at work, I found myself faced with the responsibilities of finding a home, caring for my two children and adjusting to a new job—all while coping with constant pain.

"I just have to do this one thing," I'd tell the children each time they approached me to read to them, help with homework or just talk. Lost in my own maze of coping, I was unable to reach out to them in their pain and suffering. Adding guilt to my other burdens only made the stress increase.

Then I became very ill. A combination of a very bad case of flu and infections put me in bed for a week. Each morning the children got up on their own and went to school. They came home and made their own meals. I vaguely recall being awakened and fed canned chicken soup. I drifted in a land between sleep and unconsciousness. When I was able to move from the bed and walk through the house, I discovered it in shambles. Dirty laundry and dishes; messes everywhere I looked. I didn't think I would ever be able to catch up with the housework again. The checkbook, too, had suffered. I had no paid sick leave, and the burden of managing finances without regular child-support payments forced me to return to work before I had fully recovered.

The children began calling me at work. "I'm sick; I don't feel good, come and get me; I've missed the bus—honest, Mama, I didn't hear them call my bus number!" All were a bid for the time and attention I didn't feel I could spare them. And each call meant missed work, missed pay.

The day came when they both called within five minutes. Neither child had managed to make their bus home that afternoon. Could I come pick them up? As I hurried from work it began to rain heavily. I was crying as I stopped at each school. This was all too hard, and I didn't want to do it anymore. There was no end in sight, no hope of a better life.

As we turned toward home, the clouds broke and sunshine poured onto the wet streets. A huge rainbow gleamed in the sky above us, colors brilliant and clear. It was the most beautiful rainbow I'd ever seen in my life, and my children were in awe.

"Is there really gold at the end of the rainbow?" my youngest asked.

I told him honestly I'd never seen the end of a rainbow.

"How do they know?" he asked.

"I don't know," I replied.

"Well, it looks like it ends just over that bridge," he said. "Can't we go look, Mama?"

I thought of the hundred things I needed to do. There was work to finish; there were chores and laundry to be done. I opened my mouth to say no, but when I started to speak, out came a "yes." The children shrieked with excitement. The end wasn't just over the bridge, or across the railroad, or in the field beyond that. We drove for more than thirty miles, sometimes seeing the end just ahead of us, the colors shimmering and shining, the light dancing through them. I looked at my children, their eyes shining, and at the rainbow ahead of us and kept on driving.

We laughed and talked—really talked—for the first time in

months. We talked about my accident, the divorce, their fears, their schools, their dreams. We planned future rides and projects. I felt my shoulders relax and my grip loosening on the steering wheel. My children's eyes were free of worry.

We decided to stop the chase an hour after it began. We turned to head for home. We'd found something wonderful while chasing that rainbow, something even better than that coveted pot of gold. We'd found ourselves a family again; we'd rediscovered the value of our relationship to each other. We'd remembered what it felt like to have fun. And we'd started making plans for a future that felt hopeful and full of promise.

Several years have passed, and my two children are grown. But when we are together, there is a bond between us. One of us will smile and ask, "Remember when we chased the rainbow?"

We do. It was the day we found hope again.

~Terri Cheney
Chicken Soup for the Single Parent's Soul

47

Jet

"Will you save them, Mommy?"

As I looked down into the inquisitive, trusting faces of my two sons, ages four and seven, I was touched by their undeniable, little-boy faith in me. They had not asked, "Can you save them?" They just assumed that I could. I decided to try.

The mallard nest that we had stumbled upon that spring day along the wooded shore of my father's backyard pond was abandoned and strewn apart. Only five of twelve eggs were left unbroken.

We gently gathered the smooth, creamy-white, elliptical orbs into our hands. They felt cool against my skin, which warned me that the nippy spring air had probably finished what their unknown assailant had begun during the night.

Back in our kitchen, we constructed a primitive incubator from an empty fish aquarium, clamping a reflector light to its upper rim. After placing the eggs on a towel at the bottom of the aquarium and turning on the light, we began our patient vigil. A little research told us that duck eggs take about twenty-seven days to hatch, but since we had no clue as to when the "birth" of the eggs had taken place, we didn't know how long we would have to wait.

Day after day, several times a day, their enthusiasm never diminishing, the boys checked and gently turned the eggs. As we passed day twenty-seven, the disappointment on their young faces was only too visible. Not willing to abandon hope, we continued to watch and wait.

A day or two later, our patience was rewarded. I was summoned to the kitchen by shouts of excitement. One of the eggs looked different. Its once smooth surface was now covered with dark jagged lines. When we listened carefully, we heard tiny noises confirming the life within. Slowly but surely one little mallard was struggling to make its way into the world.

After several hours of scratching and pecking, the duckling finally freed itself of the eggshell. Wet and exhausted, it collapsed and slept in the warmth of the light. By the time it awoke, it was dry, soft and fluffy. Immediately, it began to try out its spindly legs and very large feet. Before the day had ended, it was walking around, eagerly flapping its tiny wings. After eating its fill of chicken feed, it slept once again, as we looked on with wonder and pride.

In the days that followed, it became obvious that in the duckling's eyes, I was its mother. When I moved, it moved with me; when I stopped, it sat on top of my foot. When it lost sight of me, its tiny panicked peeps would fill the air.

Even though we enjoyed the enthusiastic greeting we received each morning upon entering the kitchen, it soon became obvious that we needed to make new living arrangements for our little friend. In exchange for a quiet kitchen, my husband, who through the years has patiently endured an array of orphaned critters, constructed a chicken wire pen in a remote corner of our yard, complete with a "duck house" and a tub of water.

We expected that our duckling would be thrilled to have so much space and so many amenities. Apparently, though, the adjustment from house duck to mere yard duck was not an easy one, and the duckling wasted no time letting us know how it felt about its new accommodations. In order to maintain some peace and quiet, during the day we gave the duckling free range of the yard under the watchful eyes of the boys and myself. At night, or when we were away from home, it was returned, protesting loudly, to its pen.

As the duckling grew, the soft fuzzy down that covered its body was slowly replaced by the coarser feathers of adulthood. Two things soon became obvious. The first was that our duck was a female, and second, that something about her wings was very unusual. Instead of folding neatly at her sides, her wing tips turned upside down and stuck straight out. We dubbed her Jet, because to us she resembled an airplane.

Jet assumed many roles as a member of our family. As resident comedian she was a constant source of amusement and giggles. She waddled behind whoever was walking in the yard, going as fast as she had to in order to keep up. She supplied our lawn with an abundance of fresh fertilizer. She also provided us with numerous fresh eggs, placed indiscriminately throughout the yard, though somehow we never found the courage to eat them. Jet was also an efficient bug-zapper and a terrific "watchdog." Head cocked, watching with first one eye and then the other, she was always on the alert and never failed to announce the arrival of visitors.

Jet quickly outgrew her small water tub, so we purchased a kiddy pool and propped a board on the edge to serve as a ramp. She relished her new pool and spent hours swimming, diving and flapping those misshapen, yet rapidly developing wings. As Jet reached her full physical maturity, her pool seemed suddenly small, and we knew the time had come to give her the freedom of the lake and the company of her own kind.

Wondering how long she would continue to recognize us, two quiet adults and two sad little boys loaded her into the car. As I carried her through the woods to the lake's edge, she quickly spotted her real family for the first time. I felt her heart beating wildly beneath my hands. As I placed her on the ground at our feet, the other ducks loudly beckoned to her to join them. Jet sat there, unmoving, glued to her spot in confusion. She seemed to have no clue as to what those noisy creatures were nor what she was to do. Jet had never seen a duck before!

I watched from the lake's edge as my husband and boys climbed into a small rowboat and began to paddle her out to where the other ducks had congregated. They carefully lowered Jet into the water and suddenly, with a splash, we learned another thing about her: with the right motivation, those bent wings were quite capable of flight.

And fly she did. Before the boys could get their paddles back into the water, Jet was once again on the shore, tucked safely between the feet of the only mom she had ever known.

We tried many times that day to introduce her to life on the lake, but Jet had made her choice. So we left the lake in single-file and made our way through the woods and up the hill to the car, five "ducks" in a row... all happy and relieved to be going home together.

~Lynn Pulliam
Chicken Soup for the Cat and Dog Lover's Soul

Bad Day, Good Life

This, too, shall pass.
~William Shakespeare

When I awoke at o'dark early, I never would have guessed, as I watched the falling snow, that that would be the day that changed my life—a day that would become a yardstick by which I would gauge any hard day thereafter.

The kids awoke, washed, dressed and had breakfast, and we set out for the school/workday with about six heavy, wet inches of snow already on the ground. I don't even think I realized my daughter was still wearing her tiger slippers, I was so concerned with driving on the winter country roads, but I'm sure her first grade teacher understood the harried life of a working mom.

I dropped the kids off at elementary school and headed on to work. It wasn't long before a car on the road ahead of me skidded sideways and another car, avoiding her, pushed my car into a guardrail. With a smashed fender, I trudged on to the lab. The company I worked for had been dumping chemicals into the sink, and hence the sewer, and since I knew this would kill the aerobic bacteria in the treatment plant for the town, I complained to my boss that it would be cost-effective to bulk the waste and sell it for "potpourri"—a tank load of mixture that could be refined, and not only settle the problem of dumping, but also make a few bucks for the company.

My idea didn't go over well, and I was instructed to do the dumping myself! Oh, dear. What to do? I spoke to a friend who suggested I call the health department and put a stop to this dangerous practice. Unfortunately, when I made the call, I had no idea the company recorded all incoming and outgoing telephone traffic. By the early afternoon, I was called into the personnel department and summarily fired. No severance, no consideration, no job!

I was so embarrassed about being let go, the first time this had ever happened to me, I went out with my tail between my legs, consumed with worry for my family's welfare. I drove the damaged car to the babysitter where the kids went after school, who informed me she no longer wanted to work at home and I would have to find someone else to care for my children. With the kids in the car, the snow now piled up to a good twelve inches, I drove home in the afternoon made dark by the blizzard, feeling the worst I had ever felt. What was I going to do?

No job, no babysitter, no income and two little ones to provide for soon had me crying as I drove. Of course, the kids started crying, too. We made it home to the apartment, and when I stopped to pick up the mail, there was an eviction notice in with the bills. The week before, the new landlord, who lived at a distance and had hired an incompetent to care for the property, hadn't bothered to fix the heat in my building or remove the ice from the entrance. My elderly neighbor had taken a spill, and but for one-quarter inch when she landed, would have hit her eye on the corner of the cement step. I had taken it upon myself to call and complain. He assured me he would "take care of it." Little did I know he meant removing the complainant rather than fixing the problems.

I was completely disheartened. Now, not only did I lack a job and a sitter who would watch my children while I looked for another one, but we also faced having to look for another place to live, which could likely mean another school. As we stepped out of the car, my daughter said, "Look, Mommy!" She pointed to the hood of the car, from which black smoke was pouring forth at an alarming rate. It was at this moment of my life that my attitude and entire way of being changed. I began to laugh. Then the kids began to laugh, and we stood there, in the still-falling snow laughing until it hurt.

I'm not sure what made me laugh, but I had come to the point where crying was no longer a solution and laughing at the sheer absurdity of the day was my last resort. It was at this point that we all learned the lesson of adversity: we arrived at the end of our despair and clicked over to the sheer epiphany that nothing else could go wrong, and things would just have to begin to go right.

Needless to say, we found another home, another school, another job and another sitter, one who lived right next door and became a good friend. But from that day on, every time things became difficult in the extreme, they never were more difficult than that day. I knew in my heart that if we could get through that day, we could make it in life. That one day, when I thought my world had fallen apart, became the barometer by which I measured all hard days. No matter what happened, I would immediately think back and know: if I could get through that, I could get through this and through anything else that came my way. Together we persevered and made it through life as a single mom with two kids.

~Barbara Stanley
Chicken Soup for the Single Parent's Soul

Tough Love

Small children disturb your sleep, big children your life.
~Yiddish Proverb

The feeling of terror crept back into my life. This time it was my teenage son, not my former husband. However, the same elements were in place—the gun, the ever-present fear. I sat at my kitchen table and stared into my coffee cup. The coffee was cold, and the night wore on my nerves as I waited for my son to come home.

I cupped my hands around the mug painted brightly with yellow daisies. When he was little, my son gave it to me for my birthday. He liked to give me presents—especially flowers. Clenching them in his small fist, showing a toothless grin, he'd say, "These are for you, Mama." I would get down at his eye level and hug him, then place the wilting wildflowers in a jelly jar on my kitchen table.

I poured the cold coffee into the sink. My heart broke as I remembered the last few months—when my son's anger erupted over the smallest things. "This bike is no good," he screamed as he slammed the ten-speed again and again into the ground until it lay in a crumpled heap. He had used his own hard-earned money to buy the bike, but when it wouldn't work properly, he blew up.

I cringed at his foul language, and I feared his hostility. One day in a rage, he rammed his fist through the basement door and shattered the mirror in his bedroom. He had a drinking problem, but I didn't know how to stop him.

The anger was too terribly familiar. His father had the same anger. It seethed for years under a cool exterior until he finally exploded and threatened me with a loaded gun. My former husband's life ended when he committed suicide while in jail for threatening his second wife.

Now my son had stolen a gun from our bedroom closet, and the same wrath boiled inside him.

I watched Jim, my second husband, pace the living room floor. His brow furrowed in worry. "Where is he?"

I glanced at the digital clock on the television and shrugged, exhausted with worry. "It's 1:30 and we still haven't heard from him."

Many times I'd heard the phrase, "Let go and let God." I had worried for months over how to handle my son.

I wondered if it was time to turn him over to the Lord. I decided to leave my child in God's hands instead of taking him back into mine.

I sat down at the kitchen table, bowed my head and prayed. A complete peace washed over me. "I am putting him totally and completely in God's hands," I told my husband. I crawled into bed knowing God was in control. Later, I felt my husband slip into bed.

At three A.M., the ringing phone jarred us awake. Sleepily, I answered. The police officer informed me that once again our son was in jail. This time he'd started a fight with a bouncer in a hotel lounge. When the security people found the gun on him, they called in eight police cars. I was relieved to learn the gun wasn't loaded, but it didn't make the charges any less serious.

"I have been praying about this," my husband said after I hung up, "and I feel a real peace about what I'm about to say. I don't think we should bail him out of jail again."

I swallowed past the lump in my throat. I knew, from all the times my son had been jailed for drunk driving, that my husband was right. But it was hard to turn away from my own flesh and blood. I had to put my trust in God. I would not waver.

When my son called the next morning asking us to put up bail, my husband simply said, "We are through bailing you out of jail. This time you'll have to get out on your own." My husband sighed as he hung up. "He's mad."

I often wondered how a parent could not come to a child's rescue. Yet I had to learn the hard way that if I continued to get my child out of trouble, he would never take responsibility for his own actions. And he would continue to get into trouble.

A few days later our son came home. He didn't speak to either of us except to say, "I'm moving out." He and a friend loaded his car with his belongings and left.

Six months went by before we heard from him again. He drove into the driveway with a blonde-haired girl by his side. He was smiling as they walked into the house. The four of us sat down in the living room and talked softly. I was delighted to learn he wanted to get married soon. Although I had some well-founded apprehensions about his past anger, I certainly hoped he and his future wife would be happy.

As the days, weeks and months flew by, I began to see a profound change in my married son. The angry young man who had left our home seemed to melt away as he became involved with his new family. Eventually, to my great happiness, he turned his life over to God.

At one of our first Christmases together after his marriage, my son drove to the store with my husband. The cab of the truck was almost silent except for the radio playing low. My son broke the quiet with an unexpected question. "Can you ever forgive me for the pain I put you through?" he asked.

My husband smiled and put his arm around him. "I've already forgiven you," he said, welcoming our son home with compassion, just like the father of the biblical prodigal son.

Later, our son brought a gorgeous poinsettia and set it on my kitchen table. Like a small child he said, "These are for you, Mama."

~Nanette Thorsen-Snipes
Chicken Soup for the Christian Woman's Soul

50

Little Dolly

*Every mother has the breathtaking privilege of sharing with God
in the creation of new life. She helps bring into existence a soul
that will endure for all eternity.*
~James Keller

I wish now that I could say I'd loved my daughter wholehearted-
ly right from the beginning. But when I first glimpsed Elisheva,
born six weeks early, my first thought—God forgive me—was
chicken. She was a scrawny chicken baby, the kind of baby I'd always
sneered at when one was born to other parents. I couldn't help it. My
first child, a boy, had been a golden, healthy baby who cooed and
smiled almost straight out of the womb, teethed painlessly, talked in
full sentences, read early and—at six and a half—will probably be up
for that Nobel any year now.

But my daughter was different. The first time I saw her, I literally
passed out. It didn't help that there was an IV line straight into her
forehead and what looked like a Lucite Tupperware cake cover over
her head supplying oxygen, but it might have just been from the long
labor and the fact that I'd insisted on walking rather than riding in
a wheelchair. I recovered to find three neonatal pediatricians staring
helplessly down at me, probably trying to puzzle out what to do for
a full-sized patient.

But if I thought her ruddy-yellow-skinned scrawniness was
appalling, all thoughts of chicken quickly crossed the road when, the

next morning, I first heard her cry. My only thought then—I admit, there's probably a special level of hell for mothers like me—was seagull. When the nurses paged to tell me she was awake and hungry, I heard a screeching, squawking seabird off in the distance, and as I walked toward the ICU, I realized that the noise must be emanating from my tiny bird baby. I couldn't imagine how any sound could pierce the walls of her plastic isolette, around the corner and down the hall, but she'd managed it. I walked a little slower, dreading my first physical contact with a creature who only two days earlier had been smashing my ribs from inside and parking herself on my bladder, sending me running to the bathroom every ten minutes.

Still exhausted and post-partum six weeks before I thought I'd even be feeling the first labor pangs, I didn't want or need a hungry scavenger in my life. Blearily, I made my way into the ICU. I pinpointed her by the noise rather than by any kind of visual recognition—I figured she'd gotten her looks from somewhere else on the evolutionary ladder altogether.

"Go and get comfortable," the nurse called, directing me to a rocking chair in a private playroom off the ICU. I sat in the chair, piled my lap high with pillows, and waited in dread for the baby. Soon enough, the nurse was there in front of me, carrying a pink-wrapped bundle with what looked like a sock on its head.

"What's that?" I asked.

"Stocking cap," she explained. "The volunteers made them for the New Year's babies." She showed me the glittering pompoms and gold ribbon tied around in an attempt to make the preemies' shaven heads look festive. I just braced myself to take the baby from her.

I held out my arms. "Are you ready?" she asked me. I must have nodded. "Here you go," she said, leaning over, and then, in an enchanted half-whisper, added, "Here's your little dolly." Her gentle words jarred me out of my daze; suddenly, the phrase "chicken baby" was gone. All I could hear, over and over in my mind, was "little dolly." I took a long look at the baby, brought her closer, and—unlike my son, who had always been too busy to nurse properly—she latched on immediately and began to drink.

My heart melted; I imagined I could feel its tears of relief flowing out into those first rich drops of colostrum, the early milk that welcomes a newborn after the shock of getting born. This was the milk, I realized, that would fatten her up so others, too, would recognize in her what only that nurse and I had glimpsed—a perfect dolly; my very own little baby girl, cuddling tight, a sparkling stocking cap cradling her sparse, vulnerable hair.

Some time during her first summer, as my mother and I were watching her lying on the rug kicking her legs, just for the thrill of seeing her double knees jiggle and her plump thighs wobble, my mother turned and asked, "Where did this fat, happy little girl come from?" I looked at my daughter and shrugged, pretending I'd never doubted, that, like that heaven-sent nurse, I'd been able to see through to her beauty all along.

~Jennifer M. Paquette
Chicken Soup for the Mother & Daughter Soul

51

The Potato Puppy

Pull the string and it will follow wherever you wish.
Push it, and it will go nowhere at all.
~Dwight D. Eisenhower

My four-year-old son, Shane, had been asking for a puppy for over a month, but his daddy kept saying, "No dogs! A dog will dig up the garden and chase the ducks and kill our rabbits. No dog, and that's final!"

Each night Shane prayed for a puppy, and each morning he was disappointed when there was no puppy waiting outside.

I was peeling potatoes for dinner, and he was sitting on the floor at my feet asking for the thousandth time, "Why won't Daddy let me have a puppy?"

"Because they are a lot of trouble. Don't cry. Maybe Daddy will change his mind someday," I encouraged him.

"No, he won't, and I'll never have a puppy in a million years," Shane wailed.

I looked into his dirty, tear-streaked face. How could we deny him his one wish? So I said the words that were first spoken by Eve, "I know a way to make Daddy change his mind."

"Really?" Shane wiped away his tears and sniffed.

I handed him a potato.

"Take this and carry it with you until it turns into a puppy," I whispered. "Never let it out of your sight for one minute. Keep it with you all the time, and on the third day, tie a string around it and drag it around the yard and see what happens!"

Shane grabbed the potato with both hands. "Mama, how do you make a potato into a puppy?" He turned it over and over in his little hands.

"Shh! It's a secret!" I whispered and sent him on his way.

"Lord, you know what a woman must do to keep peace in her home!" I prayed.

Shane faithfully carried his potato around for two days; he slept with it, bathed with it and talked to it.

On the third day I said to my husband, "We really should get a pet for Shane."

"What makes you think he needs a pet?" My husband leaned against the doorway.

"Well, he's been carrying a potato around with him for days. He calls it Wally and says it is his pet. He sleeps with it on his pillow, and right now he has a string tied to it and he's dragging it around the yard," I said.

"A potato?" my husband asked and looked out the window and watched Shane taking his potato for a walk.

"It will break his heart when the potato gets mushy and rots," I said and started getting out food for lunch. "Besides, every time I try to peel potatoes for dinner, Shane cries because he says I'm killing Wally's family."

"A potato?" my husband asked. "My son has a pet potato?"

"Well," I said shrugging, "you said he couldn't have a puppy. He was so disappointed, in his mind, he decided he had to have a pet...."

"That's crazy!" my husband said.

"Maybe you're right, but explain to me why he is dragging that potato around the yard on a string," I said.

My husband watched our son for a few more minutes.

"I'll bring home a puppy tonight. I'll stop by the animal shelter after work. I guess a puppy can't be that much trouble," he sighed. "It's better than a potato."

That night Shane's daddy brought home a wiggling puppy and a pregnant white cat that he took pity on while he was at the shelter.

Everyone was happy. My husband thought he'd saved his son from a nervous breakdown. Shane had a puppy, a cat and five kittens and believed his mother had magic powers that could change a potato into a puppy. And I was happy because I got my potato back and cooked it for dinner.

Everything was perfect until one evening when I was cooking dinner, Shane tugged on my dress and asked, "Mama, do you think I could have a pony for my birthday?"

I looked into his sweet little face and said, "Well, first we have to take a watermelon ...."

~Linda Stafford
Chicken Soup for the Mother's Soul 2

52

Mother's Magic

When you are a mother, you are never really alone in your thoughts.
A mother always has to think twice, once for herself and once for her child.
~*Sophia Loren,* Women and Beauty

Ken, the sixth child in our family, was born with cerebral palsy, profound deafness and mild retardation. Though my mother was extremely affectionate and loving, she never babied Ken. She expected him to do whatever we did.

I remember one Christmas we got a new swing set and slide. Ken, who was nine years old, loved the slide from the first second he saw it, but because of the braces on his legs, he couldn't manage the steps. So he spent the holidays watching the rest of us from the ground.

The first day we were all back in school, Mama put Ken in the backyard, this time without his braces, and watched him crawl right over to the slide. For the next three hours or longer, Ken climbed the ladder and fell, climbed the ladder and fell, again and again. He busted the knees out of both of his pant legs. His head was bleeding a little by one ear and so was an elbow.

The neighbor to the back of us yelled at my mother, "What kind of woman are you? Get that boy off that ladder." Mama told her kindly that if it upset her, she would have to close her kitchen curtains. Ken had decided to go down the slide, and down the slide he would go. It took a couple of days of trying before he could go up the ladder and down the slide as well as the rest of us, and another week before he could do it with his braces on.

But to this day, Ken—the boy who was not supposed to make it to his tenth birthday and is now a forty-two-year-old man who lives independently and holds down a job—approaches everything the way he did that slide so many years ago. What a gift my mother gave him that day by expecting him to be the best he could be—and never settling for less.

Mama could also make things easier for Ken. One weekday morning, the ladies of the church altar society were seated in our living room enjoying polite conversation and cups of my mother's coffee. Ken, an adult now, woke up and took his place at the head of our dining room table in the next room. Mother excused herself, served him his morning coffee and toast, then rejoined the ladies in the living room. With his breakfast Ken sat with his back to the open french doors leading into the living room and the group of ladies. However, just as he raised his coffee cup to his lips, his arm experienced an involuntary spastic movement and he threw coffee all over both french doors, one wall and himself.

Mother rushed to him finding him embarrassed to the core, his head hanging, face beet-red, apologizing over and over to her for the mess he'd made. Mama didn't miss a beat. She looked down in his cup, and seeing there was still an inch or two of coffee in the bottom, she threw the coffee on the only clean wall, and told Ken with sign language, "Looks like you missed a spot over here." Ken dissolved in laughter forgetting all about his embarrassment and the mess he'd made, and with a gentle smile on her face Mother began to clean up the mess.

Though I often feel I fall short when I compare my mothering to hers, it gives me great comfort to know that her gentle spirit is within me, somewhere—preparing me to make "mothering magic" of my own.

~Mimi Greenwood Knight
Chicken Soup for Every Mom's Soul

53

Bosom Buddies

The bust cream at $2.98 a jar hadn't worked. My friend Carol and I faithfully read the ads each month in the back of the movie magazines, showing girls with beautiful, fully developed figures. Now that we were almost fifteen, we longed to look just like them.

Scraping together our babysitting money, we excitedly sent away for two jars and eagerly awaited the mailman every day throughout June of 1955. We also staked him out because we knew this was not a purchase our mothers would approve of.

Euphoria was ours the day the jars arrived. After the recommended ten applications, like a busted (forgive the pun) balloon, euphoria dissipated into the hot July air. Well, at least for me. Carol was definitely developing, thanks to the cream or Mother Nature (who could say?) but the proof was there when she put on her bathing suit. She looked so curvy while I, her friend since first grade, was as flat as the tar patches on the hot neighborhood streets.

So one sultry July day, we opted for Plan B. Walking up to our local dime store, we made the second most important purchase of my teen life: falsies. These foam rubber answers to voluptuousness cost $1.98 a pair. Once again, a purchase to be made not with your mother, but only your best friend.

While I went to the ladies department, Carol stood guard in the aisles, lest my mom or one of her friends should come along. We had agreed upon a signal. Three coughs and the coast was clear, two coughs and trouble was near. Hearing the reassuring sound of three coughs, I handed the clerk my purchase. But wait a minute! What was that she was saying? She was out of bags and would be right back? Leaving the falsies right there on the counter in broad daylight?!

Oh, God, no! Please don't let this be happening, my young heart prayed.

Not only was it happening, but so, too, was the unmistakable sound of two coughs. Trouble, real trouble was at hand in the form of Mrs. McDoover, the neighborhood gossip, coming down the aisle. Right there and then, I promised God I'd be a missionary in China if he'd just let that salesclerk return with the bags lickety-split. And she did. Hallelujah!

Carol and I hurried home clutching the bag that held my soon-to-be new figure, well, at least the top portion of it. Once in the bedroom, I tried on my bathing suit with the falsies in place. Oh! It was so exciting! Carol assured me I looked like Marilyn Monroe or even Jane Russell. Well, maybe not that gorgeous, but very womanly, indeed.

What with the ninety-degree heat outside and no air conditioning inside, we were sweating up a storm. Hurriedly, we left for the park swimming pool. As luck would have it, this was girls' day.

We dove into the cool water and how wonderful it felt! We swam and swam, until out of the corner of my eye, I noticed something floating by. Oh, God, no! It couldn't be! Alas, it was. One lone falsie floating by without a care in the world or a matching partner, for that matter. Right then and there I knew I'd have to stay in the pool until midnight, but then I'd be late for supper, as well as grounded. Embarrassed beyond belief, I climbed out of the pool, ran into the girls' locker room and changed back into my clothes. Carol came in a few minutes later, carrying the falsie in her hand. We walked home, feeling depleted by the entire experience.

The house was sweltering, the six-inch fan blowing hot air on Mom as she sat peeling potatoes for that night's supper of potato salad and cold cuts. One look at my face and she knew the world had ended. Well, at least my little corner of it. Through tears, sobs and hiccups, the shamefaced tale was told. Reaching across the kitchen table Mom took my hand and said, "Go get my sewing basket and we'll fix things right."

That afternoon, over hot tears and cool lemonade, Carol and I learned that the quick answers the world offered to problems were often false, but love that was shared around the kitchen table was often the truest love of all.

~Alice Collins
Chicken Soup for the Girlfriend's Soul

54

Small Soldiers

When you come to the end of your rope, tie a knot and hang on.
~Franklin D. Roosevelt

I intended to move my troops to a better location, not into the line of fire. As a twenty-seven-year-old single mother of four children, I tended to think of myself as a fearless leader of my brood. And, in fact, our life often reflected the austere setting of boot camp. The five of us were crammed into close quarters—a two-bedroom apartment in New Jersey—and we lived a life of self-deprived discipline. I couldn't afford any of the niceties and luxuries other parents did, and aside from my mother, none of the rest of our family was involved in the kids' lives at all.

That left me as commander in chief. Many nights, I lay awake on my bed, planning strategies to get more things for my children. Though my children never complained about what they lacked and seemed to bask in my love, I was continually on the alert for ways to improve their simple lives. When I found a five-bedroom apartment in a three-story house—the second and third stories belonging completely to us—I leapt at the opportunity. At last, we could spread out. The home even had a big backyard.

The landlord promised to have everything fixed up for us in a month. I agreed on the repairs, paid her in cash for the first month's rent and the same in security, and hurried home to inform my troops we were moving out. They were excited, and we all camped on my bed that night, planning what we'd do to the new home.

The next morning, I gave notice to my current landlord and started packing. We loaded our boxes with the precision of a well-oiled machine. It warmed my heart to see the troops in action.

And then I realized my strategic error. I had no keys to the new house in hand, and when day after day of unreturned phone calls and fruitless searches produced no access to the house, I began to panic. I did some espionage work and called the utility company. They told me someone else had just requested new service for the same address. I'd been duped.

With a heavy heart, I looked at my children's expectant faces and tried to find the words to tell them the bad news. They took it staunchly, though I fought back tears of disappointment.

Already feeling defeated, I faced even worse obstacles. Our lease was now up on our current apartment. I couldn't afford rent on a new place because I'd paid so much for the house. My mother wanted to help, but children were not allowed in her small apartment. Desperate, I asked a fellow veteran fighter to help: a single mother of five who was struggling as much as I. She tried her best to be hospitable, but nine kids in four rooms .... Well, you get the picture.

After three weeks, we were all mutinous. We had to get out. I had no options left, no new orders to follow. We were on the run. I stored our furniture, stuffed our winter clothes in the back of our yellow Escort, and informed my small soldiers that we had nowhere to camp for the present time except in our car.

My sons, six and ten, met my gaze and listened intently. "Why can't we stay at Grandma's?" my oldest asked. That question was followed by several suggestions of others we should be able to stay with. In each case, I had to tell them the harsh truth. "People have their own lives, Honey. We have to handle this on our own. We can do this." But if my bravado appeased them, it didn't fool me. I needed strength. Where could I get help?

Knowing it was time to turn in for the night, I gathered up my troops, and we marched to the car. The children were calm and compliant, but my thoughts were engaged in fierce warfare. Should I do this to them? What else could I do?

Unexpectedly, it was my own troops who gave me the strength I needed. As we lived in our car for the next four weeks, showering at my mother's in the mornings and eating at fast-food joints, the kids seemed to enjoy the odd routine. They never missed a day of school, never complained and never questioned my judgment. They were so certain of their commander's wisdom that even I began to feel courageous. We could manage this! We parked in a different spot each night, well-lighted areas near apartment buildings. When the nights grew cold, the kids cuddled in the back seat that folded down into a bed, sharing body heat and blankets. I sat in the front, keeping watch between dozes and starting the motor every so often to run the heat.

When I had earned enough to afford rent someplace, I couldn't find any apartments that would accept four children, so we checked into a hotel. It was like being on a fantastic furlough. We were thrilled, reveling in the heat, the beds, the safety. We sneaked in our rations to cook and learned to prepare savory meals with a two-burner hot plate. We cooled dairy items in the bathtub. (Hotels have lots of ice.)

Finally, many months later, the landlord of the promised house sent me a money order refunding all that was due me, with many apologies. I used the money to find us an apartment.

That was thirteen years ago. I'm sharing command now with a husband, and we keep our children in a wonderfully large house. Every morning, when I run the inspection on my troops—taller now, looking at me eye to eye—I think back on the horrible enemy of desperation that we fought and defeated together. And then I thank God for my small soldiers: a courageous, tough little crew who never stumbled in their frightening march. Their bravery was the stuff of the greatest of heroes.

~Rachel Berry
Chicken Soup for the Unsinkable Soul

55

When All Hope is Lost

The human spirit is stronger than anything that can happen to it.
~C.C. Scott

"Don't you know? There will never be a cure!" my teenage daughter screamed from the backseat of the car.

I steadied my hands on the steering wheel while Jenna continued to rant and rave. I tried to swallow the lump in my throat. Not finding a single word that could or would change the situation, I remained quiet and tears stung my eyes. *"God, you've got to help the scientists find a cure soon. My daughter is losing all hope."*

"It's just too hard! I'm tired of feeling sick! I'm tired of being tired! I'm sick and tired of being sick and tired!" Jenna sobbed from behind. "Mom, I just don't think I can do it anymore…," she said as her voiced faded off into silence.

Jenna's words cut deep, for I knew that without hope, her heart would break. Wishing that this conversation wasn't occurring on a freeway, I fought traffic and slowly made my way to the off-ramp, checking my rearview mirror only to see the penetrating look in Jenna's eyes as she stared back at me. The unnerving silence was only interrupted by the sound of my turn signal.

It had been twelve years since Jenna truly "felt good." And for twelve years she had lived courageously, fighting her chronic disease. I understood her feelings of defeat. I too was tired of watching my daughter tend to her catheter site daily, injecting herself with the proper medications, and experiencing the unpredictable side effects. I, too, wanted to join her in screaming, "I'm sick and tired of you being sick and tired!"

Watching her in such emotional and physical pain made me ache all over. If only I could take her illness upon me, I'd give her my health and bear her infirmity. But I felt helpless not knowing how to console her.

I pulled into the first parking lot I could find. I parked the car, stepped out and then crawled into the backseat where Jenna lay motionless. I brushed her hair from her eyes hoping she'd open them and look into mine. She didn't move. For five minutes or more, I just sat and held her, praying that God would renew her strength and will to live.

What does a mother say to her child who is living a nightmare, praying that she'd someday soon wake up and it would be over? What words could bring comfort when all hope is lost?

Not knowing the answers, I spoke from my heart, hoping to reach Jenna's. "Jenna, I need you to look at me. I need to know that you really understand what I am about to say."

She turned her head towards me and opened her eyes. Immediately she began to repeat her words of hopelessness. Gently, I placed my finger against her lips.

"Honey, today you're tired and you've lost all hope. Today, you can rest in my arms and let me hope for you. You can be assured that my hope is endless and so is my love…"

"Mom," Jenna interrupted me, smiling slightly. "If you can hope for me, I guess I can too." She draped her arms around me. "Tell me again, Mom, that your hope is forever."

"It's forever, baby. My hope is forever."

~Janet Lynn Mitchell
Chicken Soup for the Caregiver's Soul

Moms Know Best

Time for Me

I've learned to take time for myself and to treat myself with a great deal of love and respect 'cause I like me... I think I'm kind of cool.
Whoopi Goldberg

Ceiling Fans

It was a usual busy Saturday afternoon when I struggled to get household chores, writing work and other miscellaneous duties completed, all while taking care of my four-month-old son, Max. I was a career woman, a writer used to being able to drop everything to work on an idea, sketch out a story or make an e-mail contact. I was also a woman used to eating lunch when I wanted, calling friends for hour-long chats at the drop of a hat, going to a movie with my husband and cleaning the house whenever the urge hit me.

But all that had changed when I found out I was going to be a mother at the ripe "young" age of forty.

In fact, my whole life changed as I fell madly in love with this little boy, my son. But I had no idea just how much time and energy this little thing could, and would, demand from me, and how crazy my new schedule would become once the word "mom" was added to my growing résumé. Even with a husband working at home, it still was an exhausting lesson in juggling priorities and multitasking.

Before I knew it, I was getting used to doing twenty things at once, before dropping into bed at 9:00 P.M. or sooner, hoping to get enough sleep to do it all over again the next day. I had always been used to staying up as late as I wanted, doing whatever I wanted. This new way of life took my breath, not to mention most of my energy, away.

One particularly hectic afternoon, I plopped Max in the middle of our king-size bed on his back so he could watch the ceiling fan while I folded laundry at the edge of the bed. At first he fussed, wanting my attention, but after a while he began staring at the blades moving round and round, and before I knew it, he was in a trance, fascinated, a slight smile frozen upon his pink rosebud lips.

He moved his gaze to the ceiling itself, nothing but an expanse of off-white textured paint, and seemed equally enraptured. I wondered what was so interesting, what fascinated him so. I decided to lay down beside him and join him to see what all the fuss was about.

Now normally my attention would be everywhere but on the present moment, especially a present moment that didn't involve doing something "constructive." I would either be going over something I did in the past, or plotting what I had to do in the future. I would be thinking about money, work, grocery shopping, losing weight, which relative had a birthday coming up. My body would be with Max, but my mind would be in a dozen other places as well.

But this time I found myself beginning to relax as we lay together on the bed, watching the whirring blades spin, feeling the soft breeze on our skin and tracing imaginary lines in the textured ceiling paint. As we lay there, we held hands and intertwined fingers, and Max gnawed on my knuckles with cool, wet gums. I kept feeling that I should get up and "do something," but Max refused to let go of my hand. He turned and looked at me with a smile that seemed to say, "Let it go for now, Mommy."

Suddenly, I felt myself totally embrace the moment. The fan, the breeze, Max's juicy wet mouth on my fingers, the laughter of our next-door neighbors splashing about in their pool. There was no thought of yesterday, or tomorrow, or even an hour from then. Only that moment.

It was as if time just opened up a huge chasm, and I fell headlong into it. The feeling only lasted a moment itself, but it jerked me back into my senses, reminding me just how much of my life I had been living in another time and place, namely the unchangeable past and the unknowable future. I lay there a little longer, just doing nothing, and doing it with every ounce of my being, for no reason other than because it was what I felt like doing. Nothing. It felt a little weird at first, but before long, I could feel every ounce of stress and strain leave my body, my mind and my spirit. I felt lighter than air.

Being a career woman and mother, heck, being a mother period, is hard, time-consuming work full of anxiety and worry over our abilities, stress over an ever-growing list of demands, and uncertainty over what lies ahead. We worry more than we should, and try to get more done than we need to, all because of the many roles we play, including breadwinner, cook, caretaker, guardian, warrior, mentor and boo-boo fixer.

But it all seems so unimportant when our own child reminds us of what really counts. Not our job performance or the current stock fluctuations. Not that promotion we missed out on, the mistake we made three weeks ago or the family reunion we have in two months. Not the three loads of laundry piled up in the hamper, the steaks that need marinating, or the e-mail that needs answering. Not how much money we make, or what kind of car we drive, or how big our house is. Not how we look or how clean our house is or what kind of clothes we wear.

What really counts is the present moment.

Fingers. Off-white textured paint. And ceiling fans.

~Marie Jones
Chicken Soup for the Working Woman's Soul

57

Freedom

My husband and I pull away from the curb, and I look tearfully through the back window as my younger child disappears into the yawning abyss of a college campus. How can I let her go? My baby, only eighteen years old, alone, halfway across the country. She tosses a wave in our direction and is gone.

My life is over. First, my son, Zack, left for school and now Nora. My nest is empty.

About fifty miles down the road, on the spur of the moment (a new concept!) my husband and I change our route and wind through the glorious Green Mountains of Vermont. We spend the rest of the day hiking and sleep that night in a charming bed and breakfast.

We do it without consulting our children. And we do it without the promise of a nearby amusement park, shopping mall or movie theater. (And we do it without the fear of anyone walking in!)

Et voilà! The end of my much-dreaded empty nest syndrome.

Now I'm convinced it's all a myth. A joke. A lie. If parents knew beforehand how delightful an empty nest really is, they'd be tossing teenagers out of their houses right and left.

I am a good mom, loving and nurturing. Sort of. I have to admit I wasn't wild about Candy Land or Suzuki violin, but I did it, and I did it well. And having devoted myself to my kids for so many years, I do occasionally have great moments of longing for those good old days.

But those moments pass the second I glance down at my car's odometer, only fifty miles added each week instead of 354. Miles of driving to and from and back and forth to every game, dance, practice, lesson or meet. And the car insurance! Without teenagers on your insurance policy, you can save enough for a trek through Nepal or a Las Vegas vacation, losses included.

Yet another bonus: When I reach for my car keys, lo and behold, they're on the hook where I last left them. In fact, all my possessions are where I last left them: my brush, my tennis racquet, my yellow sweater, my books.

I do laundry only once a week now. I watch whatever I want on TV (the remote isn't lost), and last but not least, I listen to my own music! I sleep at night not worrying about where my children are or when they might come rolling in.

Everything changes, especially your relationships. If you're married, you can rediscover why you came together in the first place. You're less judgmental, less cautious, less concerned with what you say and do since it no longer affects the children.

If you want to begin a relationship now, you might just find it easier to start one without the demands of your children coming (where else?) first. You might just discover a date prefers you with perfume instead of eau de peanut butter, and you will, I promise, discover the delight of finishing a sentence uninterrupted.

There is, as with everything, a downside to an empty nest. Those little fledglings have to fly and land somewhere, so you might need a second job to help furnish their landing pad, or to refurnish yours. Why? Because they will have carried off dishes, mops and the occasional table or chair. And if they're off to college, the cost is a killer—but the money saved on Froot Loops alone practically pays the tuition.

Since you no longer have to keep the household organized around the kids, your house can become an adult home, strewn with your own favorite toys and treasure. Oh, and if you've ever longed to sit for hours in meditation or dreamed of reading an entire book in one sitting, go for it right now.

Enjoy the freedom. It won't be long before that front door bursts open and newly hatched chicks fly in calling, "Grandma!"

~Bonnie West
Chicken Soup to Inspire a Woman's Soul

58

The Hammock

We were attending a big party at a beautiful home on Wisconsin's Lake Geneva when I saw it swaying slightly in the breeze: an inviting, big-enough-for-two hammock. I slipped in gently, relaxed a moment, then hurried back to the party.

Hurried. My whole life seemed hurried. Every minute of every day seemed pre-programmed. My whole body felt tense, yet I still hurried to work, then rushed home to take the children to baseball games, play practice and music lessons, then home to throw clothes into the washer. I hurried with my teenagers to the orthodontist, the dentist, then shopping so I could hurry home to fix supper. After dinner I'd even hurry through a storybook with my four-year-old so I could get down to my writing room to finish writing an article an editor wanted.

The speed with which life was engulfing me was giving me head-aches. It seemed that every minute of every day was programmed. My back ached, my whole body felt tense, yet I still hurried to work, hur-ried home, raced to my evening class and flopped into bed at night, too exhausted to even think.

That hammock started haunting me. Wouldn't it be nice...? I started to dream big dreams, but then I'd wonder if I could find time to relax in it if I bought one. Then one day, while waiting for my teens at the orthodontist, I saw an ad for a hammock just like the one we'd seen at the lake. On a healthy impulse, I ordered one.

When it arrived, my son Michael, age twelve, and I drilled holes in two backyard trees and mounted the screws and hooks that would support this new luxury. We did a fine job and the hammock looked marvelous and inviting.

Michael and I rewarded our efforts with an inaugural rest. Both of us plopped into the double-wide macramé rope hammock and chatted about what a great job we did. And we talked about other projects we might tackle together. A canvas swing in that tree over there? A small fence around the garden? We talked about school and then recaptured the excitement of the home run he'd hit the day before.

Then Andrew, age four, came bounding from the house with unbridled enthusiasm for his first "ride." Michael gave up his spot and Andrew climbed aboard.

The two of us stared at the leaves above us. "Mommy," Andrew giggled, "look at that squirrel!" We watched it scurry from limb to limb.

Then silence for a few minutes. I closed my eyes. A breeze was rocking me toward slumber. But not Andrew. "You know, Mom, I think those clouds are moving. There's one up there that looks like Dumbo.... See the trunk?"

"Uhhh, hummm," I answered almost unconsciously.

Andrew continued to chatter, but his little body hardly moved from the curves of my own as we snuggled in the hammock.

An hour later, I realized that I was, for the first time all summer, relaxing. Totally, completely relaxed. My headache was gone. Not only had the hammock provided a place to rest, it was the perfect place to talk to the children one-on-one. A place to open our hearts, to grow closer and to really listen.

That evening, Julia, age thirteen, spent an hour in the hammock reading. Next fifteen-year-old Jeanne plopped sideways in it to observe a colony of ants building a house directly underneath the hammock.

The next day when I returned from work, I walked right past the washing machine, grabbed a book I'd been trying to finish for over a year and headed for you-know-where.

It's funny how some rope, two wooden supports and a couple of good strong trees can change your life. Best prescription I ever took.

~Patricia Lorenz
Chicken Soup for the Working Woman's Soul

59

Paper Suits Me

During the sweltering summer of 1990, my husband, Paul, booked a hotel in Thunder Bay, Canada, that had a giant waterslide in the pool area.

Our four children screamed when they saw it. They got on their swimming suits, walked around the waterslide, and counted the ten twists and turns. I sat happily at a table with four-year-old Colleen on my lap.

"Can Colleen go down the slide with me?" Anne, our oldest at twelve, asked me.

"How can she?"

"On my lap. I'll hang on to her."

Anne took her hand as they headed for the stairs. Clare and Erin, our middle two, followed right behind.

"Be careful," I yelled.

Anne and Colleen had just finished the slide. Anne landed standing up as she lifted her sister into the air. Since there was no splash, not even a drop of water fell onto our youngest daughter's hair.

I was beginning to wish I hadn't forgotten my swimming suit. It just looked like so much fun. Like Colleen, I had never gone down a waterslide. But unlike the rest of my family, I was afraid of the water.

"Why didn't I bring my swimming suit?" I asked my husband.

"Are you thinking about going down the slide?"

"Maybe."

"Go to the front desk and see if they sell any," Paul said.

I couldn't wonder any longer. I went to the front desk.

"Ma'am, um, this might sound like a weird question, but do you sell any swimming suits?"

"Sure do. They're ten dollars," the woman behind the desk said.

"Great." I couldn't believe my luck.

"One piece or two, Hon?"

"One is fine." My bikini days had gone by the wayside after four pregnancies, stretch marks, and permanent weight gain. "What material are they made of?"

"Paper," the woman said.

Paper? The image I had of myself catapulting down the slide as my suit disintegrated was frightening to say the least. "That's okay," I said as I started walking away from the desk.

"They're very strong, Ma'am."

"Strong enough for a waterslide?"

"Yes. Look." She took the suit and pulled at the seams. The stitches didn't budge.

"Okay, I guess I'll try it," I said, as I handed over a ten dollar bill.

I went back to the room and changed into my paper suit. I inspected the texture again. It seemed strong, more like a heavy linen than paper. Just in case of any rupture, though, I wore a T-shirt over it.

"I'm ready," I said when I arrived at the pool.

My family was waiting to escort me to the steps going up to the waterslide. There were two girls in front of me and two others bringing up the rear. Paul was in the pool, anticipating my landing.

"How do you slow down?" I kept asking.

No one answered. My children glanced at each other. The eye contact with me was nonexistent.

We made it up the probably fifty steps without mishap. I didn't realize it was so high until I got to the top.

The line moved rapidly.

Anne and Colleen departed.

It was my turn now. No one was in front of me. The pounding in my chest let me know my heart was still beating.

"Do I sit?"

The attendant nodded his head.

I sat waiting for my signal to go. I swallowed the modest amount of saliva left in my mouth.

"How do you slow down?" I asked.

He looked at me strangely and said, "Just sit up straight."

"Okay," I said. I was sitting up straighter already.

"Go." The man motioned to me.

"ME? Right now?"

I was starting to sweat, but it wasn't from the heat. I looked at the long line behind me and decided it would be more embarrassing crawling over strangers and family than drowning in the three feet of water at the end.

"Lady, you can go."

I heard the words as I gingerly pushed myself down the slide.

I approached the first curve. I realized quickly and astutely that I had no control in the curves at all. I thought about swearing and then, luckily, thought again. I knew the words would echo and reverberate throughout the slide. My children would probably be traumatized for life.

I was going too fast.

Maybe if I put my legs up along the sides more, I'll slow down, I thought.

I did seem to slow down a fraction of a second. I knew I had to concentrate the entire length of the slide. The man had told me not to put my hands on the sides; I tried to keep them on my thighs, although I needed them for balance.

The bottom of my paper suit seemed to be filling with water but I didn't dare try to get it out. I pictured myself careening to the top of a curve, hanging suspended for a split second, and plopping down on my side. Or worse, I could flip over and land on my face with the water rushing up my nose.

Don't worry about the water, I told myself, as my buttocks swung from side to side.

I was weighing more with each passing second.

Paul said he would be waiting at the end for me. I hoped he

planned to catch me and keep me from going under water. I went around the S-shaped curve and saw the opening that signaled the end of the slide. I wanted to land without so much as a ripple, as Anne and Colleen had. I saw my husband standing in the water. That was my last conscious sight before feeling my body fly through the air. I hit the surface, water-filled buttocks first, with a large splash as my face and every other part of me went completely under. I was still trying to stand when my husband grabbed my arm and pulled me up.

"Are you okay?" he said.

There was a mixture of laughter and clapping around the pool.

"I'm okay," I said. "I can't believe how fast it is." I stated this fact loudly, so everyone could hear. "I felt like a rocket on that last curve."

"Mom, are you going again?" little Colleen asked.

There are some experiences in life that truly are "once is not enough." How could I say no to a four-year-old when she was almost jumping up and down?

"I think I'll go again," I said. I went back to the steps, and one of my daughters shielded me while I let out the ten pounds of water collected at the bottom of my suit. First the one side, then the other. I felt lighter already.

When the poor man saw me, he was too polite to let out a groan. And when he said go, I went. The third time I actually landed feet first, toes touching the bottom of the pool.

There was more applause from the bystanders.

After my tenth slide down, I decided to quit. The paper suit was miraculously still intact.

Paul told me later that all the people around the pool agreed that they had never seen a person go down a waterslide so slowly.

~Mary Clare Lockman
Chicken Soup to Inspire a Woman's Soul

The Amazing Technicolor Dream Table

Attitude is a little thing that makes a big difference.
~Winston Churchill

Knowing that none of my four children could be home for Mother's Day, I was in a giant funk. Jeanne had called saying her teaching job prevented her from flying home. Julia and Michael, their spouses, and my five grandchildren, who all lived nearly one hundred miles away, planned to celebrate Mother's Day with me later in the week when I was in Madison giving a speech. And Andrew, my youngest, who was still in college, had just finished his finals and was busy working at a new job on campus.

So there I was, alone and lonely when I awoke on Mother's Day. After giving in to a few weepy moments before I got out of bed, I told myself that if I kept busy all day I wouldn't have time to continue my pity party. I got up, fixed my favorite French vanilla tea and enjoyed a huge mug of it out on the deck.

The day before, I'd scraped all the chipped varnish off the octagon-shaped wooden picnic table. I used my electric sander to sand the top smoother than a granite headstone, then painted it with white acrylic primer. As I drank my tea I decided to paint the second coat brown to match the deck floor when I got home from church.

Church that morning was not a very spiritual event for me as I sat there with all those grandmothers, mothers and children. Youngsters clamored to sit next to their honored mothers. I was sad and embarrassed to be sitting there alone, and glad that I'd picked a seat way in the back.

When Father Bob asked all the mothers to stand for a special blessing, my eyes filled with tears. Then I caught myself. No! I will not give in to this self-pity stuff. I will do something to brighten my life and get out of this depressing mood.

I looked up at the stained-glass windows and marveled at the many colors—bright red, yellow, turquoise, orange and many shades of green and blue. That's it! I thought excitedly, I'll paint the picnic table in multicolored stripes! I couldn't wait for the last song to finish.

At home I changed into my paint clothes and grabbed the box of acrylic paints. I counted the wood slats in the picnic table. Nineteen. I chose twenty small bottles of brightly colored paint, allowing one for the trim. Everything from bold primary colors of red, blue and yellow to pink, lavender, aqua, orange, purple, sage, berry and sand. I lined them all up and decided which colors would look good next to which colors and then numbered the bottles from one to twenty.

I started with purple and a small paintbrush. Hey, this purple is the exact same color as that suit I bought for Jeanne when she lived in California! Jeanne loved it and wore it often, and I saw her in it again some ten years later!

When I dipped my brush into the soft chocolate brown, I thought of the brown walnut vanity I'd purchased for ten dollars at an estate sale in Denver in 1969 and refinished right in the middle of our tiny apartment living room. When my second daughter, Julia, was in sixth grade, I'd moved the vanity with the huge round mirror into her room as a special surprise. She loved it, took it with her to college and has since passed it on to her daughter.

The next color was bright Wisconsin Badger red. Boy, if that didn't remind me of Michael, my third child, who proudly wore the red University of Wisconsin Marching Band uniform for five years.

Football Saturdays and post-season bowl games made wonderful adventures for Michael and me.

Next came a doublewide bright yellow center stripe, the same as Arizona State's school colors where my youngest child, Andrew, was a junior. The yellow patch also reminded me of the scorching Arizona sun the day I said goodbye to Andrew when I took him to campus his freshman year.

On that beautiful sunny Mother's Day, as I painted that picnic table, each color provided me with spectacular Technicolor memories of each of my children—memories that will live in my heart and on my deck forever.

~Patricia Lorenz
Chicken Soup for the Christian Soul 2

Gotta Watch the Fish Eat

What you do today is important because you are exchanging
a day of your life for it…. let it be something good.
~Anonymous

I did something very daring today. I said, "No." I was at a meeting where I was asked to serve on a committee that would require numerous Thursday evening meetings. And I said, "No."

I declined politely, even graciously, but it wasn't enough. The others just looked at me, waiting. Three long seconds, four, five. Waiting, waiting for my important excuse. They couldn't move on until I had explained my answer.

"You see," I continued, "I really want to be home to tuck the kids in bed at night." Most of the others around the table nodded in understanding. "Well," the chairperson offered, "we can make sure we're done by 8:30, so you can be home in time to tuck the kids in." The others murmured in affirmation, and turned back to me, expectantly, waiting for my response.

"Well," I explained, "that's right when we are watching the fish eat." The others weren't impressed. "You see," I continued, "on Thursdays, after I've quizzed the children for Friday's spelling tests, we watch the fish. It's just an important time in our family's week. It seems to set the tone for the next day, and when I'm gone on Thursday nights, Fridays just don't go as well." My words sounded rather weak and almost silly as they tumbled out. No one said, "Oh, of course, Cheryl, we understand!" They were still waiting.

Now, I could have added, "But, you see, I've got a book manuscript due to the publisher in two months that I have got to work on." That would have been sufficiently important. After all, that's my career. They would have nodded in understanding, and quickly moved on. But the truth is, I'm not writing between 7:30 and 8:30 P.M. on Thursday evenings. I'm being Mom. I'm reviewing spelling words for Friday's tests. I'm checking math answers. I'm making sure permission notes are signed, book reports are written and weekly assignments completed. And when school work is done, and the children have brushed their teeth and gotten into their PJs, the family gathers on the couch in front of the aquarium to watch the fish eat. We feed the fish every night, of course. But on Thursdays we make an effort to sit together as a family and watch them. This is when I heard about Blake's plans to be a paleontologist. It's when I learned about how Bryce handled the bully on the playground. This is when Sarah Jean explained why she doesn't want to wear bows in her hair anymore.

The committee members were still looking at me. Feeling guilty, I almost changed my mind to say, "Okay, I'll do it." But I didn't. Because my reason for saying no is important. On Thursday evenings, we watch the fish eat.

~Cheryl Kirking
Chicken Soup for Every Mom's Soul

Getting Away

$\mathcal{I}$ don't get out much. Like most moms, I'm too busy doing mom stuff to take time for myself.

It wasn't always like this. Before I had kids, I had a career. Though I spent more hours nurturing my professional image in those days, it still seemed there was time left over for me. I'd make time to rejuvenate at a spa or unwind on a daylong shopping spree. Relaxing was a crucial component to the corporate image I was polishing.

Now, the only thing I polish is the furniture.

Having swapped the corner office at work in order to write from the corner bedroom at home, I now consider a trip to the grocery store without the kids to be a getaway. The business lunches I enjoyed at fancy restaurants were so long ago that the navy blue business suit I'd worn to them has gone out of style. I've cashed in the career and all the perks that come with it.

Oh, I'm not complaining. This is exactly where I want to be. So you can imagine the emotional tug-of-war I felt when my literary agent phoned to say that the publisher of my first book was sending me on an all-expense paid publicity tour from coast to coast!

At first the whole idea of a business trip seemed almost scary to me. The last time I was away from home all night I was giving birth. It's been a decade since I've gone anywhere without stuffing Goldfish crackers and an Etch-A-Sketch into my bag for the ride. I'd have to step out of my comfortable role as mother and step into the role of— what?—businessperson? Out of my Reeboks and into heels? Out of the laundry room and into television studios? Can I pull that off? I wondered. Won't they catch on and realize I'm just a mom?

But then I pondered the benefits of the trip. I'd be flying alone, dining alone and sleeping in luxury hotels alone. For an entire week, it would be just me. No school lunches to pack. No baseball practice. No four o'clock panic over what to make for dinner. I started to plan all the adult things I'd be able to do. I could visit each city's famous museums and stare as long as I wanted at each masterpiece without having to divert my eyes to keep tabs on my boys. I would browse through shops instead of racing through them, shouting, "Don't touch!" to my guys. And I would "dine" instead of "eat." It was beginning to sound better and better.

Finally, after making sure the refrigerator was full and the hamper was empty, I was on my way. As the plane took off, it also took my breath away. I was, for the first time in thirteen years, on my own—if only for a week. The curious thing about the trip was this: Instead of feeling like an adult, I actually felt more like a child! I could stare out the window of the plane in awe of the billowy clouds without having to tend to someone else. I could think uninterrupted thoughts. I didn't have to make my bed. I could drop my towel on the floor in the hotel bath and someone else would pick it up. I could order anything I wanted off the menu and not worry if I had enough money to pay the tab.

Even dessert. Twice if I wanted to.

Instead of driving my kids to school and practice and trying to stay on schedule, I had personal author escorts in every city who chauffeured me around. They were being paid to keep me on schedule. While they concentrated on the road I could take in the scenery, the flowers and the people—all things you miss when you're the pilot instead of the passenger.

But San Francisco's cable cars and Seattle's Space Needle left me missing my family. Flying over Mount St. Helen's and seeing New York's skyline on approach to JFK are sights that should be shared. The guy in the seat next to me was snoring.

During a layover in Denver, I watched an exhausted mother

chase her toddlers through the terminal. She apologized as they knocked my luggage over. "It's okay," I smiled. "I'm a mom, too."

But after days without doing any mom stuff I didn't feel like one. I had morphed into this other person, but the spell was starting to wear off. I knew I'd be turning back into a pumpkin soon, and the weird thing was, I was looking forward to it.

It became clear to me that for moms, coming home is what getting away is all about. Whether it's cruising the Caribbean or cruising the aisles of the grocery store alone, I know now how important it is to get away.

When I returned home my children looked angelic. The exploding hamper was a challenge, not a chore. I looked forward to filling up the empty refrigerator. I was refreshed. I was home.

A week later, up to my ears in mom stuff, I decided to write another book.

~Kimberly A. Porrazzo
Chicken Soup for the Working Woman's Soul

A Mother's Wisdom

*The willingness to accept responsibility for one's own life
is the source from which self-respect springs.*
~Joan Didion

63

May Basket

"Hey, do you know what? Today is May Day!" my sister announced. "Do you remember the May Day baskets we used to make with colored paper and paste?"

Childhood memories and warm feelings engulfed me as I recalled that my sisters and I would run around our neighborhood delivering the not-so-perfect baskets brimming with spring flowers. We would place the handmade treasures on a doorstep, knock on the door, then scurry away as fast as our legs could carry us. It was delightful to peer around a bush and watch our friends open their doors and pick up the colorful gift, wondering who had left it out for them.

I distinctly remember the May Day of the year that I was in fifth grade. That year I was faced with a challenge involving one of my dearest friends. She lived right across the road from our family, and we had walked together to school nearly every day since first grade.

Pam was a year older than I, and her interests were starting to change from the interests that we had shared together. A new family had recently moved into our small town, and Pam was spending more and more time at their house. I felt hurt and left out.

When my mother asked me if I was going to take a May Day basket to Pam's house, I responded angrily, "Absolutely not!" My mom stopped what she was doing, knelt down and held me in her arms. She told me not to worry, that I would have many other friends throughout my lifetime.

"But Pam was my very best friend ever," I cried.

Mom smoothed back my hair, wiped away my tears and told me that circumstances change and people change. She explained that one of the greatest things friends can do is to give each other a chance to grow, to change and to develop into all God wants each of them to be. And sometimes, she said, that would mean that friends would choose to spend time with other people.

She went on to say that I needed to forgive Pam for hurting me and that I could express that forgiveness by giving her a May Day basket.

It was a hard decision, but I decided to give Pam a basket. I made an extra special basket of flowers with lots of yellow because that was Pam's favorite color. I asked my two sisters to help me deliver my basket of forgiveness. As we watched from our hiding place, Pam scooped up the flowers, pressed her face into them and said loudly enough for us to hear, "Thank you, Susie, I hoped you wouldn't forget me!"

That day, I made a decision that changed my life: I decided to hold my friends tightly in my heart, but loosely in my expectations of them, allowing them space to grow and to change—with or without me.

~Sue Dunigan
Chicken Soup for the Girlfriend's Soul

64

I Love My Body... Now

It has been about five years since I've worn a swimsuit. I've been overweight since elementary school, and I've had a poor body image ever since I can remember. I've spent much of my life feeling bad about my body, avoiding mirrors, leaving dressing rooms in tears, and mentally beating myself up over what I look like. I was so ashamed of and embarrassed by my body that I hated to let even my husband see it. I would try to hide myself if he came into the room while I was showering or getting dressed.

When I found out I was pregnant, I was certain that having a baby would be the end of any chance I might have had of eventually being happy with my body. I cringed every time someone mentioned my growing belly. I knew it was all part of the childbearing deal, and that everyone else knew that. But for someone who has spent most of her life feeling embarrassed and self-conscious about her girth, suddenly having strangers and friends commenting on it can be pretty painful.

We had moved and I needed a full-length mirror for the new place to help me when getting ready in the mornings, but my husband kept finding little excuses not to buy one. So when I did catch a full view of myself at nine months pregnant, I was shocked and dismayed. And he admitted that this was why he had been avoiding buying the mirror—not because of what he thought of my appearance, but because of what he knew I would think.

My baby girl was born in July of 2000. She is, without question, the most amazing thing that has ever or will ever happen to me. I am simply astounded when I look at her and realize that she is what I felt moving inside of me all those months. Here is a beautiful, wonderful little person. She is perfect. I love her perfect little hands, little round eyes, little legs, little feet, little pinchable bottom and little mind that I can see developing along with her body. Every day I can see how she is changing and growing as a separate human being, yet I still feel as if she is somehow a part of me. I love her and love being her mother with every fiber of my being.

And here's what I've come to realize. This wonderful little person grew inside of my body. My body provided the ingredients that became her. It then sheltered her, protected her and provided every single thing her body used to develop and become her. It wasn't something my mind did. For the first weeks, my mind wasn't even aware of the process my body was carrying out. I didn't will her into being, and it had nothing to do with my intelligence, determination or perseverance. It was my body that did everything. Then, when her body was ready to leave the protection of mine, mine did just what it was supposed to do. Without any instructions or experience, it went into action and delivered life into the world.

Yet the process wasn't over there. Once my baby was born, my body continued to provide for her. It immediately began producing exactly the kind of food she needed as a newborn. I didn't study medicine or take the right pill or eat a certain food to cause it to do this. It simply did. And three days later, when she was ready for a new and different food, my body provided it. For six months after, my body continued to provide all the nutrients and antibodies she needed, complete and perfect for her, and in just the right amount. In short, my precious daughter's very existence is a function of my body.

My body just gave me the greatest gift I've ever received. How could I possibly dislike it now? I look at my stretch marks and I see a visual reminder of what has happened, a reminder I'll be able to carry with me my whole life. I don't look in the mirror and see fat anymore; I see an amazing and wonderful life grower. I'll never look anything remotely like a super model. My society and culture will never declare me a beautiful woman, and men will never turn and watch me go by or whistle as I pass. There will always be people who will look at my body and consider it average, unattractive, even ugly. Frankly, I don't care. Those people don't know or understand what makes a person, or a person's body, beautiful and wonderful. This is my body. And I love it… now.

~Regina Phillips
Chicken Soup for the Mother & Daughter Soul

65

Pearls of Time

Faith makes things possible, not easy.
~Author Unknown

I hadn't intended to isolate myself in my bedroom for three days, but the unexpected death of a dear friend had devastated me. I was a new Christian, unprepared for the questions and doubts that overwhelmed me.

The door opened and my husband, Jeff, came near.

"It's going to be okay," he said softly, stroking my hair.

I buried my head in his shoulder. I didn't understand this grief. Life seemed so perfect until this happened. One minute Jeff and I were rejoicing in the news of my pregnancy, the next, we were grieving over the loss of a friend. The future was an uncertain destiny, and how was I, a Christian and expectant mother, supposed to view life's sorrows and triumphs?

"I'm so confused," I confessed, lifting my tear-streaked face. "I wish God would just give me a simple answer. A vision of how to journey through life as a Christian woman."

Just then, the doorbell rang. Jeff kissed the top of my head, then left to answer it. When slow-moving footsteps returned to the doorway, I was surprised to find my elderly neighbor, Sarah, appraising me. I yearned for the wisdom her blue eyes held behind wire-rimmed glasses.

"I missed your visits to me these past days," she said, shuffling over to sit beside me. "I thought you might've been experiencing morning sickness, but then I learned your friend died."

I didn't say a word. Sarah was the godliest woman I had ever met. She rarely left her home unless it was an emergency. I suppose she figured this was an emergency.

"How do I look today?" she surprised me by asking.

"Beautiful," I answered, assessing her pale blue dress and pearl necklace. "I've never seen that necklace before. It's lovely."

"You have one too," she said, lifting a finger to point at my collarbone. "Only it's a spiritual one unseen by human eyes." She reached behind her neck and unlocked the necklace. Holding it between her fingers, she rubbed the pearls gently. "This necklace was handed down to me as a reminder of the heavenly necklaces women wear." Patting my knee, she continued, "God instilled in women an incredible sense of caring and compassion, Karen. We are the nurturers, the vessels of life. We take care of our husbands, our children, our houses, and sometimes we feel as though everyone's emotional well-being depends on us."

She paused, handing me a tissue, then smiled. "Long ago, when I was a child, an elderly woman told me that she believed there's a special blessing for women—a 'pearls of time' necklace that we're born with. During our lifetime, the pearls that adorn our necks represent momentous events in our lives."

Moved by her words, I instinctively touched my neck, as if I could sense adornment there.

"But," she emphasized, holding the necklace for me to see, "the most important part is the clasp that holds it together. That represents Jesus. Like a perfect circle—from beginning to end, He's with us. Holding us firmly in life's tragedies or triumphs. We only need to remember and trust in that." She sighed, slipping the necklace back on and waiting for me to speak.

Speechless, I absorbed her words, allowing them to soothe my soul. "I don't know what to say," I whispered.

"Don't say anything, then," she chuckled, standing up. "I'm just fulfilling the scripture in Titus 2:4 for older women to be holy, so that they can teach the younger ones. One day you will, too. Right now, you're a young, uncertain Christian woman, but you have a teachable spirit and a great desire to obey God. That's a winning combination."

We embraced, and I inhaled the familiar scent of lilac soap. "Thank you, Sarah. Thank you."

"You don't have to thank me, honey," she said, "but I do have to go. My son is waiting." She was almost out of the doorway when she stopped briefly and turned to me. Lifting her hand, she brought my attention to her neck. "Just remember, dear."

"I will," I promised, walking over to help her down the stairs.

As I watched the car disappear around a curve, I suddenly felt renewed. "Thank you, Jesus," I murmured, closing my eyes. "Thank you for answering my prayers." When I reopened them, my vision was clear.

Four years later, I clutched the hand of my three-year-old daughter Abigail as we stood beside Sarah's hospital bed. "You're going to get better," I told her, watching in despair as her face grew paler.

"I'm not worried, dear," she grinned, squeezing my hand. "I'm looking forward to seeing the Lord."

"But we'll miss you," I blurted, clutching her hand. "I love you! You've not only been my friend, but you've been a godly teacher to me. I'll miss our talks, our laughter, our—"

"Shhh," she smiled, meeting my eyes. "You'll do just fine without me." She pointed to a small box lying on the bedside table. "Take that. Open it tonight with Abigail. It'll help both of you. Now, promise me."

"I promise," I said, slipping the box into my purse.

We said our tearful goodbyes, each being a little more lighthearted for Abigail's sake, but we both knew it would be the last time we'd see each other.

Later that night, after receiving the news that Sarah had passed away, I snuggled with Abigail on the couch. She curled into my side, her silky hair brushing against my cheek. "Open it, Mama," she said, curiously touching the box.

Through tear-filled eyes, I lifted the lid and found the pearl necklace that Sarah had modeled for me four years before.

"It's beautiful, Mommy," Abigail exclaimed, gently touching the shimmering treasure. "But why do I still feel so sad? Sarah said it would help us."

Her question tugged at my heart, but I was prepared. "Well, honey," I said, touching her soft cheek with my fingertips. "This necklace was handed down to me as a reminder of the heavenly necklaces women wear...."

~Karen Majoris-Garrison
Chicken Soup for the Christian Soul 2

66

"One Day, You'll Look Back on This..."

"**I** can't go to school like this!" I wailed as I stared into my mirror, hating my face, my body and life in general. A river of salty tears traced a path down my cheeks. Summoned from the kitchen by my shrieking, my mother appeared at my side a second later.

"What's the problem?" she asked patiently.

"Everything... just everything!" I complained and continued to stare horrified into the mirror.

At almost thirteen, the problems that I felt I had were overwhelming. I had a hideous new crop of angry, red pimples that had erupted on my forehead and chin overnight—every night. My hair suddenly looked greasy all the time, even though I washed it every second day. My aching tummy signaled that my newfound "friend" was about to visit once again, causing my jeans to fit too snugly and make me appear as though I had been eating nothing but hot fudge sundaes. And to top it off, my chewed-up fingernails were torn and bloody, since biting them seemed to go along with the way I worried about how other people perceived me. But everything that was bothering me wasn't just on the surface—I also had a broken heart. The guy I had been going out with had recently dumped me in favor of an older, more developed girl. Everything combined, I was a physical and emotional wreck.

"Come on, now, Honey. Try not to cry," my mother said with

a smile. "I remember what it was like to be your age. It was awkward and frustrating, and I got my heart stomped on, too, but I came through it—and so will you! It's not as bad as you think, and once you get to school with all your friends, you'll forget all about your pimples and what's-his-name, and one day you'll look back on this and wonder why you were ever so upset."

Convinced that she didn't know what she was talking about, I gave her a dirty look and headed off for school, greeting my girlfriends on the sidewalk while my mother waved encouragingly from the front door. Later, as much as I hated to admit it, I found out that my mother was right. As I spent time with my friends who were going through the same things that I was, my mind wasn't on my troubles anymore, and soon I was laughing.

When I returned home later that day, I was in a much better mood and because I had put my best foot forward, my mother rewarded me with a bag of goodies she had purchased from the drugstore. On my bed was a bag that included shampoo and conditioner, some acne medication, a gift certificate to a hair salon and, surprisingly, some hot, new shades of nail polish.

"What on earth is this?" I asked bewildered, thinking that my mother had to be out of her mind if she thought I was going to flaunt my gnarled nails.

As it turned out, she had a plan. I thought that it was cruel at the time, yet it turned out to be highly effective. I wasn't allowed to have any of the stuff in the bag, nor was I allowed to keep my ever-so-important stick of concealer. The deal was that for each week that I didn't bite my fingernails, one item of my choice would be returned to me. Desperate to retrieve my makeup and to get my hands on everything in the drugstore bag, I concentrated heavily on my schoolwork, instead of biting my nails and worrying about what people thought of me. Over the next few weeks, I was thrilled to watch my nails grow. By the time I earned the certificate to have my hair cut and restyled, my nails were so long that my mother also treated me to a manicure while we were at the salon. And as time wore on, I began to see that I was getting through the rough spot, just as she had promised I would.

I liked that I received so many compliments on my hands and hair, but more than that, I was proud of myself for sticking with the deal and improving myself in the process—so proud, as a matter of fact, that I failed to notice my acne slowly clearing up. And I couldn't have cared less about what's-his-name. He quickly became a distant memory as I began to date many different boys, some of whom broke my heart and others whose hearts I broke.

Though it certainly wasn't my last acne outbreak, bad hair day or crushed spirit, I did learn something. I will hold with me forever my mother's words of wisdom: "One day you'll look back on this and wonder why you were ever so upset."

Years later, after several ups and downs in my life, I look back and realize that I did come through it all and I am the better for it. I only hope that if one day I have a daughter who is experiencing the struggles of adolescence, I will be as understanding, helpful and creative as my mother was with me.

~Laurie Lonsdale
Chicken Soup for the Girl's Soul

67

Calling Mr. Clean

I got the blues thinking of the future, so I left off and made some marmalade.
It's amazing how it cheers one up to shred oranges and scrub the floor.
~D.H. Lawrence

Maybe it was nesting on steroids. Possibly it was my less-than-neat twin toddlers. Or perhaps it was a compulsive desire to maintain the illusion of order in my life. Whatever the reason, during my last pregnancy I just could not stop thinking about cleaning things. I just couldn't get enough of All Things Immaculate.

So when I saw the sponge, yellow, five inches thick and really squishy looking, I had to have it. Had to have it in a way only a pregnant woman has to have something. It's bizarre, but I actually salivated when I saw it. Had I ever seen anything more useful, more amazing? And for a mere ninety-nine cents! Who could pass up such a bargain? Certainly not pregnant old Pavlovian me.

Myriad cleaning endeavors starring the sponge and myself tap-danced glitzily around in my head. I would try it out first as my own personal bath implement. Unfortunately, it made a squeaky noise as I pulled it across my skin, so I had to nix that idea. I used it to clean the bathtub instead. After that, I couldn't stop thinking about it. I'd giddily daydream, planning our next encounter. Maybe tonight it would be the bathtub again. Or the kitchen floor. Or maybe even the car.

And it didn't stop with the sponge. Other cleaning implements, things that I hadn't glanced at in years, let alone used, became tantalizingly attractive to me. The white scouring brush under the sink. Brillo pads. Bottled cleaning products. I couldn't keep my hands off them.

At the supermarket, instead of standing pondering ice cream bars in the frozen foods aisle as usual, I stood transfixed by Ajax, Soft Scrub and Pine Sol. Mr. Clean winked seductively at me, and I fantasized about just how sparklingly clean I could get my bathroom faucet if only I brought the burly fellow home with me.

I scoured the finish off the linoleum in the kitchen one night. I washed the car every day for a week. Masked and gloved, I obsessively sprayed, spritzed, rubbed, wiped, waxed and polished my way through my last trimester.

And then I had my baby boy, and the romance was over. Whatever hormone it was that caused my sponge fetish thankfully exited my body with my son, leaving me once again a comfortable slob, unconcerned about suds and sparkling appliances. The scrub brush got tossed back under the sink with a shrug; the brigade of impulse-purchased cleaning supplies was relegated to the back of the linen closet. I stopped returning Mr. Clean's calls. The wonder-sponge sulkily disappeared into the basement. I wondered, perplexed, just what I'd seen in the thing when I stumbled upon it about a year later. I held it in my hand and tried to rekindle the old flame. Nothing doing.

And then a couple of days ago, we were at Sam's Club, and there it was. Another sponge. A big, meaty, make-everything-sparkling-clean yellow sponge. My heart skipped a beat. I could practically taste the bone-tingling satisfaction of a cleaning job done right. I started to drool.

And that's when I knew.

That sponge and I were going to be very busy for the next nine months.

~Karen C. Driscoll
Chicken Soup for Every Mom's Soul

68

Second Skin

My favorite pair of old jeans will never fit me again. I have finally accepted this immutable truth. After nurturing and giving birth to two babies, my body has undergone a metamorphosis. I may have returned to my pre-baby weight, but subtle shifts and expansions have taken place—my own version of continental drift. As a teenager, I never understood the difference between junior and misses sizing; misses clothing just looked old. Now it is all too clear that wasp waists and micro-fannies are but the fleeting trappings of youth. But that's okay, because while the jeans no longer button, the life I exchanged for them fits better than they ever did.

For me, this is a barefoot, shorts and T-shirt time of life. I have slipped so easily into young motherhood; it is the most comfortable role I have ever worn. No tough seams, no snagging zippers. Just a feeling that I have stepped out of the dressing room in something that finally feels right.

I love the feel of this baby on my hip, his soft head a perfect fit under my chin, his tiny hands splayed out like small pink starfish against my arms. I love the way my eight-year-old daughter walks alongside us as we cross the grocery store's sunny parking lot. On gorgeous spring days, the breeze lifts her wispy ponytail, and we laugh at how the sunshine makes the baby sniff and squint. I am constantly reaching out to touch them, the way a seamstress would two lengths of perfect silk, envisioning what might be made from them, yet hesitant to alter them, to lose the weight of their wholeness in my hands.

On those rare mornings when I wake up before they do, I go into their rooms and watch them sleeping, their faces creased and rosy. Finally, they squirm and stretch themselves awake, reaching out for a hug. I gather them up, bury my face in them and breathe deeply. They are like towels just pulled from the dryer, tumbled warm and cottony.

Sometimes, I follow the sound of girlish voices to my daughter's room, where she and her friends play dress-up, knee-deep in garage-sale chiffon, trying life on for size. Fussing and preening in front of the mirror, they drape themselves in cheap beads and adjust tiaras made of sequins and cardboard. I watch these little girls with their lank, shiny hair that no rubber bands or barrettes seem able to tame. They are constantly pushing errant strands behind their ears, and in that grown-up gesture, I see glimpses of the women they will become. I know that too soon these clouds of organdy and lace will settle permanently into their battered boxes, the ones that have served as treasure chests and princess thrones. They will become the hand-me-downs of my daughter's girlhood, handed back to me.

For now, though, my children curl around me on the sofa in the evening, often falling asleep, limbs limp and soft against me like the folds of a well-worn nightgown. For now, we still adorn each other, and they are content to be clothed in my embrace. I know there will be times that will wear like scratchy wool sweaters and four-inch heels. We will have to try on new looks together, tugging and scrunching, trying to keep the basic fabric intact. By then, we will have woven a complicated tapestry with its own peculiar pattern, its snags and pulls and tears.

But I will not forget this time, of drowsy heads against my shoulder, of footy pajamas and mother-daughter dresses, of small hands clasped in mine. This time fits me. I plan to wear it well.

~Caroline Castle Hicks
A Second Chicken Soup for the Woman's Soul

69

Three Words

Think left and think right and think low and think high.
Oh, the thinks you can think up if only you try!
~Dr. Seuss, Oh, the Thinks You Can Think!

As I stood outside the arena on that bitter February day, I had no idea of the warmth that I would find inside. Before entering the building to join 5,000 people, I slipped a three-word sign on my baby's stroller. I very much wanted to connect with the people inside. I hoped that someone would read my sign and welcome us into their community.

Nine months earlier, I had given birth to my third child, Jimmy. He was a beautiful baby in every way. On his second day of life, I was told he had Down syndrome. I read everything I could get my hands on about Down syndrome and received encouragement from other parents. Jimmy was nine months old when I read that Toronto and Collingwood, Ontario, were hosting the Special Olympic World Winter Games. I wanted to go with my baby and get a peek into our future. Before leaving the house, I raced down to the basement and made a three-word sign out of white felt and red marker.

When Jimmy and I entered the arena, we took a seat alongside the boards. Within minutes, my sign was being noticed. Parents squeezed my hand and told me of the challenges and unbelievable joys I would know. Athletes came over to meet my baby and wish him luck. Volunteers who travelled thousands of miles to be a part of the games attached their country's pins to the little square of felt. It was also noticed by a crewmember from The Sports Network (TSN), and by Frank Hayden, the founder of the Special Olympics movement worldwide.

It was Frank Hayden who put my little, three-word sign into a context I never imagined. He told the Canadian Parliament and the news media that it was the "defining moment" of the games and of his thirty-year career as a sports scientist. He said, "Thirty years ago, even ten years ago, would a mother have walked into a public place and proudly announced that her child had a mental disability? She was looking toward the future, not with fear and trepidation, but with great expectations."

Last July I received a beautiful letter from an artist in Ottawa. He had been commissioned to create a logo for the ninth Special Olympic Canadian Summer Games in Sudbury, Ontario. Bernard Poulin wrote, "You and your child have been my creative muses. The 'challenge sign' on your baby's chest said it all." Poulin created a circular logo that he says "reminds us of the hearts and souls of the parents who fuel the dreams of the athletes, who are supported and encouraged by the organisation." Poulin added, "It exists because in a crowd at the Centennial Arena in North York, Ontario, a proud mother and a beautiful child challenged the world with their daring."

The impact of the three words on that makeshift sign continues to amaze me. It said only, "Future Special Olympian."

~Jo-Ann Hartford Jaques
Chicken Soup for the Canadian Soul

70

The Story of Mary the Maid

*No matter how calmly you try to referee, parenting will eventually produce
bizarre behavior, and I'm not talking about the kids.*
~Bill Cosby, Fatherhood, 1986

When I was growing up in Delaware, my dad was a Jewish communal worker, and my mom a professional Hebrew teacher. They were truly pillars of the community. Nevertheless, my mom took great pride in keeping a balbatisch (dignified, decorous) house, and training her daughters to do the same. It was her custom to clean windows, for example, the way most housewives did in those days. She would open the double-hung window, climb halfway out, and sit on the sill facing inward. Lowering the window onto her thighs to pin her in place, she would proceed to clean with huge sweeping motions with her arm. This meant she had to ignore the fact that she was dangling out over the street, and could fall two stories onto hard cement with one false move.

One day, my dad came home from work unexpectedly and saw her suspended in space, with her posterior hanging out. He was not amused. He thought it undignified for the wife of the executive director of the Jewish Community Center to be seen in this activity, and he considered it dangerous to boot. He really was quite upset by it, and he told Mom in no uncertain terms that she must get someone to help her. In vain, my mother protested that a maid would cost money, that no one could do the job as well as she, that she did not mind doing her own housework, and all of that. My father persisted until my mom reluctantly capitulated and agreed to hire a maid.

She was as good as her word. She told my father a week later that she had found a suitable candidate through Sylvia Rosenbaum, who lived across the street. Mary was a Polish woman with a long name consisting of a string of unpronounceable consonants. A divorced woman, she was the sole support of her two sons. The older was a no-goodnick who had a drinking problem and had recently joined the Marines, which she hoped would do him some good. The younger boy got good grades, and she was praying that he would get a college scholarship. Mother and her new assistant got along just fine from the start.

We never got to meet Mary because she came after we left for school and work, and she was gone by 3:00 P.M. Every Thursday, however, my father would leave a ten dollar bill to pay her wages, and every Thursday night the house would sparkle, for Mary was a whirlwind with a mop and pail. Even mother admitted that her preparations for the Sabbath on Friday were much easier now that Mary was here.

All went well for the better part of the year, with Mother periodically updating us on Mary's life and activities. We felt as if we knew her and her sons, and we were liberal with our advice about how to handle them. Then one day my father came home looking glum. There had been a domestic disaster, a broken boiler, an exploded carburetor; I don't remember exactly what it was. But it was something that would be expensive to fix, and money was tight.

"How much do you need, Harry?" asked my mom.

"Four hundred dollars at least," was the reply.

My mother got a thoughtful look on her face, then excused herself from the dinner table and ran upstairs. She returned with a huge wad of ten dollar bills that she pressed into my father's outstretched hand. "What's this?" asked my father in bewilderment, looking down at almost fifty bills. Looking like the cat that swallowed the canary, and chortling in utter triumph, my mother exclaimed, "That's Mary the maid!!"

We rather missed Mary, from then on, and not a peep was heard from my father.

~Naomi Bluestone
Chicken Soup for the Jewish Soul

71

A Fib and the Matinee

I was six years old and my sister, Sally Kay, was a submissive three. For some reason, I thought we needed to earn some money. I decided we should "hire out" as maids. We visited the neighbors, offering to clean house for them for a quarter.

Reasonable as our offer was, there were no takers. But one neighbor telephoned Mother to let her know what Mary Alice and Sally Kay were doing. Mother had just hung up the phone when we came bursting through the back door, into the kitchen of our apartment.

"Girls," Mother asked, "Why were you two going around the neighborhood telling people you would clean their houses?"

Mother wasn't angry with us. In fact, we learned afterwards, she was amused that we had come up with such an idea. But, for some reason, we both denied having done any such thing. Shocked and terribly hurt that her dear little girls could be such "bold-faced liars," Mother then told us that Mrs. Jones had just called to tell her we had been to her house and said we would clean it for a quarter.

Faced with the truth, we admitted what we had done. Mother said that we had "fibbed." We had not told the truth. She was sure that we knew better. She tried to explain why a fib hurt, but she didn't feel that we really understood.

Years later, she told us that the "lesson" she came up with for trying to teach us to be truthful would probably have been frowned upon by child psychologists. The idea came to her in a flash ... and our tender-hearted mother told us it was the most difficult lesson she ever taught us. It was a lesson we never forgot.

After admonishing us, Mother cheerfully began preparing for lunch. As we munched on sandwiches, she asked, "Would you two like to go to the movies this afternoon?"

"Wow! Would we ever!" We wondered what movie would be playing. Mother said "the matinee." Oh, fantastic! We would be going to "the matinee"! Weren't we lucky? We got bathed and all dressed up. It was like getting ready for a birthday party. We hurried outside the apartment, not wanting to miss the bus that would take us downtown. On the landing, Mother stunned us by saying, "Girls, we are not going to the movies today."

We didn't hear her right. "What?" we objected. "What do you mean? Aren't we going to the matinee? Mommy, you said we were going to go to the matinee!"

Mother stooped and gathered us in her arms. I couldn't understand why there were tears in her eyes. We still had time to get the bus. But hugging us, she gently explained that this was what a fib felt like.

"It is important that what we say is true," Mother said. "I fibbed to you just now, and it felt awful to me. I don't ever want to fib again, and I'm sure you don't want to fib again either. People must be able to believe each other. Do you understand?"

We assured her that we understood. We would never forget.

And since we had learned the lesson, why not go on to the matinee? There was still time.

"Not today," Mother told us. We would go another time.

That is how, over fifty years ago, my sister and I learned to be truthful. We have never forgotten how much a fib can hurt.

~Mary Alice Dress Baumgardner
Chicken Soup for the Mother & Daughter Soul

72

Adam's Apples

After all, there is but one race—humanity.
~George Moore

One afternoon, my son came home from school with a puzzled look on his face. After asking him what was on his mind he said, "Are all people the same even if their skin color is different?"

I thought for a moment, then I said, "I'll explain, if you can just wait until we make a quick stop at the grocery store. I have something interesting to show you."

At the grocery store, I told him that we needed to buy apples. We went to the produce section where we bought some red apples, green apples and yellow apples.

At home, while we were putting all the groceries away, I told Adam, "It's time to answer your question." I put one of each type of apple on the countertop: first a red apple, followed by a green apple and then a yellow apple. Then I looked at Adam, who was sitting on the other side of the counter.

"Adam, people are just like apples. They come in all different colors, shapes and sizes. See, some of the apples have been bumped around and are bruised. On the outside, they may not even look as delicious as the others." As I was talking, Adam was examining each one carefully.

Then, I took each of the apples and peeled them, placing them back on the countertop, but in a different place.

"Okay, Adam, tell me which one is the red apple, the green apple and the yellow apple."

He said, "I can't tell. They all look the same now."

"Take a bite of each one. See if that helps you figure out which one is which."

He took big bites, and then a huge smile came across his face. "People are just like apples! They are all different, but once you take off the outside, they're pretty much the same on the inside."

"Right," I agreed. "Just like how everyone has their own personality but are still basically the same."

He totally got it. I didn't need to say or do anything else.

Now, when I bite into an apple, it tastes a little sweeter than before. What perfect food for thought.

~Kim Aaron
Chicken Soup for the Preteen Soul

73

Mirror, Mirror

As a student in the sixties, Janelle had traveled to Denver in search of the promised "Rocky Mountain High." She found it in some poetic scribbles on a powder room wall in Larimer Square, in these famous lines by Edna St. Vincent Millay:

> *My candle burns at both ends;*
> *It will not last the night;*
> *But, ah, my foes, and, oh, my friends—*
> *It gives a lovely light!*

The times were risky and the dangers real when she first read, memorized and adopted this simple poem as her credo.

In the shop next door she had come upon an old candleholder with a twisted brass ring. The ring held a candle before a curved reflector in a special way that allowed the candle to burn on both ends—thereby doubling the illumination. Janelle seized the odd lantern, paid too much for it and declared it her magic mirror. When faced with trouble or indecision, Janelle lit both wicks. Gazing into her distorted image above the dual flames, she reflected upon her options until a decision, or sense of inner peace, came to her.

Inner peace had become a rare commodity in Janelle's life. Like the candle burning at both ends, she habitually drove herself to the ragged edged of her time and energy, reaching her daily objectives with the help of caffeine and nicotine. Food came at random, as time allowed; rest came when the body could push no more. She often laughed about her schedule and quoted the poem that reflected her own race to achieve goal after goal without ever asking "Why?"

With time, Janelle finished college and swiftly soared to successful heights in her career. Marriage followed and, some years later, a family of two adorable babies brought her near-perfect joy. She pushed onward, mixing career with motherhood, and still kept a perfect house. She cut back on her caffeine and nicotine during her pregnancies, but almost as soon as each baby bounced beautifully into the world, Janelle returned to her subsistence on coffee and cigarettes.

As the evidence against smoking mounted, her husband hinted that her health was in jeopardy. Her mother nagged. When her friends began to kick the habit, one by one, Janelle—quoting her poem—consulted her meditation mirror, which reflected the candle burning at both ends. Gazing into the strangely quivering reflection from the distorted glass, she considered the brief span of our lives and weighed the boost from her friendly stimulants against her own mortality and quality of life. To continue smoking meant accepting the health threats in exchange for the promise of staying thin and enjoying chemically induced energy boosts. She repeated yet again, "This candle does indeed give a lovely light," and with that thought chose to continue her dubious lifestyle.

She proclaimed to friends and loved ones that she had made a conscious choice to smoke. It was her decision and her business. And smoke she did—at her desk, in the car, on the boat, in the house—even while she cooked, cleaned and read. The only time she did not smoke was when she tended the children, for somehow she could not totally shake the possibility that the smoking might not be good for them.

One day, as she drove home from work, a cigarette wedged between her fingers as she maneuvered the curves toward home, a voice came over the radio. "So you have chosen to smoke and to risk dying from lung cancer?" the voice asked.

"I surely have," Janelle sang out and took a deep drag from her cigarette.

The radio voice continued. "Did you know that 50 percent of the children whose parents smoke will also smoke?" The voice paused, then continued, "How many of your children have you chosen to die from lung cancer?" Janelle gulped and choked on the smoke in her lungs.

Janelle slammed the radio knob to quiet it, then quickly hit it again to bring it back, but the dial had moved and she could no longer find the awful man's voice. Tears stung her eyes as she desperately searched the stations.

Shaking, she pulled into the driveway. Her husband would arrive with the children in a few minutes. She had to pull herself together before they got there. From habit, she pulled deeply on the cigarette in her hand, now barely more than a filter, and the hot air burned her throat as it lunged into her chest. She flicked the butt to the driveway and ground it with the toe of her high-heel shoe.

Dropping her purse on the kitchen counter, she fled to the quiet of her office. There, she sat before the mirror and lit the two-ended candle. Staring into her own reflection, she repeated the question posed by the radio. If smoking parents caused half of their children to smoke, then odds were that one of her two would smoke—or maybe neither, or... maybe both. Even after she had preached to them so often against it. She shook her head. The cold, inescapable reality dawned on Janelle—because of her example, one or both of her beautiful children might smoke.

Janelle imagined she heard the mirror ask, which child will you choose to die? And she began to cry as she had not cried in years.

When her sobbing finally ceased, she wiped her eyes, leaned forward and with a breath, extinguished the flames from the candle. Taking the twisted brass ring, she pulled until it turned and the candle, squatty from the dual flames, stood upright. Never again, she swore, would her candle burn at both ends. Her children would die someday, as we all do—but not from lung cancer, not from smoking.

Janelle was quieter than usual as she served dinner to her family that night. Afterward, she took the little ones aside, sat down with them and asked, "If I promise to quit smoking, will you promise never to start?"

Two warm hugs embraced her in an indelible promise. Janelle choked back the tears as she began a difficult but rewarding path toward a smoke-free life.

Janelle smoked two more cigarettes—but not until seven years later, and none since. Now, the magic mirror, silenced forever, has moved to the attic, to lie among other relics of the past. The candle retired, never again to burn from both ends.

What Janelle would not or could not do for herself, she did for her children. They have since grown up and made their own choices. Neither child smokes.

~Joy Margrave
Chicken Soup to Inspire the Body and Soul

Famous Last Words

It takes a long time to grow an old friend.
~John Leonard

O h those dreaded words! But here was my trusted, very best friend calling me and telling me that she was fixing me up on a blind date. A blind date! Was she out of her mind? We were juniors in high school and she and I had been the best of friends since first grade. We had grown up together, shared our secrets, shared our parents and had laughed and cried together. Did she want to end our friendship here and now? She must have been crazy thinking that she was going to fix me up with her boyfriend's friend. She had never even seen this guy and here she was insisting that we were going to double date and go to Disneyland. And the date was tonight! Was she crazy? I was not going to go out with some strange geek, and I was especially not going to be stuck with that geek at Disneyland for hours and hours. Couldn't we go to a movie instead? At least if we were going to a movie, it would be dark and I wouldn't have to talk to him or look at him.

My friend, Sue, and I had a huge fight. She insisted that I was going on this date, and I insisted that there was no way that I was going. Back and forth we argued. She said that I was just being stubborn—like that mattered. She said that if I didn't go, she couldn't go—like guilt was going to make any difference to me. Who cared? We were at a complete impasse.

I decided to talk to my mother. I knew she would be on my side and back me up. She always did. To my surprise my mother told me that she thought I should go. I couldn't believe my ears. What was my mother doing on Sue's side of the argument? My mother said that I really enjoyed going to Disneyland and, since Sue was going, too, she knew that I would have a good time. Sue and I always had good times together. Then, after the date, we could talk on the phone for hours and hours going over all of the details again and again. After all, it was only for one short evening. My mother said to me, "You're just going to Disneyland—you're not going to marry the guy!"

Famous last words! Not only did I go to Disneyland on that blind date, but four years later I did marry that very same guy! And now, some thirty years later, my blind date, Frank, our three sons and I still tease my mother about her famous last words. And I am still the very best of friends with Sue—who is more like a sister to me than a friend. We still share our secrets and our memories and she still tells me that I am stubborn. Well, we all know which one of us is the stubborn one—and it's not me! She never gives up until she gets her way. And after all of these years she still gives me a hard time about not wanting to go on that blind date. Who knew it would turn out the way that it did? Thanks, Sue.

~Barbara LoMonaco
Chicken Soup for the Girlfriend's Soul

Always Believe in Miracles

Where there is great love there are always miracles.
~Willa Cather

The year was 1924, and it was a few days before Christmas. Outside, a blinding snowstorm raged around the typical city row house into which my family had moved from the country only two months earlier. We hadn't yet become acquainted with any of our new neighbors.

I didn't see the snowflakes making frosty designs on my window, nor was I aware of my mother's lonely vigil by my bedside. I was a little girl of five, deep in a feverish coma, and had the only case of the dreaded diphtheria in Philadelphia.

Two weeks earlier, my illness had been diagnosed by the neighborhood's family doctor, whose office was a well-worn room in the basement of his home at the corner of the block. Immediately, my father and older sister had been given shots of antitoxin and shipped off to relatives until the danger passed. My mother, refusing to trust her child to a strange hospital, in a strange city, stayed behind to nurse me at home.

The city posted yellow warning signs on our front and back doors announcing a contagious disease. To make doubly sure no one other than the doctor approached, a policeman stood guard, twenty-four hours a day, outside each door. It was also their duty to see that my mother remained inside. Mail was laid on the doorstep, and the officer would tap on the door, then move back some distance to see that my mother opened the door only a crack and quickly took the mail inside.

In those days, Christmas shopping didn't begin in October, nor were toys given in the abundance popular today. A week or so before was time enough to prepare, and the tree was to be decorated by Santa Claus when he came on Christmas Eve. This year, in my family, it was different. With the sudden onset of diphtheria, no thought had been given to Christmas. My getting well was all that mattered.

Late in the afternoon of December twenty-third, the policeman tapped on the door. There was a letter on the stoop from my mother's sister. She was Catholic, and she'd enclosed a small bag of medals with her letter. "I can't be with you," she wrote, "but I want to help. My priest has blessed these medals. The bag is never to be opened, just pin it on your little girl's nightgown and believe."

My mother, willing to try anything, pinned the medals to my gown, but with little hope, as she looked down at my drawn cheeks and proceeded to apply cool compresses to my forehead. My eyes remained closed. During his visit, the doctor's face was grave, and he only shook his head sadly before taking his leave.

Late the next afternoon, my mother heard a faint call. Rushing into my room, she burst into tears of joy. The fever had broken and my eyes were open! Uncomprehending but overcome with gratitude, she fell to her knees and hugged me, but her relief was suddenly shattered when my first words were, "Mama, it's Christmas Eve. What is Santa going to bring me?"

"No, no!" she cried. "Honey, you've been sick a long time, but it isn't Christmas Eve yet." But try as she might, she could not persuade me to think otherwise, and I fell asleep that night with sugarplums dancing in my head.

Downstairs, my mother was frantic. She told me years later how she even considered putting on some of my father's clothing and trying to sneak out to the corner store to get me a few toys, but of course she didn't. Come morning, all she could do was hope to convince me that Christmas was yet to arrive.

Christmas morning came, and I awoke with the usual childish anticipation. My mother, exhausted with heartache, was still half-asleep when the policeman gave his familiar tap on the door. Wearily, my mother opened it, and then gasped in surprise. On the doorstep was a large country basket filled with a Christmas dinner for two and an assortment of toys for a five-year-old girl. My mother's eyes silently questioned the policeman, but he only smiled and shrugged his shoulders. There was no answer there. Where had this spirit of Christmas come from? Would she ever know?

I recovered fully, unaware that two miracles had occurred that Christmas. My father and sister returned, and we settled into life in the city. As the years passed, my mother made a lasting friendship with one neighbor in particular, a friendly Irish woman and busy mother of six. Although they were close friends for years, it was only much later that my mother finally discovered the secret of the second Christmas miracle. Her friend with the thick, Irish brogue and smiling eyes—at the time a complete stranger—was the one who had understood, as a mother, the awful predicament my mother faced and cared enough to leave that wonderful Christmas basket on our doorstep. Thanks to her, I still believe in Santa Claus! You just have to know where to look for him.

~Gerrie Edwards
Chicken Soup for Every Mom's Soul

Moms Know Best

The Bond Between Mother and Child

*I've said it a thousand times and I'll say it again:
There is no job more important than that of being a parent.
~Oprah Winfrey*

76

A Mother Is Born

Faith and doubt are both needed, not as antagonists,
but working side by side to take us around the unknown curve.
~Lillian Smith

My first child, a daughter, was born on July 27, 2000, and I found I was completely unprepared. I thought I was ready for her birth. I had read my books and articles on childbirth and baby care; I had bought everything on my shopping checklist. The nursery was ready for use, and my husband and I were anxiously awaiting her arrival. I was prepared for wakeful nights, endless diapers, sore nipples, crying (both hers and mine), and the feeling that I can't get anything done. I was prepared for sitz baths and hemorrhoids.

What I wasn't prepared for was the way the entire world looked different to me the minute she was born. I wasn't prepared for the fact that the sheer weight of my love for her would reduce me to tears on a daily basis. I didn't know that I wouldn't be able to get through my first lullaby to her because I wouldn't be able to sing through my tears. I didn't know that the world would suddenly become unbelievably beautiful and yet infinitely scarier. I didn't know that it would seem like a new place had been created inside of me, just to hold this incredible love.

I had no idea what it would feel like when the nurse wheeled my daughter in to me saying, "She's looking for you," and the way the image of her deep-blue eyes looking right at me would be seared in my heart forever. I didn't know that I could love someone so much it literally hurts, that a trip to Wal-Mart would make me feel like a protective mother bear guarding her cub, or that my first trip to the grocery store without her would break my heart.

I didn't know that she would forever change the way my husband and I look at each other, or that the process of giving birth to her and breast feeding her would give me a whole new respect for my body. No one told me that I would no longer be able to watch the evening news because every story about child abuse would make me think of my daughter's face.

Why didn't anyone warn me about these things? I am overwhelmed by it all. Will I ever be able to leave her and think of anything but her, or see a crust in her eye or spot on her skin that doesn't make me nervous? Will I ever be able to show her and express to her just how deep and all-encompassing my love for her is? Will I ever be able to be the mother I so desperately want her to have?

I have heard it said, and I now know that it is true, that when a woman gives birth to her first child, there are two births. The first is the birth of the child. The second is the birth of the mother. Perhaps that is the birth that is impossible to prepare for.

~Regina Phillips
Chicken Soup for the Mother & Daughter Soul

77

Love and Water

ama died just days before my eleventh birthday, and my destiny careened dramatically from snuggly to loose-ended. Overnight, my childhood vanished. In the coming months, Dad met Dot at work and began seeing her regularly. A year later, they married.

So much. So quickly. Another woman moving into our house stirred anew my still-fresh memories of Mama. At the same time, Dot inherited a brood of three children, ages five, eight and eleven.

When alone, I listened to an old recording of "You'll Never Walk Alone," and I was convinced my mama sang those words to me from the other side. Yet in moments of grief I wondered, How can she walk with me now? My child's heart yearned for a mother's touch.

"Do you want the kids to call you Mama?" Dad asked Dot one day. Something in me wanted her to say "yes."

Dot looked troubled for long moments, then said, "No. That wouldn't be right."

The no felt like a physical blow. Blood's thicker'n water, came my grandma's favorite litany. I'd not, until that very moment, grasped its meaning. My stepmother's answer seemed proof that blood was thicker, that I was merely Daddy's "baggage"—proof that, to her—despite the fact that she introduced me as "my daughter"—I was biologically not.

I was of the water. So I distanced myself.

My sulky aloofness hid a deep, deep need for acceptance. Yet no matter how churlish I became, Dot never hurt me with harsh words. Ours was, in those trying days, a quiet, bewildered quest for harmony.

After all, we were stuck with each other. She had no more choice than I.

I visited Mama's grave every chance I got to talk things over with her. I never carried flowers because fresh arrangements always nestled lovingly against the headstone, put there, no doubt, by Daddy.

Then, in my fourteenth year, I came in from school one day and saw my newborn baby brother, Michael. I hovered over the bassinet, gently stroking the velvety skin as tiny fingers grasped mine and drew them to the little mouth. I dissolved into pure, maternal mush. Dot, still in her hospital housecoat, stood beside me.

In that moment, our gazes locked in wonder. "Can I hold him?"

She lifted and placed him in my arms.

In a heartbeat, that tiny bundle snapped us together.

"Like your new coat?" Dot asked that Christmas as I pulled the beautiful pimento-red topper from the gift package and tried it over my new wool sweater and skirt.

In a few short months, Dot had become my best friend.

At Grandma's house one Sunday, I overheard Dot tell my Aunt Annie Mary, "I told James I didn't think it was right to force the kids to call me Mama. Irene will always be Mama to them. That's only right." So that's why she'd said "no."

Or was it? Blood's thicker'n water. Was Grandma right? Was that always true in matters pertaining to familial loyalty? I shrugged uneasily, telling myself that it didn't matter anyway.

The following years, Dot embraced my husband Lee as "son," she soothed me through three childbirths, and afterward spent full weeks with me, caring and seeing to my family's needs. Between these events, she birthed three of her own, giving me two brothers and a sister. How special our children felt, growing up together, sharing unforgettable holidays as siblings.

In 1974, Lee and I lived two hundred miles away when a tragic accident claimed our eleven-year-old Angie. By nightfall, Dot was there, holding me. She was utterly heartbroken.

I moved bleakly through the funeral's aftermath, secretly wanting to die. Every Friday evening, I dully watched Dot's little VW pull into my driveway. "Daddy can't come. He has to work," she said. After leaving work, she drove four hours nonstop to be with me each weekend, a trek that continued for three long months.

During those visits, she walked with me to the cemetery, held my hand and wept with me. If I didn't feel like talking, she was quiet. If I talked, she listened. She was so there that, when I despaired, she single-handedly shouldered my anguish.

Soon, I waited at the door on Fridays. Slowly, life seeped into me again.

In 1992, Dad's sudden auto accident death yanked the earth from beneath me, and I lapsed into shock, inconsolable. My first reaction was that I needed Dot—my family.

Then, for the first time since adolescence, a cold, irrational fear blasted me with the force of TNT. Dad, my genetic link, gone. I'd grown so secure with the Daddy and Dot alliance through the years that I'd simply taken family solidarity for granted. Now with Dad's abrupt departure, the chasm he left loomed murky and frightening.

Had Dad, I wondered, been the glue? Did glue equate genetic, after all?

Terrifying thoughts spiraled through my mind as Lee drove me to join relatives. Will I lose my family? The peril of that jolted me to the core.

Blood's thicker'n water. If Grandma felt that way, couldn't Dot feel that way, too, just a little bit? The small child inside my adult body wailed and howled forlornly. It was in this frame of mind that I entered Dot's house after the accident.

Dot's house. Not Dad's and Dot's house anymore.

Will Daddy's void change her? She loved me, yes, but suddenly I felt keenly DNA-stripped, the stepchild of folklore. A sea of familiar faces filled the den. Yet, standing in the midst of them all, I felt utterly alone.

"Susie!" Dot's voice rang out, and through a blur I watched her sail like a porpoise to me. "I'm so sorry about Daddy, honey," she murmured and gathered me into her arms.

Terror scattered like startled ravens.

What she said next took my breath. She looked me in the eye and said gently, "He's with your Mama now."

I snuffled and gazed into her kind face. "He always put flowers on Mama's grave ...."

She looked puzzled, then smiled sadly. "No, honey, he didn't put the flowers on her grave."

"Then who ...?"

She looked uncomfortable for long moments. Then she leveled her gaze with mine. "I did."

"You?" I asked, astonished. "All those years?" She nodded, then wrapped me in her arms again.

Truth smacked me broadside. Blood is part water. Grandma just didn't get it.

With love blending them, you can't tell one from the other.

I asked Dot recently, "Isn't it time I started calling you Mom?"

She smiled and blushed. Then I thought I saw tears spring into her eyes.

"Know what I think?" I said, putting my arms around her. "I think Mama's looking down at us from heaven, rejoicing that you've taken such good care of us, doing all the things she'd have done if she'd been here. I think she's saying, 'Go ahead, Susie, call her Mom.'"

I hesitated, suddenly uncertain. "Is that okay?"

In a choked voice, she replied, "I would consider it an honor."

Mama's song to me was true: I do not walk alone.

Mom walks with me.

~Emily Sue Harvey
Chicken Soup for the Grieving Soul

78

My Original Role

When I stopped seeing my mother with the eyes of a child,
I saw the woman who helped me give birth to myself.
~Nancy Friday

"Don't stay out too late," my mother says, handing me her car keys.

"Do you want to wait up for me?" I ask her.

She shrugs. "I won't be able to sleep anyway."

When I left home to come visit my mother, I was a mature woman. But once I enter my mother's house, I revert to my earliest, most practiced role, that of daughter.

Every mother knows so much more than her daughter. Every mother sees the beauty, the secret hollows and lost potential of her daughter. The mother saves these insights like precious unread love letters. She prays that somehow, someday her daughter will ask her just how much she knows. I, too, am a mother. I know the exact words that could change my daughters into happier women. And like my own mother, I wait helplessly for them to open their ears to me.

I return to my mother's house before midnight. Though my old friends were yearning to go to another jazz club, I felt my mother waiting for me. She opens the door before I even knock.

"I have something to show you," she says. I follow her into the breakfast room.

"Look at this," she says, pointing to a photo of a beautiful woman sitting coquettishly under a tree. Her lipstick is a taunting red, her hair a provocative black. "This was taken when I was in nurse's training," my mother says. I see her secret smile, her joy in how beautiful she was.

I sit down and study the picture, knowing that she had already lost her mother and her first husband, that deep sorrow stretched underneath her beauty. Then my mother spreads more pictures. Me at age five, playing jacks on the front porch. Me and my daughters sitting in a mimosa tree.

"No one can hurt you as much as your own daughter can," my mother says as she hands me another photo, one of my wedding. "I knew you were making a big mistake," she says, jabbing her finger at my ex-husband's picture.

Before when my mother made remarks like this, I resented it. But this visit, I listen. I allow the words to soak in. I hear their translation: "I love you. I think of you all the time. You are so important to me." Has she been speaking in a foreign language all these years, so I never noticed the real meaning of her words?

I call home to check on my fifteen-year-old daughter.

"Hi, how are you?" I say.

"Fine," she answers.

"How was your day?"

"Okay."

I know when she is done talking to me, she will call her friends and they will laugh and chat for hours. I feel like a thirsty woman, wanting too many drops of water.

"Want some coffee, dear?" my mother asks, when I get off the phone.

I take the coffee, made the way she likes it, too strong. We sit together on the sofa, and she asks me if I eat properly.

I want to answer, "Yes," in a voice crisp and clipped as my daughter's.

I take a deep breath before I answer. "Yes," I say, "I eat properly."

"Do you get enough rest?" she asks.

My friends and I talk about money, work, relationships, children.

No one else asks me these basic questions: Am I surviving? No one dares get so deep, so primal.

In the beginning, the mother is the everything, the arms and the heart and breath of her daughter. The mother is the leader, the model. She takes a step, and her daughter follows. But gradually, the child pushes away from her mother. Like a swimmer, kicking off from the side of the pool, the child moves herself into deeper water.

I know that moment, standing alone at the edge of the pool, watching my daughter swim faster and farther. It is a moment of "hallelujah" success and heartbreaking loneliness. To be a good mother means to lose your child to the world.

My mother's child has returned. I am old enough to allow her to renew our original bond, my original role in life. I am old enough that I truly treasure having a mother.

~Deborah Shouse
Chicken Soup for the Mother & Daughter Soul

79

Happy Father's Day!

hile Mrs. Berry stood at the front of the class talking about an assignment, Elizabeth stared dreamily out the window. With fewer than two weeks left in the school year, she couldn't seem to concentrate. Visions of swimming, trips to the beach and endless days of pure fun filled her head. *Would Mom make us go to that awful camp again this year? Even worse, would she have Mrs. Pulowski, who always smelled of garlic, babysit us again?* Elizabeth wrinkled her nose at the thought.

Mrs. Berry's voice interrupted her daydreaming. "Elizabeth! Perhaps you would care to join the rest of the class?"

Elizabeth snapped to attention and tried to stay focused while Mrs. Berry described the Father's Day cards they were supposed to make. Although Elizabeth's mom said that most holidays were made up by greeting-card companies so they could sell more cards, Elizabeth thought they were more fun than ordinary days.

Mrs. Berry passed out construction paper and pieces of fabric that had been cut into the shape of neckties. They were supposed to fold the paper in half to make a card, then paste the necktie to the front. She wrote the message that was supposed to go inside on the blackboard. Dutifully, Elizabeth folded her yellow piece of paper in half, but stopped and frowned at the blue necktie-shaped fabric she had been given. Taking her scissors out of her desk, she began to cut the fabric. It was hard because the scissors were dull, so she struggled for a few minutes, trying to get the right shape. By the time the rest of the class was writing their message on the inside of the cards, Elizabeth was still working on the front of hers, but she didn't mind. She was almost always among the last to finish. Mrs. Berry said it was because she spent so much time daydreaming.

When Elizabeth finally did look at the message on the board, she noticed something else written next to it. She felt her face grow warm—she hadn't heard Mrs. Berry's explanation that anyone who didn't have a father could make a card for a grandfather or an uncle. She had messed up again. Mrs. Berry was going to be upset.

As her teacher walked up the aisle, Elizabeth tried covering her card with her arm, but Mrs. Berry gently lifted it so that she could read it. Elizabeth sat very still, waiting for her to say something, but when she looked up she saw a tear roll down Mrs. Berry's face. That's when she knew she had really messed up. She had never made Mrs. Berry so upset that she cried.

When the class was dismissed for the day, Elizabeth waited until all the other kids left so that she could apologize.

"I'm sorry for not listening," Elizabeth said. "I'll make another card if you want. I'll do it at home and bring it in tomorrow. I promise."

"What are you talking about?" asked Mrs. Berry.

"My Father's Day card. I know you're upset because I didn't do it right."

"Elizabeth, that was the best card in the whole class. It was so sweet it made me cry."

"You cried because it was sweet? You really think it was the best one?"

Mrs. Berry just nodded.

Elizabeth was so happy that she ran out of the classroom.

When her mom came home from work that night, Elizabeth decided it would be okay to give her the card early, since it was the best one in the class.

On the front of the card was a drawing of Elizabeth's mom, with the blue piece of fabric cut to look like a bow in her hair. Inside the card she had written:

Dear Mom,

I know you work really hard to be both a mommy and a daddy. I want to thank you and wish you a happy Father's Day!

Love,

~Elizabeth

When her mom read the card she started crying, just like Mrs. Berry had.

"Are you crying because it's sweet?" asked Elizabeth.

Her mom just hugged her and cried some more.

~Hazel Holmes
Chicken Soup for the Single Parent's Soul

80

Saying I Love You

Love is a fruit in season at all times, and within reach of every hand.
~Mother Teresa

When I was a new mommy, I invented a quiet little signal, two quick hand squeezes, that grew into our family's secret "I love you."

Long before she could debate the merits of pierced ears or the need to shave her legs, my daughter, Carolyn, would toddle next to me clasping my finger for that much-needed support to keep her from falling down.

Whether we were casually walking in the park or scurrying on our way to playgroup, if Carolyn's tiny hand was in mine, I would tenderly squeeze it twice and whisper, "I love you." Children love secrets, and little Carolyn was no exception. So, this double hand squeeze became our special secret. I didn't do it all the time—just every so often when I wanted to send a quiet message of "I love you" to her from me.

The years flew by, and Carolyn started school. She was a big girl now, so there was no need for little secret signals anymore... or so I thought.

It was the morning of her kindergarten class show. Her class was to perform their skit before the entire Lower School, which would be a daunting experience. The big kids—all the way to sixth grade—would be sitting in the audience. Carolyn was nervous, as were all her little classmates.

As proud family and friends filed into the auditorium to take their seats behind the students, I saw Carolyn sitting nervously with her classmates. I wanted to reassure her, but I knew that anything I said would run the risk of making her feel uncomfortable.

Then I remembered our secret signal. I left my seat and walked over to her. Carolyn's big brown eyes watched each of my steps as I inched closer. I said not a word, but leaned over and took her hand and squeezed it twice. Her eyes met mine, and I immediately knew that she recognized the message. She instantly returned the gesture giving my hand two quick squeezes in reply. We smiled at each other, and I took my seat and watched my confident little girl, and her class, perform beautifully.

Carolyn grew up and our family welcomed two younger brothers, Bryan and Christian. Through the years, I got more experienced at the mothering game, but I never abandoned the secret "I love you" hand squeeze.

Whether the boys were running on the soccer field for a big game or jumping out of the car on the day of a final exam, I always had the secret hand squeeze to send them my message of love and support. I learned that when over-sentimental words from parents are guaranteed to make kids feel ill at ease, this quiet signal was always appreciated and welcomed.

Three years ago, my daughter married a wonderful guy. Before the ceremony, while we were standing at the back of the church waiting to march down the aisle, I could hardly look at my little girl, now all grown up and wearing her grandmother's wedding veil, for fear of crying.

There was so much I wanted to say to her. I wanted to tell her how proud of her I was. I wanted to tell her that I treasured being her mom, and I looked forward to all the future had in store for her. However, most important, I wanted to tell her that I loved her. But I was positive that if I said even one word, Carolyn and I would both dissolve into tears.

Then I remembered it—our secret signal. I left my place and walked back to Carolyn. As the organist began to play *Ode to Joy*, I took Carolyn's hand and quickly squeezed it twice. Our eyes met, and she returned the signal.

There were no tears, there were no words exchanged, just a secret "I love you" that I created one sunny afternoon, when I was a new mother.

I am no longer a new mother... but a new grandmother. Today, I was strolling with my little grandson, Jake. His tiny hand was holding on to my finger, and I couldn't help remembering his mother's hand in mine over thirty years ago. As we walked, I gave his hand two quick squeezes and whispered, "I love you." He looked up and smiled.

··~LindaCarol Cherken
Chicken Soup for Every Mom's Soul

81

A Gift of Faith

Growing up in suburban Baltimore, my brother, sister and I were typical kids. What set us apart from the other children in the neighborhood was our Irish Catholic upbringing. We were the "Catholic school" kids. All of our friends went to the public school. They got to ride the school bus. They got new clothes every fall. They always talked about people we only knew from their yearbooks. And they definitely weren't forced to go to Mass every Saturday night!

Some of my friends went to church with their families. I even went with them a few times, but I often found myself defending my Catholic beliefs. Many times I'd come home and ask my mother questions such as why we prayed to the Blessed Mother.

My younger brother, Chris, questioned our religion for different reasons. A sensitive kid, he was always disturbed by news reports of violence and famine. As a result, the question he would often ask my mother is, "How do you know there is a God?"

My mother enjoyed these conversations. She would sit for hours in her rocking chair, happy to share her beliefs, and hoping to provide comfort and strength to her children as they grew into independent young adults. Her faith was always evident. She lived her life the way she thought God wanted her to. That is one reason why she was okay with the thought of dying. She often said, "When it's my time, it's my time. It's not up to me." She accepted God's will for what it was.

Her faith sustained her through every challenge in life. It wasn't until the Persian Gulf War that I realized how powerful that faith could be. Fresh out of college and a young army officer, I had no idea what a war would be like. When I was deployed to Saudi Arabia, my mother sent me a card that read, "God grant me the serenity to accept the things I cannot change, the courage to change the things I can and the wisdom to know the difference." I kept that card next to my pillow so it would be the last thing I'd see at night and the first thing I'd see in the morning.

After I had my own children, I started to realize how special the relationship between a mother and her children is. I had always loved my mother, but once I became one, I began to really appreciate her. When I was younger, I had sworn I'd do something more than "just" be a mom, which seemed so trivial, so unimportant. As events unfolded, however, I found myself making sacrifices for my family. I learned how powerful a mother truly is.

My mother and I talked about that when my three girls were little. We talked about everything. She really was my best friend. We'd end our conversations with her saying, "Mother loves you." I'd answer it with, "Daughter loves you." She knew how I felt because she had lost her own mother shortly after my older sister, Kathy, was born. It made my mom sad that she never told her mother how much she appreciated her. Ironically, I never fully understood the depth of the pain she felt after her mother died until she herself passed away in May 1997.

I was living in Indiana at the time, thirty-one years old and pregnant with my fourth child. I was looking forward to having the baby because I knew my mother would come and cook for me. I even told that to my husband the Thursday night before Memorial Day weekend, after a long day of morning sickness and taking care of my three small girls. As soon as I said it, the phone rang.

My brother-in-law was calling to tell me my mother was in the intensive care unit. Her heart had stopped as she was working out that afternoon at the health club. At fifty-seven, she was in pretty good shape. She and my father enjoyed an active social life and, though she had been on heart medication for years, she never let it slow her down.

Fortunately, a doctor, an off-duty firefighter and a nurse happened to be working out at the club and were able to revive her with CPR. She had no recollection of her ordeal and seemed fine to everyone who spent the weekend visiting her in the hospital. On Monday, they moved her to a private room with a phone, giving me an opportunity to talk with her. I teased her because she didn't remember seeing any white lights at the end of the tunnel. She assured me that if she had to go, that was the way she wanted to do it because she didn't feel anything, and it happened quickly.

"At least hold off till this baby is born," I remember saying to her, half-joking, half-serious.

Her response: "When it's my time, it's my time. I'm ready if the Lord wants me."

"That's great for you," I said, "but none of us are ready for you to go yet."

What she said next were the last words I remember her saying to me. They were the beautiful culmination of thirty-one years of my Irish Catholic upbringing all summed up in a humorous, heartfelt flubbing of the lines: "May the road rise up to meet you, may the wind be always at your back, and may God hold you in the palm of his hands, until we meet again." We said goodbye, hung up, and I knew I'd never talk to her again. Daughter loves you, I thought.

She was scheduled for an operation on Tuesday morning. If all went well, she'd be released on Wednesday. Unfortunately, my father got a call around six in the morning on Tuesday. Her heart had stopped again. He and Chris rushed to the hospital and were led to a waiting room. They waited until a nurse named Bobbie came out and said to my brother, "Are you Chris?"

Days later I called Bobbie to hear her tell the story. My mother's heart had stopped, and the hospital staff had rushed in to revive her. She had been gone for about forty-five minutes. "We didn't want to stop. She was too young," Bobbie told me. Certainly, all hope was lost; still, they had persisted. Suddenly, my mother's eyes opened! She reached up and grabbed Bobbie's arm, looked into her eyes and said with great urgency, "There is a God! I saw his face! Tell Chris, there is a God!" And then, my mother was gone.

Our mother, who constantly reaffirmed our faith in life, did so even more in death. When I heard the story, I remembered the many times I'd seen my mother praying the Rosary, sometimes even using her fingers to count the Hail Mary's. So many times she had asked for the Blessed Mother's intercession, "Holy Mary, Mother of God, pray for us sinners, now and at the hour of our death." Her prayers were answered. Mary's gift to our mother was our mother's gift to us—the gift of faith. There is a God.

~Kelly E. Kyburz
Chicken Soup for the Grieving Soul

82

The Mother's Day Gift

It was a beautiful spring day in early May when I picked up my two little daughters from my mother's house. I was a single working mother and Mom was kind enough to babysit for me. Putting a roof over my children's heads and food on the table were major expenses and ones I worked very hard to cover. The bare essentials were the focus of my paycheck.

Clothes, gas money and an occasional repair of our car left little for discretionary spending. Thankfully, I had a wonderful mother who was always there for us.

As we were driving home, Debbie, my six-year-old kindergartner, asked if we could go shopping for a Mother's Day present for Grandma. I was tired and had many things to do at home, so I told her I'd think about it, and maybe in the morning we would. Both Debbie and her four-year-old sister, Cindy, decided that was a definite plan, and they were very excited about it.

After putting the girls to bed that night, I sat down and went over my budget. Putting money aside for the rent, gas for the car and new shoes Cindy needed, I had fifteen dollars for food till the next payday in two weeks. Grandma's present would have to come from the food money.

The girls were up bright and early the next morning and willingly helped me clean and dust—the usual Saturday chores. The talk centered on what gift we should get for Gram. I tried to explain that we didn't have much money to spend, so we would have to shop carefully, but Cindy was so excited she had a list a mile long.

After lunch we drove to town. I had decided that the only place we might find something I could afford was at the five-and-dime. Of course, this being Debbie and Cindy's favorite store, I immediately made a hit with them. We walked through the store, carefully going up each aisle looking at anything that might be appropriate. Cindy thought Grandma might like a pair of shoes too, (we'd found her a pair of blue tennies for $1.99) but Debbie saw a white straw hand-bag she said would be, "Just perfect for Grandma to take to church!" Again I explained that we only had a few dollars to spend, so we would have to look further.

After going past most of the counters, we came to the back of the store and were ready to turn down the last aisle when Debbie stopped and pulled me over to a display of small potted plants. "Mom," she said, tugging on my arm. "Look, we could get Grandma a plant!" Cindy started to jump up and down with excitement. "Can we?" she asked. "Grandma loves flowers!" They were right. Mom had a beautiful flower garden and had vases of cut flowers in the house all summer. There was a large selection of plants in 2" pots for fifty cents. We could even pick out a pretty, little pot and some potting soil and plant it for her. That decision made, we now had to select just the right one. They finally settled on one with shiny green leaves with white variegations—a philodendron.

That was a special Mother's Day. Both the girls helped repot the little plant and eagerly told their grandmother all about it. Grandma was pleased and placed it on her kitchen windowsill over her sink, "Where I can watch it grow while I do the dishes!" she told them.

The little plant thrived under Mom's caring hands, and my sister and I got many a cutting from it over the years. Time sped by, and the girls grew up to be lovely young women, married and had babies of their own.

One day when Debbie and Cindy stopped by to visit, Deb spotted my philodendron that was hanging and twining all around my kitchen window. "Mom, is that plant new?" she asked. Both girls wanted to know what kind of plant it was and where I bought it. I explained that you just had to break off a short stem from one and place it in a glass of water and let it root. Grandma always had several glasses with philodendron rooting in them, sitting on her kitchen windowsill. Didn't they remember that they had given Grandma that philodendron for Mother's Day all those years ago?

"You're kidding," they both said in wide-eyed wonder. "You mean this is all from that same little plant?" I assured them it was and suggested they go ask Grandma for some cuttings and start their own plants.

Later that day, Cindy called to let me know she and Debbie had gone to visit Grandma, and both of them now had several pots with philodendron planted in them. "Grandma had loads of them, most of them with real long roots," she said. "And Mom, did you know that she still has the original plant Debbie and I gave her for that Mother's Day when we were little?"

It was just a little Mother's Day gift—a very inexpensive gift at that—but now forty years later, we see the beauty of it. A philodendron is like a human family. You break off a little stem from the mother plant and reroot it somewhere else. And it grows and spreads in its own unique pattern that still somehow resembles the plant from which it came. As our family goes its different ways, the philodendron we all have has become a symbol for us of how connected we all are. Through its silent daily reminders, the philodendron has brought us closer together as a family.

Mom and Dad currently live in a Care Center close to me. The largest remnant of that philodendron plant now graces my front entry, and yes it is still giving of itself. I always have a vase with snippets of its rooting in my kitchen for the homes of my granddaughters. These plant snips are the descendants of that one little plant bought from the Five and Dime by two children for a long-ago Mother's Day gift.

~Joan Sutula
Chicken Soup for Every Mom's Soul

83

In Mom We Trust

The truth will set you free, but first it will make you miserable.
~Attributed to James A. Garfield

My mom embarrassed me. In fifth grade, she was the mom interrupting sex education with my birthday cupcakes. In seventh grade, she picked up the phone and told me it was bedtime at 9:30 on a Friday night when I was on the phone with Eric, the cute boy in art class. And after Sam stood me up on the night of winter formal, my mom stormed into his work and made a scene, demanding he pay for my unused dress and shoes. Although (I must admit) it would have been classic to see the look on his face had I been there, I was furious with her for making matters even more humiliating. Mom was always there to serve and protect. She was like a superhero who just seemed to make everything worse.

During the middle years when every month brought changes in bra size, boyfriends and hair color, my mom was as impossible to hide from as puberty. She was like a supernatural force, a divine spirit with psychic abilities. If I made any sort of mistake, she knew about it before I walked through the front door. She had a sixth sense, and it wasn't fair. My friends could experiment and lie and be out past curfew, and their parents would never in a thousand years catch on. As for me, if I were to even sample a beer or inhale one drag of a cigarette, my mom knew. As a result, by high school I had learned that it was best for me not to lie—after all, I knew better. I had a mom who knew everything, anyway.

And then there was a night when I couldn't be honest. All my friends were making a journey down to Mexico for the evening. The boy I especially liked invited me to come along. He was older and had a car. I really, really wanted to go. I had resisted in the past, but this time I found myself agreeing to the invitation. (My parents thought I was spending the night with my best friend.) We went, and it was fun and dangerous and stupid, and GREAT! Luckily, we made it home safely that night, and I spent the night at a friend's house. His parents weren't home, but if they had been, I have a feeling they wouldn't have cared that ten high-schoolers were gathered in their living room after a night in Tijuana. They were the type of parents who just didn't seem to care all that much about anything, which at the time I thought was pretty cool.

The morning after my little rebellious experience, my dad opened the front door to greet me.

"Hi Bec," he cheered. My mother put down her dishtowel and kissed me on the cheek. I waited for her to notice something different about me, something that might lead her to believe that I had been up to no good.

"I'm gonna take a shower now," I began.

She didn't say anything. She just hugged me tightly and asked me not to forget to clean my room. I spent twenty minutes in the shower wondering what I should do. My mom would surely figure it all out sooner or later. Should I tell her?

I decided to stay rigid. I was a good little actress. I could cover for myself if I needed to. A lie (just this once) couldn't hurt anyone. When I came down for breakfast, I waited for the inquisition, but to my surprise, it never came. Mom's crystal ball must have been cloudy that day, and for once, she didn't suspect a thing. I was in luck. I was relieved. I was shocked. I was guilty.

My conscience caught up with me after a few days. I couldn't stand it anymore and I told Mom everything, every detail. She cried, of course, scared for my life, afraid of what could have happened to me, and through her gentle tears she grounded me—for an entire month! Why, might you ask, did I tell her? Trust me, I asked myself that same question every day of that miserable month. I could have gotten away with it. I know that for a fact—or do I?

Sooner or later she would have probably found out about everything. And if that had happened, she would have not only grounded me, but would have lost all of her trust in me, as well. You see, after the Mexico incident, after I had confessed and then served my sentence, I eventually earned back my parents' trust. In return, I was given a later curfew, not to mention more privileges.

I didn't tell my parents everything after that. Instead, we had a system. I told Mom and Dad where I was going, when I would be back and the important things that were happening in my life. It turned out that superpsychic mom was cooler than I had originally thought. I liked that she cared about me and my life, and I really liked being able to share with her.

Over the years, Mom's embarrassment factor has dimmed like an old night light, but she remains the raging superhero she always was. Even though I'm living one hundred miles away, she brings me soup if I'm sick, helps with my work when I'm swamped and makes sure that boyfriends are treating me right. She still has her crystal ball on hand and will often call me on a bad day to cheer me up even before I tell her that I was just fired, dumped or just plain lonely. She has grown to be my best friend, and even though I don't live at home anymore, I still confide in her and tell her everything. Well—almost.

~Rebecca Woolf
Chicken Soup for the Teenage Soul on Love & Friendship

84

My Name Is Mommy

t's only been ten years. Yet, as I stand in the vestibule of the posh country club, staring at the picture, all I can think is where did the time go? The girl in the picture is smiling. A wide I'm-ready-to-take-on-the-world smile of an eighteen-year-old with her whole life ahead of her. I read the caption under the picture: "Cheerleading, Varsity Track, DECA, Choir." And under that, the phrase "In Ten Years I Will Be ...." The handwriting that completes the phrase is still the same. It says, "I will have a doctorate in marine biology and be living in either North Carolina or California."

That's it.

Nowhere does it say, "I will be pregnant with my sixth child and getting ready to celebrate my tenth wedding anniversary." Yet, that's what it ought to say because that is where I am ten years after high school graduation.

The girl in the picture is me. A hardly recognizable me. Over the years, I traded in the eighties "big" hair for a more easily maintained style. I exchanged the now outdated, but then trendy, clothes for never-go-out-of-style jeans and whichever-my-hand-grabs-first-out-of-the-drawer shirts. I somehow lost the fullness to my face and the tight skin around my eyes. As I creep toward twenty-nine, these things don't bother me—the inevitable, the getting older. But the caption does bother me for some reason—"I will have a doctorate in marine biology ...."

What was I thinking? Did I really think I could accomplish such an extravagant goal? I guess I must have. Ten years ago. Funny, I remember loving science in high school—anatomy, chemistry, botany, the whole nine yards—but marine biology? I don't even have pet fish!

I enter the main room, where the class of '87 high school reunion is already in full swing. I am wary, uncomfortable in the outrageously expensive maternity outfit I bought especially for the occasion. I search the crowd of some two hundred people for a familiar face, but I moved six hundred miles away just after graduation, married and hadn't seen these people for ten years. When I received the invitation, it hadn't seemed so long ago. For some reason, now it feels like an eternity.

At first, faces look vaguely familiar, then names start popping in my mind like kernels of popcorn. A girl from my cheerleading squad, Debbie, yes Debbie! Gosh, she looks so chic! And... it's all coming back to me now. Over there is Brett What's-His-Name. He still looks the same, just older, just like the rest of us. Somewhere in this crowd are the girls I'd been best friends with, the girls I had once confided my deepest secrets to, my dreams, my desires. Here are the boys I once dated and fancied myself in love with for a few days or weeks.

Memories I didn't know I remembered surface, one by one, dripping a name to match a face here, then trickling more there, then flooding me with snapshot memories of classes, football games in the rain, dates and dances, musicals and plays, lunches at McDonald's on one dollar and ten cents, my first car, parties and friends. Suddenly, I don't feel so out of place. I even see a few protruding bellies that rival mine.

I take a deep breath and smile at the first girl, or should I say woman, who catches my eye. I remember her. We never did get along well, but what the heck, it has been ten years. We are all grown up now, right?

I take a step closer and yell over the eighties music and chattering noise, "Hi, Kirsten!"

She searches my face, trying to place me in her own memories. Maybe I have changed that much. She finally gives up, and her eyes float down to my name tag, then snap right back to my face as her mouth drops open. "Oh, my gosh!"

I say, "How are you?" with a huge smile I practiced for just such an occasion as this.

"Oh, my gosh!" she repeats and calls me by my maiden name, a name I haven't thought of as belonging to me for nearly ten years. "You look sooo different!" she exclaims, looking me over, the way a female will do only to another female. "Are you pregnant?" she asks.

I nod and say, "Six months."

"Don't you already have like a million kids?"

Do I detect a condescending note in her voice? "Just five," I answer, my eyes dancing over the crowd for a more friendly reception. I spot a girl I'd known since grade school. "Nice seeing you again, Kirsten," I call over my shoulder as I move away.

I start having fun, reminiscing with old friends I'd once shared everything with. Each conversation started with, "Oh, my gosh! You've changed sooo much, blah, blah, blah. You look fabulous!" And then, "What have you been doing?"

I listen as these once-great friends—now strangers—gush on and on about fun-filled college years, fantastic careers, outstanding salaries, dreams of corporate ladder climbing, travel, big-city life in Chicago, New York, Los Angeles, Atlanta. I am reacquainted with friends who have become doctors, lawyers, engineers, teachers, accountants, scientists, actors, etc.

And then they turn back to me and say, "What have you been doing? Where did you go to college?"

This is where my smile starts to feel forced. "I didn't go to college," I say. "I got married. We started a family right away." They tell me how great they think it is that I am what they call a stay-at-home mom. How they can't believe I have five kids, am expecting a sixth and still have my sanity. How I must really have my hands full and how busy I must be.

I smile and think, They have no idea what they are talking about. I smile through their caustic teasing about birth control and planned parenthood. I smile through their sly speculation of what a stud my husband must be. I smile and smile and smile. I feel myself sinking. I entered the room as a mom, but now I am nothing but a mom. I never thought of myself that way before.

I return to the vestibule and stare at the picture again. What happened to the girl I once was? Or better yet, where is the woman I almost was? The marine biologist, living on the ocean, sun-kissed face, salt-bleached hair?

At one time, I was filled with such dreams, such goals. I wanted to make a difference; I wanted to be successful; I wanted to be rich .... I wanted to have it all.

I think about this all the way back home on the plane to Maryland, where I now live, getting more of that awful sinking feeling in the pit of my stomach, the kind that makes you want to cry in self-pity. Then I see something.

I see a woman holding a baby.

The baby is not yet a year. He's wild-eyed, clutching his ear with one hand, the other hand wrapped around his mother's neck in a white-knuckled grip. The mother is rocking gently back and forth in her seat, singing softly, patting lightly, face calm, soothing her baby. I watch. I can't take my eyes off her. The baby's eyes begin to droop, then close; his body relaxes.

It's something I've done a hundred times, a thousand, maybe, rocking my baby, one of them, any of them, all of them. An earache, a stomachache, a nightmare, a boo-boo, a fight, something I could always fix with my rocking chair and my arms.

Suddenly, I realize I do still have dreams, just different ones. I dream of seeing the bottom of my laundry basket, an empty kitchen sink, a freezer that is always stocked, a toothpaste-free bathroom counter, a bathroom without a miniature potty right next to the big one, stairs that don't have a gate at the top and bottom, every sock in my house reunited with its mate. And I know when I have accomplished these goals, I'll sit down and cry.

It occurs to me that, over the years, I have gone through an unseen but tremendous transformation. I have learned to love construction paper; crayon-colored birthday cards; sun catchers made from wax paper; autumn-colored leaves; Christmas decorations of cotton balls, glitter and too much glue; Dixie cups full of dandelion tops and assorted weeds on my table; refrigerators covered in papers, and pictures with "I Lov U Momy" scrawled beneath.

I've learned to see swing sets as lawn ornaments, exclaim with genuine enthusiasm at the sight of a hot-air balloon or a helicopter flying low in the sky, offer up a cheek for a sticky-faced kiss and then beg for another.

I do make a difference—in the lives of my children. I have awesome responsibility—making major decisions that will shape the lives of five—almost six—individuals. I am rich—in love and family.

I do have it all. Or all I need to have.

The plane lands, and the passengers make their way down the gateway. I walk slowly, waddling really, lugging my carry-on, while my mind switches back into mommy mode, as my thoughts race through all I must do once I get home. The dishes and the laundry and the groceries and the ....

"Excuse me, ma'am." I turn toward the voice behind me, a gentleman, his hand outstretched. He asks, "Can I give you a hand with that bag?"

I smile broadly. "I'd rather you carry this baby. My back is killing me."

He laughs. "Is this your first?"

We are coming through the gate now, and I spot my family waiting to meet me, five little faces lighting up at the sight of me, and my heart swells with love. "Not hardly," I say and gesture with my free hand.

He says, "Your life must be pretty hectic."

To this I respond, "It's pretty wonderful."

~Stacey A. Granger
A 6th Bowl of Chicken Soup for the Soul

85

This Is the Best Day of My Life

The purpose of life, after all, is to live it, to taste experience to the utmost,
to reach out eagerly and without fear for newer and richer experiences.
~Eleanor Roosevelt

Being a mother of five children who were all born within seven years tells me I am either very crazy or I love being a mother. For me it is the latter. From the moment I felt the first baby moving within my womb I was hooked. I knew my calling in life. I went to college; I did all the things that the modern woman is told to do. But, all I really wanted was to be a full-time domestic goddess (as Roseanne Barr used to say.)

For many years I was a full-time mother; however, I did have to supplement my husband's income to make ends meet. So I would tend and fall in love with yet more children. Not children that I gave birth to, but working mothers' children. I loved those kids like my own. This allowed me to stay home with my own and share my love for others' children. A working mom is a happy mom when her kids are happy. Well, I did my very best to make sure that their kids were happy.

When my last child started school, I decided that I would substitute teach at the local schools. I loved it. Again I was allowed to be home with my kids when they were at home. What I didn't realize was that I would be able to go on field trips with my own children. I would have freedom that I hadn't had in a long time. I had never been able to do this when I ran home daycare. I felt that it was a fair trade-off to be home with my kids.

My son, who was eight at the time, brought home a note for a field trip to be signed. For years I had always checked the "No" box where they ask for chaperones. He pleaded with me to go. I already had a substitute job scheduled for that day. I thought about it for a while and I checked the "Yes" box. Jonathan was thrilled to say the least. I quickly notified the teacher that I wouldn't be able to sub on that day, and she would have to find someone else. She wasn't thrilled but she understood.

The field trip day arrived. We were going to ride the "Bell Carol" steamboat down the Cumberland River and then walk to the Spaghetti Factory for lunch. The anticipation was just about to kill my son. He beamed with pride as we walked into the school building together. He introduced me to his class. I was so touched by his tender words and pride in me.

The bus ride from LaVergne, Tennessee, to downtown Nashville is about thirty minutes on a good day. This can be a very long time with ninety-plus kids on a bus. Jonathan wanted me to sit by him. I chose not to be the disciplinarian to the children that I was sitting by that day. I let the teachers and their aides do that. I focused my entire attention on my son, and we talked the entire ride. We talked about many fun and silly things. I listened while he talked. Our eyes met, and he looked deep inside mine and said, "Mama, this is the best day of my life." My heart was filled with true joy. A soft tear or two rolled down my face and Jonathan asked me, "Mama, don't cry; Mama, why are you crying?" And I answered, "Because you have made this one of the best days of my life."

The true joy of motherhood comes from the simple things that we do for and with our children.

~Dian Tune Lopez
Chicken Soup for the Working Woman's Soul

Chapter
9

Moms Know Best

Letting Go

Sometimes the best way to hold onto something is to let it go.
~Author Unknown

86

The Gift

The willingness to accept responsibility for one's own life
is the source from which self-respect springs.
~Joan Didion

When I was a child, Mom taught me to question everything. She was a mother who never minded the eternal "why." She made me consider the possibilities myself, jumping in only when my maturity or knowledge couldn't encompass the entire issue.

When I wanted to do something, I had to review all possibilities within my limited scope. "What would you feel like if someone did that to you?" was a question always asked when I reacted to an issue or event. She guided me, made certain I attended church and Sunday school and had a solid background of character and morality.

On my thirteenth birthday, all that changed. Entering my teens was heady in itself but attained an even higher ranking when Mom called me into her room after school.

"Anne," she told me, patting the bed beside her, "I want to talk to you."

"What's up?" I asked easily, self-assured in my new-found teen status.

"I've spent the last twelve years giving you a sense of values and morals," she began. "Do you know the difference between right and wrong?"

"Yeah, sure," I replied, my grin slipping slightly at this unexpected opening.

"You've now entered your teens, and life, from this point, will be much more complicated," Mom told me. "I've given you the basics. Now it's time for you to begin making your own decisions."

I looked at her blankly. What decisions?

Mom smiled. "From this time on, you'll make your own rules; what time to get up, when to go to bed, when to do your homework, and who you select as companions and friends will be your decision now."

"I don't understand," I told her. "Are you mad at me? What did I do?"

Mom put her arms around me, hugging me close. "Everyone has to begin making her own decisions in life sooner or later. I've seen too many young people let loose from their parents make horrible mistakes, usually when they're away at college and no one is there to give them guidance. I've seen them go wild, and some have ruined their lives forever. So I'm going to give you your freedom early."

I stared at her, dumbfounded. All sorts of possibilities occurred to me. Staying out as late as I wanted, parties, no one to tell me I had to do my homework? Super!

Mom smiled again as she stood and looked down at me. "Remember, this is a responsibility. The rest of the family will be watching. Your aunts, uncles and cousins will be waiting for any possible misstep. You'll have only yourself to blame."

"Why?" I asked, elated that she trusted me so much.

"Because I'd rather you make your mistakes now, while you're at home and I can advise and assist you," she replied, hugging me. "Remember, I'm always here for you. If you want advice, or just to talk, I'm available any time."

With this she ended the conversation and the birthday proceeded pretty much as the previous ones had, with cake, ice cream, presents and family. I knew quite well she wasn't stepping out of my life entirely, merely giving me space in which to stretch my wings and prepare for the flight I'd someday be taking.

During the coming years, I made my share of mistakes, the same ones all teenagers do. I neglected my homework periodically, stayed up late occasionally, and once attended a party I had reservations about. Mom never berated me for them. When grades slipped, she quietly pointed out that my chances for the university I wanted to attend would slip as far as my grades did; the lower they were, the poorer my chances of acceptance. If I stayed up late, she cheerfully chided me for my sour mood. After the party she simply asked me what I would picture those friends doing in ten years. Did I wish to share this future with them? Undoubtedly, I did not. When I saw this, I invariably altered my behavior to compensate. She was always ready with advice on how best to mend the tears in the fabric of my life. I never resented her as so many teens do. In fact, this brought us much closer.

A few years ago, I took my daughter into my room on her thirteenth birthday. We had a similar talk. We, too, have remained close during her teens. My son had a similar discussion with his dad at the same age. My children made many of the same mistakes that are the milestones of growth and maturity, but many others they passed by because they thought about it and came to us to discuss it first. They looked at us as mentors rather than jailers, and we've all been better for it. The continuity of life and wisdom has remained unaltered in this family for years and if I'm not available, my children will seek out my mother for advice.

Honor, love and respect for the wisdom of experience are valued in our family because of the wise words of my best friend, my mother.

~Anne Lambert
Chicken Soup for the Mother & Daughter Soul

87

A Mother's Love

When I think of Clara Harden's family, happiness is what comes to mind. The sounds of laughter always greeted my visits.

Their lifestyle was so very different from mine. Clara's mother believed nurturing the mind was more important than trivial chores. Housekeeping wasn't a high priority. With five children ranging in age from Clara, the oldest at twelve, to a two-year-old baby, this lack of order sometimes bothered me but never for long. Their home was always in some state of chaos with at least one person's life in crisis, real or imagined. But I loved being part of this boisterous bunch, with their carefree, upbeat attitude toward life. Clara's mother was never too busy for us. She'd stop ironing to help with a cheerleading project, or switch off the vacuum cleaner and call us all to trek into the woods to gather specimens for a child's science project.

You never knew what you might do when you visited there. Their lives were filled with fun and love—lots of love.

So the day the Harden children stepped off the school bus with red, swollen eyes, I knew something was desperately wrong. I rushed to Clara, pulled her aside, begging to hear what had happened but not prepared for her answer. The night before, Clara's mother had told them she had a terminal brain tumor, with only months to live. I remember that morning so well. Clara and I went behind the school building where we sobbed, holding each other, not knowing how to stop the unbelievable pain. We stayed there, sharing our grief until the bell rang for first period.

Several days passed before I visited the Harden home again. Dreading the sorrow and gloom, and filled with enormous guilt that my life was the same, I stalled until my mother convinced me that I couldn't neglect my friend and her family in their time of sadness.

So I visited. When I entered the Harden house, to my surprise and delight, I heard lively music and voices raised in animated discussion with lots of giggles and groans. Mrs. Harden sat on the sofa playing a game of Monopoly with her children gathered round. Everybody greeted me with smiles as I struggled to hide my bewilderment. This wasn't what I had expected.

Finally Clara freed herself from the game, and we went off to her room where she explained. Her mother had told them that the greatest gift they could give her would be to carry on as if nothing was amiss. She wanted her last memories to be happy, so they had agreed to try their hardest.

One day Clara's mother invited me for a special occasion. I rushed over to find her wearing a large gold turban. She explained that she'd decided to wear this instead of a wig now that her hair was falling out. She placed beads, glue, colored markers, scissors and cloth on the table, and instructed us to decorate it, while she sat like a regal maharaja. We turned the plain turban into a thing of gaudy beauty, each adding his or her own touch. Even as we squabbled over where the next bauble should be placed, I was conscious of how pale and fragile Mrs. Harden appeared. Afterwards, we had our picture taken with Clara's mother, each pointing proudly to her contribution to the turban. A fun memory to cherish, even though the unspoken fear of her leaving us wasn't far beneath the surface.

Finally the sad day arrived when Clara's mother died. In the weeks that followed, the Hardens' sorrow and pain were impossible to describe.

Then one day I arrived at school to see an animated Clara laughing, gesturing excitedly to her classmates. I heard her mother's name mentioned frequently. The old Clara was back. When I reached her side, she explained her happiness. That morning dressing her little sister for school, she'd found a funny note her mother had hidden in the child's socks. It was like having her mother back again.

That afternoon the Harden family tore their house apart hunting messages. Each new message was shared, but some went undetected. At Christmastime, when they retrieved the decorations from the attic, they found a wonderful Christmas message.

In the years that followed, messages continued sporadically. One even arrived on Clara's graduation day and another on her wedding day. Her mother had entrusted the letters to friends who delivered them on each special day. Even the day Clara's first child was born, a card and poignant message arrived. Each child received these short funny notes, or letters filled with love until the last reached adulthood.

Mr. Harden remarried, and on his wedding day a friend presented him with a letter from his wife to be read to his children, in which she wished him happiness and instructed her children to envelop their new stepmother in love, because she had great faith that their father would never choose a woman who wouldn't be kind and loving to her precious children.

I've often thought of the pain Clara's mother must have experienced as she wrote these letters to her children. I also imagined the mischievous joy she felt when she hid these little notes. But through it all I've marveled at the wonderful memories she left those children, despite the pain she quietly suffered and the anguish she must have felt leaving her adored family. Those unselfish acts exemplify the greatest mother's love I've ever known.

~Pat Laye
Chicken Soup for the Mother's Soul 2

88

Who'll Water My Teardrops?

I do't believe that life is supposed to make you feel good, or to make you feel miserable either. Life is just supposed to make you feel.
~Gloria Naylor

My daughter's tears started as we drove out of our driveway and down our neighborhood streets toward the highways that would take us over nine hundred miles to Colorado and her first year of college. These were the streets she and I had traveled hundreds of happy times, going here or there, many times sharing thoughts and laughter. How perceptive she is, I have often thought, at reading people and situations, getting to the core of any matter, and putting into words the clarity of her thoughts. She is so much more capable of this than I was at her age.

Now she could not find the words to say why she was crying on an occasion that should have been mostly happy. I thought she should be feeling the excitement of beginning a life for herself away from home—that she would be exhilarated at the prospect of being on her own and free from her parents' constant scrutiny. What went wrong?

Was she crying because she would be away for an extended period for the first time, because she would be leaving her friends, familiar places and faces, and her family or because she was leaving her best friend and first love, a young man she met months ago? This was the loss that seemed to have the greatest impact on her at this time.

I hoped the long trip would be another happy time for the two of us when we could talk freely and deeply for the two days we would be on the road. Her sorrow made it difficult to converse about the good times of the past and the new experiences she could look forward to. Though the tears eventually subsided, there would be no bonding on this day, and my chance to impress her with my best worldly advice had passed. Mostly we shared silence.

The next day when the mountains came into view and loomed larger so, too, did the reality of her future in this beautiful country. As the mountains grew, so did her anticipation and her spirits. We exchanged superficial talk.

Finally, we were on campus, and she was moving into her room, unpacking and settling in. She and her roommate seemed to hit it off right away. Both liked thick, gourmet coffee and country music; both were messy and had to set the alarm clock on the other side of the room to get out of bed in the morning. I never thought I'd see these habits as positive traits.

The orientation schedule was informative but grueling and kept both of us tuned into surviving the present. There were meetings for parents only, for students only, and for both parents and students together. I learned that this university is one of the top-ten party schools in the nation, that sexually transmitted diseases are epidemic and that two-thirds of the freshman class is on academic probation after the first midterms. Why did we agree to let her go to school here?

It was difficult for us to find our way around a six-hundred-acre campus where most of the buildings looked the same and where I needed my glasses to read the building names. Our differing methods of finding our way caused more friction between the two of us than anything else. I was into map reading, and she was into following her nose on the random chance that it would take her to the right building.

On the final day of orientation, registration was thoroughly frustrating, even maddening. It seemed as though none of the classes she wanted to take were open, and there were long lines for every step of the registration process. There was one advisor for approximately fifteen students. Only through her perseverance and willingness to wait for hours the next day to meet alone with an advisor did she get the classes she wanted.

With a gentle nudge she made it clear that it was time for me to leave her on her own. Now the excitement was hers, and a lump settled in my throat and tears came to my eyes. If I was going to impart any great new wisdom, it would have to be done in the few minutes of our leave-taking. What could I say that hadn't already been expressed?

I told her of a time when she was very young. She and I went shopping at a large department store, and I was trying on clothing. She walked out of the dressing room leaving me in a state of undress and unable to go after her. By the time I got my clothes back on, she was gone. After frantically searching for what seemed like an eternity, I found her sitting quietly in the mall security office. It was a nightmare that seemed to describe this moment aptly. When she leaves me today, I will want to run after her. I still want her to stay with me, safe and secure. Now I am emotionally undressed; I cannot chase after her. She will be more content without me than I think she should be.

As I gave her a final hug, I could not hold back the tears.

"I love you," I said.

Out of nowhere she said, "Will you water my teardrops?" This is our name for the plants she has sitting in the windows of her bedroom. The delicate vines cascade to the floor nearly covering one wall; the small, circular leaves and the fragile, lavender flowers resemble teardrops. We both knew what she was asking. Would her room be there when she returned, the same as she left it? Would her family be there for her as we always had been in the past? Would we drive and laugh and confide on the same familiar streets that surround the only home she has ever known?

Yes, we'll water your teardrops.

She turned toward her new life, and I turned toward home. As the mountains diminished in my rearview mirror, so, too, did her presence. I became lonelier and emptier until the plains flattened my emotions. I managed to hold myself together for nearly twenty-six hours until the familiar sights of home brought cascades of tears.

Without her our streets are silent; our house is empty; my stomach is hollow.

Who'll water my teardrops?

~Win Herberg
Chicken Soup for the Mother & Daughter Soul

89

Can I Come with You?

Your children need your presence more than your presents.
~Jesse Jackson

"Why are you going out again? Can't I come with you? I don't want you to go. I want you to stay home with me."

Words of love from my ten year old.

My older children used to say the same things, used to cry when they were babies, when I would leave them for an evening; used to beg, when they grew older, to tag along wherever I'd go.

"We'll be good. We won't make any noise. We promise."

Sometimes their demands would annoy me. Why couldn't they stay home with someone else for a while? The things I had to do weren't fun things. Alone I could finish more quickly and get home sooner, and then play with them.

I tried reasoning, explaining. "But we want to be with you," they insisted.

So they came. Everywhere. To the grocery store, the bank, the library, the movies. Anywhere I went, there they were, right by my side.

Most times I didn't mind, but there were days I ached for moments alone. Driving in the car, I would turn on the radio and a song would come on, one that I loved and I'd turn up the volume and a little voice would interrupt. "What does 'Go Children Slow' mean, Mommy?" "What town are we in?" "Did I tell you what happened yesterday?" And the song would be long over by the time the story was told.

In restaurants, I'd be listening to a friend, hoping my son and daughter would talk to each other, which they did. They always tried to be polite. But there were important questions, legitimate interruptions. "Mommy, do they put celery in the egg salad in this place?" "Can I have a vanilla milk shake?" "Will you go to the bathroom with me?" And I'd wish for a time when I could finish a sentence, have a complete thought, eat one entire meal without interruption.

It was my attention they wanted. My opinion and presence they craved. I was the audience they played to day after day. I became accustomed to their stories, their interruptions. Their fresh observations enriched me. "Why is that man called a waiter, Mom, when we're the ones doing the waiting?" "How come that sign says, 'dressing room' when everyone goes in to undress?"

As they grew older, their questions became less entertaining and more annoying. The early teenage years were accompanied by a litany of demands and complaints. "How come everyone else can go out on a school night and I can't?" "No one else has to be home by eleven o'clock. Don't you trust me?"

Then, most of all, I wished they would be quiet, find something else to do, someone else to listen to them. Why did even the simplest things have to turn into confrontations? Couldn't they ever just leave me alone?

Now, too often, they do.

"How was your day?" I'll ask my seventeen-year-old son, when he comes home from work. "Where did you go? What did you do?"

"We hung doors somewhere. It was no big deal, Mom. It was just work."

Just work. This isn't fair. I want detail. I want texture. I want to know what he does twelve hours a day. I want to hear about his friends, listen to his stories.

"How was your trip, Mom? What did you see? Did you have fun?" he used to ask only a few years ago. "What did you do at night?

Did you go out? Did you miss us?" The endless questions always answered, always explained.

"Are you going out again tonight?" I find myself saying.

"Can't you stay home sometime? You'll be leaving for college in three weeks and I already miss you now."

Why didn't someone tell me this was going to happen? Everything is reversed. Now I'm the one tagging along, saying, "I miss you." "When are you coming home?" Marking it on the calendar when he has a day off.

Mornings when I drive my daughter to work, if a song she likes comes on the radio, she turns up the volume and I know better than to talk. She loses herself in the music. She doesn't want to hear what I have to say. And I understand.

But underneath the understanding, there's this feeling, this growing awakening: This is how she felt, how my son felt years ago. Afraid that something—some song, some play, some activity, some person—would come along and take me away from them. She shouldn't like that song more than she likes me, a child thinks. She shouldn't be able to have fun without me. So the child complains and the child imposes. Here I am. Look at me.

Here I am. Look at me, this adult wants to say. But of course I don't. I simply understand a little better when my ten-year-old sulks when I am someplace she can't be. Finally, after all these years, I am beginning to understand why children cry when they are left behind.

~Beverly Beckham
A 6th Bowl of Chicken Soup for the Soul

Warm Rocks and Hard Lessons

For weeks, I had noticed the small but wiry gray tomcat, with the split ears and the fighting spirit of a tiger, hanging around our yard. Since we lived in the country, far from any neighborhoods, I wondered how he had found his way to our house. Of course, we'd broken our don't-ever-feed-strays rule when we saw that he was hungry.

"Maybe we should take him to the animal shelter," my husband suggested. But the cat was wily, eluding our best efforts to catch him.

One day, I found the tomcat high in a box in the storage shed. This time, he didn't slink away when I approached. I climbed up to see four kittens sucking greedily, kneading their mother's stomach with tiny paws. Our "tom" was a "thomasina!"

"Well, it looks as if we have a new cat," I told the family. "Now, all we need to do is to find a feminine name for her."

Our two teenagers rose to the occasion. "Louella," they said, and it stuck.

Lou was a good mother. I moved her kittens into a more comfortable box in our garage. When she wanted some time away from her family, she would query me earnestly about my appropriateness as a kitten-sitter, all the while anxiously eyeing her babies. After I reassured her that I would babysit, she would go off on her own for an hour or so, looking refreshed when she returned.

The kids begged me to keep the kittens. They named one, a striped gray like his mother, Reuben Caine, after a Joan Baez ballad. Reuben's sister, who looked nothing like the rest of her family—a blue-eyed beauty who could have passed for a full-blooded Siamese—the kids named Lotus. I relented, saying we could keep those two, but I drew the line at the third and fourth kittens. These were placed in the arms of a gentle mother and kids who saw our ad in the paper.

Kittens grow up quickly, and, soon, we had both of them altered. Lotus enjoyed going off on her own in the pastures and farmlands that surrounded our acreage, but Reuben gloried in being the only son, clinging to his mother in a shameless show of dependency. Having grown to a great length, far exceeding his diminutive mother, he had a habit of stretching himself out on the hood of our car and allowing Lou to bathe him from head to toe.

Our kids were growing up, too, making noises about launching their own lives, considering schools and jobs. I hovered in the background, asking vague questions about appropriate apartments, laundry facilities, security and all the other things mothers worry about. In truth, I was scared to death at the thought of them on their own. How will they ever set their alarm clocks and get up in time for class or for work when I have to call them at least four times every morning? And who will turn off their radios at three in the morning when they finally fall asleep?

One day in late summer, I was watching Lou groom the heir apparent, now an enormous creature whose body dangled off the front of the car. Reuben Caine was in his usual ecstatic pose, eyes closed in bliss, legs stretched out so Mama could properly bathe every inch of him. What a ridiculous sight, I thought.

And, as if she heard me, Lou stopped her vigorous licking and regarded Reuben. Was she having an epiphany? Her One and Only opened his eyes in amazement. What had interrupted the ablution? Then, the kind little mother cat did an amazing thing. With one swoop of her paw, she knocked her enormous son off the car. Thud! Dazed, he looked up at Louella. It must be a mistake, you could see him thinking. But the usual adoring expression on his mother's face was replaced by a snarl. Reuben slunk off and hid. After that, Louella treated her son as she would any other adult feline. She was polite, unless he tried to invade her space. I made a mental note.

When autumn came, I watched my kids pack. "I can't find my new Rolling Stones tape," my son complained.

"My luggage won't fit into my car," my daughter said, with just the right amount of pathos in her voice. "Do you think Dad could make a rack or something?"

"Dunno," I said lightly, as I went downstairs and resurrected my easel from the storage room. I had a few days until my teaching duties called me back to work. Striking matches, I heated the caps on the tubes of oil paints that had been stuck for years. Rose madder. Yellow ochre. Burnt sienna. Titian red. The names of the colors seduced me, and the scent of the linseed oil and turpentine took me back to studio classes in college when I had finally learned to shut out everything but the brush, the paint and the blank canvas before me. Now, I stopped listening to the house noises, stopped thinking about how much they would soon change when the kids were gone. Instead, I tuned my ear to the distant fields. A crow called, his voice accentuating the silence. Dipping my brush into the paints, I gazed at the landscape outside my window and started to paint. I don't know how the cat crept into the painting, but there was Lou, sitting among the gold grass of autumn, the picture of feline grace and serenity. I couldn't help but wonder if she was grateful that we, with the help of our veterinarian, had arranged for her mothering days to end.

• • •

Our children left home, made a few mistakes, called home and didn't call home.

And the world did not end.

And Louella, freed from motherly duties, found time to luxuriate on the sun-warmed rocks in front of our house. She also had a habit of wandering alone each evening to the western slope of our acreage and sitting there until dark. "Lou's watching the sunset again," my husband would remark as he came home from work. And I, needing a break from grading stacks of papers, would pause for a moment, rub my eyes, and join Lou to watch the landscape give up its color and turn into a serene study of twilight—mothers enjoying the peace that comes when one phase of life ends and a new one begins.

~Joan Shaddox Isom
Chicken Soup for the Cat Lover's Soul

91

Crossing Over

The best conversations with mothers always take place in silence,
when only the heart speaks.
~Carrie Latet

It was a cool autumn day. Clouds overshadowed the canopy of blue, as if God wanted to hide the sun's great splendor. The winds whispered by as leaves rustled to the ground.

A day to remember, that was. The day young women everywhere wait their whole lives for, and I knew in my heart I would treasure those moments forever.

Before me stood a young man with whom I had shared my vast secrets and enchanted moments. I had whispered promises in his ear and did my best to fulfill them. I had never trusted anyone with the key to my heart until he entered my life. Now, I knew the only safe place for this key to remain was with him.

This was a first for both of us. We gazed nervously in each other's eyes, waiting for the other to make the first move. I was unsure if we were ready for this. Making a hasty decision like this could be so devastating to our lives.

We stood there in silence for what seemed an eternity. Echoes from the past rang endlessly in my mind. The laughter and tears we had shared will forever be held in a special place in my heart. My emotions were so vulnerable at that point. Part of me wanted to run and hide, and the other said, "Go ahead. It's time."

Then just as if he were reading my mind, he gently grasped my hand, sending a cold chill up my spine and erasing all my doubt. With his soft voice, he whispered, "It's time."

I stood back to take one last glance at him to remember how he looked before we took this major step. Never again would I look at him as I do now. Things would be different once we crossed over; we couldn't look back.

Once again our eyes met. If only we could cease time and steal those moments away in our hearts forever. Neither he nor I would ever feel as we did then. There's only one first time for everything, and this was it.

I wrapped my arms around him and playfully kissed the tip of his nose, then I whispered softly in his ear, "I love you." Then it happened—the moment we both had been waiting for.

I'll never forget that day or the silly grin on his face afterward. Tears streamed down my face as he crossed the street to step onto the big yellow school bus. Then he turned to me and said, "Bye, Mommy. I love you."

~Angela Martin
A 6th Bowl of Chicken Soup for the Soul

92

Peace for Pickles

She just appeared one day, looking sad-eyed and mournful, peering in through the patio door. Her silky fur was jet-black, and her eyes were as big as saucers. I gazed at her and spoke the thought that was running through my head: "My, you are in quite a pickle." This beautiful, regal cat was definitely pregnant. Her stomach was bulging, and she appeared ready to give birth any day.

I was in a pickle, too. I had lost my father after caring for him through a long illness. My grief enveloped me like a black cloud. I sure didn't have the energy to take care of a cat. And a pregnant one at that. But I found myself pouring a bowl of milk and setting it outside. She'll be gone by morning, I thought. Pulling my bathrobe closer around me, I trudged back up the stairs.

The next day she reappeared. What is she doing back here? I can barely take care of myself right now, let alone a needy cat. But I couldn't turn away. I found an old basket and arranged a soft blanket inside. I walked outside, and she backed up about ten feet, watching me with wary eyes. I set down the basket and went back in the house.

Remembering my dad's kind and caring ways was the only comfort I had at the time. He loved animals and had a soft spot for all strays. When I was a little girl, our house was a revolving door for abandoned cats and dogs. I could at least try to take care of her. Dad would like that. But only until I found out where she lived.

I had seen a black cat in our neighborhood, so I assumed she was someone's pet. On one of my furtive runs out to the mailbox in my worn-out bathrobe and slippers, I saw my next-door neighbor.

"Hi, how are you?" he asked.

"Fine," I said as I ran my hand through my uncombed hair. "Can I ask you something? A black cat has been coming around my backyard. Do you know where she lives?"

"That cat has been around for years. Everybody feeds her, but as far as I know, she doesn't have a home."

"Thanks," and I shuffled back inside with the mail.

She must have had a hard life surviving on her own all those years.

"Okay, Dad, you must have guided her to my door. I'll take care of her," I spoke aloud.

I could almost hear him ask what I was going to call her.

"I'm going to name her Pickles."

I went upstairs to comb my hair. Looking in the mirror, I saw a wrinkled, creased face. I wish somebody would take care of me. Sadness etched the corners of my eyes, and my shoulders sloped with grief. The coolness of the water felt good as I ran a washcloth over my face. I changed out of my tired old bathrobe and put on jeans and a sweatshirt.

Over the next few days, Pickles came to drink the milk and eat the food I put out for her, but then would disappear. Each day, I eagerly searched the basket for some sign of the new life Pickles was carrying. One morning, I saw a tiny black kitten curled up inside. Then I heard the screech of brakes.

"Oh, no!" I cried out. There in the street was Pickles, running right in front of a car. She was carrying a solid gray kitten by the nape of its neck. Bounding across the yard, she deposited it in the basket and took off again. She made three more trips for a total of five kittens.

I made my way around the side of the house to get a closer look. I longed to hold Pickles and snuggle her close, but her years of living in the wild made her wary of human contact. I peered into the basket and watched as she licked and cleaned each kitten. They're finally here!

Since Dad had died, I had no one to take care of. Now, I couldn't wait to get up in the morning. The kittens needed me. I was showering, dressing and even making my bed. I began to say hello to the neighbors when I went out for the mail, wearing real clothes instead of pajamas and a robe.

And, when I looked out through the patio door, I sure didn't feel alone when six pairs of hungry eyes stared back at me. I sat with the kittens for hours. It was fun watching them roll around on top of each other and play hide-and-seek under the edges of the blanket. I even started to laugh again, surprising myself with that sweet, familiar sound. While Pickles watched from a distance, I stroked each furry little ball and soothingly crooned, "It's okay, Pickles. I won't hurt them. They're so cute, with their soft fur and big eyes just like yours. Look at this one with the black-and-white mask on her face. She looks like a little bandit. And this solid black one looks just like you."

Pickles seemed to understand my contact with the kittens was necessary, and it sure did my heart good. Sometimes, though, the sad tears would flow as I thought of how much I missed my dad. Then Pickles would look at me with those big eyes that seemed to say, "Everything's going to be all right. You take care of me, and I'll take care of you."

When the kittens were old enough, I found homes for four of the five. The antics of every kitten endeared each one to me, but the solid gray one stood out among the rest. He was soft and cuddly, and I decided to keep him. When he stood up and stretched his paws against the door, he looked just like a bear, so that's what I called him.

I guessed Pickles was around nine years old and had obviously borne many litters. She was an excellent mother, but she looked exhausted after feeding, cleaning and tending to her offspring. Now that the rest of the kittens were in new homes, I knew there was one more thing I had to do. Pickles needed to be spayed, and Bear neutered, too, when he was old enough. Dad always told me how important that was.

I thought it would be easy to take her to the vet, but no matter what I tried—and I tried one thing after another for days—she wouldn't go into a plastic cat carrier. Unsure of what to do next, I sent up a silent plea to my dad. Dad, I need your help. I want Pickles to live in peace. Please show me what to do.

I picked up the phone and called the vet's office. After explaining my dilemma, they said they had a metal cage I could borrow, which had a trapdoor used most often to catch wild animals that needed medical care.

I retrieved the cage and then carried it out to the backyard as I talked to Pickles, who sat in the corner watching me. "Look at this one, Pickles. It's much bigger, and you can see through it. When you go inside, the door will shut behind you, but don't be afraid."

I placed a piece of chicken in the corner of the cage, with the metal door propped open. All Pickles had to do was approach the bait. What happened next seemed like a miracle. Although she had struggled and resisted my attempts to get her into the carrier for days, now, with a slow, steady gait, Pickles walked straight inside, almost as if guided by a loving hand. Her weight pressed down on the spring, and the door shut.

She sat inside, a calm emanating from her. I marveled at her acceptance and surrender. Is that what it takes? I wondered. Acceptance? Allowing others to help? Maybe that's what had been lacking in my own life.

I brought her home from the vet the next day and let her out of the cage. She took a few steps, then turned and looked at me. Our eyes locked, and I saw the beginning of my own newfound serenity reflected in hers.

The gentle, guiding hand that showed Pickles the way to peace had shown me the way to acceptance—the first step in my journey back from grief.

~B. J. Taylor
Chicken Soup for the Cat Lover's Soul

Chapter
10

Moms Know Best

Gratitude

Loving a child is circular business....
The more you give, the more you get,
the more you get, the more you want to give.
~Penelope Leach

Graduation Message

I'm a divorce lawyer. At times, I feel as if I've heard and seen it all. But ten years ago, a woman walked into my office with a whole new agenda, and neither my life nor my practice has been the same since.

Her name was Barbara, and as she was shown to my office, wearing a rather "plain Jane" outfit, I guessed her to be about nineteen and fairly innocent.

I was wrong. She was thirty-two, with four children between the ages of three and nine. I've heard many brutal stories, but the physical, mental and sexual abuse that Barbara had suffered at the hands of her husband made me sick to my stomach.

Yet she finished a description of her circumstances by saying, "Mr. Concolino, you know, it isn't all his fault. My children and I have remained in this situation by my choice; I take responsibility for that. I've known the end to my suffering would come only when I decided I'd suffered enough, and I've made that decision. I'm breaking the cycle."

I'd been practicing law for fifteen years at that point, and I've got to admit that in my head, I was getting great pleasure from thoughts of nailing that guy to the wall.

"Do you believe in forgiveness, Mr. Concolino?" she asked.

"Yes, of course," I said. "I believe what goes around comes around, and if we try to do the right thing, good comes back to us. The clients of mine who have withheld forgiveness have withheld it only from themselves."

Those words were so common for me that they practically spoke themselves. And yet, if anyone had cause to be full of rage, Barbara did.

"I believe in forgiveness, too," she said quietly. "I believe that if I hold on to anger at my husband, it will only fuel the fire of conflict, and my children are the ones who will get burned."

She gave a tremulous smile. "The problem is, kids are very smart. They can tell if I haven't truly forgiven their dad ... if I am just saying words. So I have to really release my anger. And here is where I need a favor from you."

I leaned forward across my desk.

"I don't want this divorce to be bitter. I don't want all the blame put onto him. The thing I most want is to truly forgive him, and to have both you and me conduct ourselves accordingly." She paused and looked me in the eye. "And I want you to promise to hold me to this."

I've got to say, this request was against my best lawyerly business advice. But it fit my best human advice, hand in glove.

"I'll do my best," I said.

It wasn't easy. Barbara's husband had no interest in taking the high road. The next decade was marked with his ugly character assassinations of her and repeated periods of nonpayment of child support. There were even times she could have had him thrown in jail, but she never would.

After yet another court session that went in her favor, she caught me in a corridor. "You've kept your promise, Bob," she said, and she laughed. "I admit that there have been times I've wanted to curse you for making me stick to my beliefs. I still wonder sometimes if it's been worth it. But thanks."

I knew what she meant. In my opinion, her ex continued to violate normal standards of decency. Yet she had never responded in kind.

Barbara ultimately found and married the love of her life. Although matters were settled legally, I always enjoyed getting her Christmas card, hearing how the family was doing.

Then one day I received a call. "Bob, it's Barbara. I need to come in and show you something."

"Of course," I said.

Now what? I thought. How long is this guy going to keep at this? How long before she finally cracks?

The woman who walked into my office was lovely and poised, full of so much more confidence than she had possessed ten years earlier. There even seemed to be a bounce to her step.

As I stood to greet her, she handed me a photo—an eight-by-ten taken during her oldest son's senior year in high school. John was wearing his football uniform; his father stood to his left rigidly and coldly. The boy himself was looking proudly at his mom, who stood close to him, a warm smile on her face. I knew from her Christmas letters that he had graduated from a very well-respected private high school.

"This was after he caught the winning touchdown in the championship game," she grinned. "Did I mention that game gave their team the number-one ranking in America?"

"I think I heard something about it," I smiled.

"Read the back," she said.

I turned the photograph over to see what her son had written.

Mom,

I want you to know that you have been the best mom and dad a boy could ever have. I know because of how Dad worked so hard to make our lives so miserable. Even when he refused to pay all he was supposed to pay for school, you worked extra just to make sure none of us missed out. I think the best thing you did was what you did not do. You never spoke bad about Dad. You never told me he had other "new" kids to support; he did.

With all my love, I thank you for not raising us in a home where the other parent was the bad one, like with my friends who went through divorces. Dad is and has been a jerk, I know it, not because of you, but because he chose to be. I do love you both (you would probably still slap my behind if I said I didn't love Dad), but I love, respect and admire you more than anybody on the face of the earth.

Love,

~John

Barbara beamed at me. And we both knew it had been worth it.

~Robert A. Concolino
A Second Chicken Soup for the Woman's Soul

94

My Mother

My mother kept a garden,
A garden of the heart,
She planted all the good things
That gave my life its start.

She turned me to the sunshine
And encouraged me to dream,
Fostering and nurturing
The seeds of self-esteem.

And when the winds and rain came,
She protected me enough—
But not too much because she knew
I'd need to stand up strong and tough.

Her constant good example
Always taught me right from wrong—
Markers for my pathway
That will last a lifetime long.

I am my mother's garden.
I am her legacy,
And I hope today she feels the love
Reflected back from me!

~Staci Warren
Chicken Soup for the Teenage Soul on Love & Friendship

95

Mother's Hands

Love is patient, love is kind. It does not envy, it does not boast,
it is not proud. It is not rude, it is not self-seeking, it is not easily angered,
it keeps no record of wrongs....
~1 Cor. 13:4-5

Night after night, she came to tuck me in, even long after my childhood years. Following her longstanding custom, she'd lean down and push my long hair out of the way, then kiss my forehead.

I don't remember when it first started annoying me—her hands pushing my hair that way. But it did annoy me, for they felt work-worn and rough against my young skin. Finally, one night, I lashed out at her: "Don't do that anymore—your hands are too rough!" She didn't say anything in reply. But never again did my mother close out my day with that familiar expression of her love. Lying awake long afterward, my words haunted me. But pride stifled my conscience, and I didn't tell her I was sorry.

Time after time, with the passing years, my thoughts returned to that night. By then I missed my mother's hands, missed her good-night kiss upon my forehead. Sometimes the incident seemed very close, sometimes far away. But always it lurked, hauntingly, in the back of my mind.

Well, the years have passed, and I'm not a little girl anymore. Mom is in her mid-seventies, and those hands I once thought to be so rough are still doing things for me and my family. She's been our doctor, reaching into a medicine cabinet for the remedy to calm a young girl's stomach or soothe a boy's scraped knee. She cooks the best fried chicken in the world... gets stains out of blue jeans like I never could... and still insists on dishing out ice cream at any hour of the day or night.

Through the years, my mother's hands have put in countless hours of toil, and most of hers were before perma-pressed fabrics and automatic washers!

Now, my own children are grown and gone. Mom no longer has Dad, and on special occasions, I find myself drawn next door to spend the night with her. So it was that late one Thanksgiving Eve, as I drifted into sleep in the bedroom of my youth, a familiar hand hesitantly stole across my face to brush the hair from my forehead. Then a kiss, ever so gently, touched my brow.

In my memory, for the thousandth time, I recalled the night my surly young voice complained: "Don't do that anymore—your hands are too rough!" I reacted involuntarily. Catching Mom's hand in mine, I blurted out how sorry I was for that night. I thought she'd remember, as I did. But Mom didn't know what I was talking about. She had forgotten—and forgiven—long ago.

That night, I fell asleep with a new appreciation for my gentle mother and her caring hands. And the guilt I had carried around for so long was nowhere to be found.

~Louisa Godissart McQuillen
A Second Chicken Soup for the Woman's Soul

One Rose

Biology is the least of what makes someone a mother.
~Oprah Winfrey

M otherhood took me by surprise. One day I was a single woman living at the beach with a ten-year career as a flight attendant, and the next, a wife and mother of four. And it happened almost that quickly.

I met and married my husband within months of meeting him. I had gone to visit my grandmother in the hospital and was introduced to her surgeon, my soon-to-be spouse. I had learned a year before meeting him that I was not able to have children on my own. So, upon learning that he had two sons that he was moving in with us, life seemed like an episode from Ozzie and Harriet (updated to include my keeping a solid career.) His sons were nine and ten when their mother put them on an airplane from the East Coast and "shipped" them to the West Coast, having very limited contact with them for the next eight years. My husband left their mother when they were only two and three years old, so we were all literally strangers under one roof. Ironically, no sooner had I married my husband, then I became pregnant with our own child. The day after his sons moved in with us, our son was born (a month early.) Three children within two days! Two years later, I gave birth to our second son.

I remember times when I would be so overwhelmed that I could only tell myself over and over, "One day they will thank you." I don't remember a lot of those tumultuous years. There was a lot of chauffeuring to and from Little League games, a lot of getting up at three in the morning to get to ice hockey practice by five, banquets, PTA meetings, and "short order" cooking. I remember witnessing the growing pains of two young men going through adolescence. Their father was often away, their biological mother completely out of the picture, their two half-brothers often felt like an annoyance to them, and their stepmother never seemed able to meet their needs. Yet, I knew in my heart that one day they would look back and realize that I did love them as my own and that I did my best.

When my older stepson graduated from high school, his biological mother decided to finally pay a visit. The graduation ceremony was held outside at dusk, and my husband and his "ex" stood together and watched with pride as "their" son received his diploma. My other stepson stayed by their side. I stood off a slight distance away with our two sons. There was a strange twist to this graduation ceremony. The principal of the high school delivered a speech that included a theme of "giving a rose to the person who has meant the most to you in your life." I found that odd, but each graduating student held in their hands one red rose. Upon receiving their diplomas, each student walked up to the person and handed them their rose. To this day I will never forget the feeling of holding that rose in my hands.

~Jolie "Jes" Shafer-Kenney
A 6th Bowl of Chicken Soup for the Soul

97

Mothers Deserve More than One Day

Unfortunately, many people focus on Mother's Day as the best chance to make their mom feel important. It's funny how holidays work. Sure it's great to remember special people on their birthdays, our faith at Christmas or Hanukkah, and our parents on Mother's and Father's Day. But what about the special things our loved ones bring us throughout the year?

As with many auto-racing fans, I was introduced to the sport by my parents. My father was an open-wheel fanatic, attending the Indianapolis 500 every year. My stepfather was a NASCAR fan, and Charlotte—the hometown of many in the sport—is where he wanted to retire.

I was fortunate, you see. I was gifted with my mother's addiction to speed and driving ability while I inherited my father's sense of direction. Yes, he finally found his calling as the navigator for Mom when they did road rallies.

When she wasn't busy erasing the tread of an innocent set of Goodyears, my mother loved to watch auto racing. Early on she was a big A. J. Foyt fan. Foyt's fiery temper and passion for winning was what caught her eye. Coincidentally, May, the month we pay "tribute" to our mothers, is also the month when the Indianapolis Motor Speedway comes alive. Foyt owns a piece of Indy car history, winning four Indianapolis 500s. Although Foyt turned out to be a heck of a choice, Mom usually loved to cheer on the underdog. When watching NASCAR, she spent her time booing the Richard Pettys and Darrell Waltrips, legends of the sport. She preferred to cheer for the Eddie Bierschwales and Chad Littles—two drivers with many years of racing experience and no victories.

I lost my best friend, auto racing lost its biggest fan and the cops their most elusive target in 1994, but her memories still live on. The first race I attended after my mother's death, the 1997 NASCAR Busch Series race at Daytona, Chad Little started forty-second out of forty-five cars. As the cars were heading into turn 3, about to take the white flag signaling one lap to go, the impatience among the leaders took its toll. All heck broke loose, and all I could see was smoke and spinning cars.

Then, like a Hollywood production, Little's red and yellow #23 emerged unscathed from the chaos. As Little came to the start/finish line to take the white and yellow flags, I couldn't help but scream to my stepfather, "He's going to win, he's going to win!" The next two and a half minutes seemed like an eternity as Little followed the pace car at fifty-five miles per hour to complete the final lap of the race.

While my stepfather and I had cried a river by the time Little took his first checkered flag, I couldn't help but crack a smile. That was my sign. My sign Mom was still watching.

All of my mom's passion and love for the sport of auto racing was sent to me from above that day. I was hooked. I became a Chad Little fan in February 1995. Shortly thereafter, I got to know his family and began writing for his Web site. The experience helped me get to where I am today. I get paid to cover the sport I love. I get paid to write a story like this, a story about how much I appreciate my mother each and every day.

Thanks, Mom.

~Roy Lang III
Chicken Soup for the NASCAR Soul

98

Mini Massage Therapists

t had been a long and exhausting day. My husband was out of town for the third night in a row, the house was a mess, the phone kept ringing, laundry and papers were everywhere, my six-year-old twins were screaming, and my head was pounding. It was a reality-based type of day with no dreamy visions of being the perfect mother with a beautiful, spotless home, laundry all neatly folded in drawers and children playing angelically side by side.

My pleas of "Stop fighting, you two!" "Please stop running in the house!" and "Please play quietly!" went unheeded.

"Mom, Jake came in my room!"

"I did not!"

"Yes, you did ... Mom—he's not listening!"

"You're not the boss of me!"

"But it's my room!"

"So what! Who do you think you are, Princess Tara or something?"

"Mom, Jake is calling me Princess Tara again! Mom!"

I screamed, "Stop it, you two!" Rather than quiet them, my loud reprimand caused their voices to escalate.

"BUT MOM, I TOLD HIM TO GET OUT OF MY ROOM!"

"BUT MOM, SHE COMES IN MY ROOM SOMETIMES WHEN I TELL HER NOT TO ...."

I asked my children to work it out between themselves and

decided to find a quiet room for a few moments. Within a minute they burst in.

"Mom, she won't share her Disney characters even though she's not playing with them."

"That's because you didn't share your markers with me the last time I asked you."

"Well, you shouldn't have lost your markers. It's your own fault if you didn't take care of them, right, Mom?"

"Mom?"

"Mom?"

I gathered my children and whispered, "Jake and Tara, let's go hug each other quietly for a few moments. I don't feel very well. I'm also feeling sad right now. I love you both so much, and I would love a very special hug from each of you."

Their response was quite different than when I had shouted at them to quiet down. With rather serious looks on their faces, they asked, "But why are you sad, Mom?"

"I don't really know," I replied. "I just know I need some quiet time and some extra special love from both of you right now."

"Okay, Mommy," they whispered. They each took one of my hands, led me to my bed, fluffed up my pillows and told me to lie down. With a big hug and some "I love you's," they said, "Okay, Mommy, you just relax here a few minutes." As they walked away, I heard a lot of excited, conspiratorial whispers.

A few minutes later they were back. Jake brought me a glass of water. Tara brought me my favorite flannel pajamas. I smiled at both of them, took a drink of the water and put my pajamas on. They turned the lights down low, told me to relax on my bed, and started to give me a back scratch. I thought about nothing and simply enjoyed the feel of their four little hands.

Next, they massaged me—first my back, then my legs and arms. My body was sinking into the bed, and I felt totally at peace. They slowly massaged my feet and neck. I felt truly pampered. They then rubbed my temples with their thumbs and massaged my forehead.

All the anxiety of the day dissipated. The messy house and to-do lists became inconsequential.

"You are the most special mom in the world," Tara whispered as she worked.

"This is what you do for us every night, Mommy. Tonight's your turn," Jake said affectionately.

Were those really the same children I had spent the day with?

Just when I thought my special treatment was over, they took turns brushing my hair. I was in heaven. I relished every moment and smiled to myself, thinking, Who really needs a spotless house and folded laundry?

Tara and Jake whispered to each other, ran into the bathroom, returned with my favorite lotion and slowly massaged my feet again as the peach-scented aroma filled the room.

What did I do to deserve this? I felt more relaxed than I had in a long time. As I thought it over, I realized that rather than scream for quiet or holler that I expected better behavior, I had simply taken a moment to share my need with my children. I had asked for some special nurturing, and thankfully, they were loving enough to give it.

~Marian Gormley
Chicken Soup for Every Mom's Soul

Patches

My mother had a slender, small body, but a large heart—a heart so large that everybody's joys found welcome in it, and hospitable accommodation.
~Mark Twain

It was such an exciting time of the year, for me especially. Christmas was just around the corner, the signs of which were already appearing at the malls, and my baby shower was just a week away. Mom was worried about how many people would actually come, considering Christmas was so close. She had worked so hard on planning the perfect baby shower for her first grandchild. She was so tickled, I laughed just watching her trip all over herself planning it.

She had really hoped I would find out the gender of the baby so she could have a pink or blue shower, whichever was applicable. She also wanted to include that tidbit of information within the invitations; at both of her showers she had received a lot of boy items, and of course, she had had two girls.

I knew Mom had gone over her budget on the shower, especially with Christmas right around the corner. I made her promise that she would not buy a shower gift in addition to all she had done. I was worried about the money, but I also had another reason. I had not found out if it would be a boy or a girl, and I wanted Mom to be the one to pick out the special "coming-home outfit" for my child.

December nineteenth, what a day it had been! I will never forget that day or that date. I felt like I had been opening presents for hours, and what wonderful presents I had received. The generosity of my family and friends overwhelmed me. As I replaced the top of the box on what I thought was the last gift, I was handed one more. I hadn't seen that one. Where had it been? It wasn't wrapped with traditional baby shower paper; it was wrapped with beautiful Christmas paper adorned with angels singing hymns, the words written in gold so delicately on the paper. There was no gift tag attached, but there was a Christmas card. "To my daughter ...," it read. Mom had promised not to buy a shower gift, but I had said nothing about a Christmas gift! I gave her one of those "I'm going to kill you" looks, and she just sat there, smugly smiling.

"This one is from my mom," I announced as I opened the gift. Inside was a quilt. I tried to smile as I held it up for all to see, hoping Mom couldn't see my face. She would know my smile wasn't genuine; she could read me like a good book, cover to cover. The quilt was not very pretty, you see. It was not a "baby quilt." It wasn't made of pink, blue and yellow materials; it didn't have bunnies or bears. It was just a patchwork quilt sewn of materials that were of all different colors and patterns. Holding the quilt up, I noticed a note tucked in the bottom of the box.

Not realizing the note was intended to be private, I set the quilt aside, picked up the note and began reading it. Mom had made the quilt for me. The unmatched materials were remnants of my life she had saved over the years. She had cut swatches of material from items dating back to my first Christmas dress and as current as the shirt I wore to the doctor the day I found out I was finally pregnant. She had accumulated "patches" of my life for all those years to make this quilt for my child.

By the time I finished reading Mom's letter telling of the "patch" of her old robe—I remembered it well; it was fleece and I used to insist she wear it so I could lay my head on it when she rocked me—and the "patch" of Dad's flannel shirt I used to put on after my bath, and each and every other "patch" and its meaning, there was not a dry eye in the dining room. I picked up the quilt and held it against me and I cried. To think, just seconds before I had thought it ugly. It was beautiful. It was the most beautiful quilt I had ever seen. This quilt was made of my life and with my mother's love. She had sewn her love into every stitch. To think my mom could sew!

The quilt now hangs on my son's wall. It is a reminder of my life, my mother's love and the wonderful Christmas present I received at my baby shower.

~Cathy Novakovich
Chicken Soup for the Soul Christmas Treasury

I Am My Mother

I swore it would never happen. In fact, I spent most of my life trying to make sure it wouldn't happen. And yet it crept up on me when I wasn't looking.

I am now officially my mother.

Don't get me wrong: My mother is a wonderful, smart, funny, loving, sweet woman, and I love her dearly. But I swore I'd never be like her.

How could I ever be so cruel as to not let my five-year-old child eat sugared cereal every morning for breakfast? How could I even think about banning cartoons from my children's lives? And how could I ever be so heartless as to not allow my child dessert until she had eaten something healthy first?

Then there were the teen years. What kind of mother imposes a curfew on her teenage daughter, I asked. Didn't she trust me? And what was the idea of making the boys I went out with come inside to meet her and Dad before I could leave? They weren't going out with my parents so why should they have to meet them?

Never would I subject my children to these atrocities.

My children, I vowed, would be allowed to survive on chocolate bars and, of course, sugared cereal. They would watch TV until their eyes popped out if that is what they so desired. Curfew? Not in my house! My children could stay out all night, and the next day, too, if they wanted, and I would applaud their independence and trustworthiness.

My children would have such a cool and hip mom that they would probably invite me to their parties, and all of the other kids would say, "Cool! There's that awesome mom! Boy, are her kids lucky!"

I also planned on never worrying. I watched my mother worry about me, about my sisters, about everything it seemed, and I knew I would never be like that. I told her often that she had no need to worry about me—I'd be home by midnight, maybe 1:00 A.M., and everything would be fine. There was no need to worry—the car has only a few dents in it, and nobody was hurt. What's to worry about? Why worry about my friends? They are very nice people who simply happen to have spiked hair, tattoos and pierced body parts. No need to worry. I could handle myself.

I planned on never worrying like that with my children. I planned on being hip and cool. I would, of course, always dress in the most recent fashions, and never, ever, wear "mom" clothes. I would be so hip that my children's friends would think I was one of them.

Yes, that was my plan. To be the coolest, hippest mother around. To enforce only one rule in my house—there are no rules. I was planning on a complete revolt from my upbringing; I was planning on giving my children everything I was so brutally deprived of.

But something happened along the way.

I had a child of my own.

On the day I brought my little girl home from the hospital, I made my husband throw out all the remaining sugared cereal. When she started eating solid food, I never gave her anything sweet until she had something healthy first.

And she has yet to see a cartoon on TV.

She hasn't hit the teen years yet, but I shudder to think of all the things she will want to do, and all of the things I won't let her do. I've already decided she'll have an 8:00 P.M. curfew and not be allowed to date until she's eighteen. Of course, I reason, this is all for her own good, and so she'll understand and meekly go along with my rules. Or not.

I'm already worried.

But she will always be showered with love, affection and adoration. She already loves to read books, and she has a penchant for broccoli and other vegetables. Okay, maybe not the veggies, but the rest is true.

As for me, I've finally admitted that my mom was pretty great after all. Even though I was deprived of so many wonderful, glorious things as a child, I turned out okay. And I have a feeling that my little girl will, too—although she'll probably grow up planning all her life not to be like me. I only hope I can be as good a mother to her as my mother was, and is, to me.

~Anne Tews Schwab
Chicken Soup for the Mother & Daughter Soul

Mother to Mother

Adoption is when a child grew in its mommy's heart instead of her tummy.
~Author Unknown

I sit in the audience with the other parents, beaming at our children filing into their seats. My little ones' black hair and sienna skin make exclamation points among the other, pastel angels forming the pageant choir.

The chorister raises her arm, and the pianist comes in with the downbeat. So do some of the kids—a bit early. In cherubic fervor, their words spill out, "I am a child of God ...."

Oh, how I wish both of you could see this. They're perfect. Just perfect.

I often send this silent message to my children's birth mothers. I long to comfort and reassure them, to share with them the unspeakable joy their babies have brought into my life. I long to tell them their precious ones are beautiful and bright, healthy and strong.

"...and he has sent me here ...." I can almost distinguish Shyloh's sweet voice in the choir.

Just the other day, she asked, "Mommy, why is my hair black? Yours isn't."

The answer came easily to me. "To make you look beautiful, Shyloh, just like your mother in China." And typically Tiggerlike, she bounced away, grinning in satisfaction.

I hope you find peace in your decision to share this happy girl with me.

"...has given me an earthly home, with parents kind and dear ...." I catch the eye of my Samoan daughter, Whitney, whose hair is a shining cape flung across her shoulders and whose voice rings loudest of all the angels. She's singing with all her young heart.

She's adjusting, Mama. I grin through my burning eyes. Your daughter's finally joining in. So is little Luke.

My grateful tears plop down to bless the slumbering head of Whitney's contented baby brother, asleep on my lap.

What sacrifices these women made for their children, their difficult choices possible only because their powerful mother-love transcended all else. And what joy their decisions continue to bring into my life.

Whoever you are, wherever you are and whatever your circumstances, I hope your intuition calms you and tells you all is well.

Mother to mother, I wish I could wrap my arms around them this holiday season—those selfless birth moms—and assure them of my appreciation for these beautiful children of ours. More than anything, I wish I knew how to express the gratitude in my heart.

"...I am a child of God, and so my needs are great ...." Their angelic voices supplicate and saturate the auditorium and reach into the depths of my consciousness.

And—with sudden, deep conviction—I do know how, the only way that makes sense: I'll continue to love and cherish their little ones with all my being.

That will be thanks enough.

~Annette Seaver
Chicken Soup for the Soul: The Book of Christmas Virtues

More

Chicken Soup for the Soul®

...

Chicken Soup for the Soul

Share with Us

We would like to how these stories affected you and which ones were your favorite. Please write to us and let us know.

We also would like to share your stories with future readers. You may be able to help another reader, and become a published author at the same time. Please send us your own stories and poems for our future books. Some of our past contributors have launched writing and speaking careers from the publication of their stories in our books!

The best way to submit your stories is through our web site, at

www.chickensoup.com

If you do not have access to the Internet, you may submit your stories by mail or by facsimile.

Chicken Soup for the Soul
P.O. Box 700
Cos Cob, CT 06807-0700
Fax 1-203-861-7194

Chicken Soup for the Soul

of the Soul

Chicken Soup for the Soul: Woman to Woman

Women Sharing Their Stories of Hope, Humor, and Inspiration

978-1-935096-04-7

Women have always been wonderful sources of inspiration and support for each other. They are willing to lay bare their souls and share their experiences, even with perfect strangers. Put two random women together in a waiting room, on an airplane, in a line at the supermarket, and the sharing begins, often at the deepest level. This new volume includes the 101 best stories and poems in Chicken Soup's library for women of all ages, written by women just like them.

Check out our other
books for

Chicken Soup for the Soul

for the Soul.

Woman to Woman

Our **101** BEST STORIES

Women Sharing Their
Stories of Hope, Humor,
and Inspiration

Jack Canfield
& Mark Victor Hansen

Edited by Amy Newmark

Women

Enjoy these additional fine books for Moms from

Chicken Soup for the Soul

Chicken Soup for the Woman's Soul

Chicken Soup for the Mother's Soul

A Second Chicken Soup for the Woman's Soul

Chicken Soup for the Parent's Soul

Chicken Soup for the Expectant Mother's Soul

Chicken Soup for the Christian Family Soul

Chicken Soup for the Mother's Soul 2

Chicken Soup for the Grandparent's Soul

Chicken Soup for the Christian Woman's Soul

Chicken Soup for the Mother & Daughter Soul

Chicken Soup for Every Mom's Soul

Chicken Soup for the Grandma's Soul

Chicken Soup for the Single Parent's Soul

Chicken Soup for the Mother and Son Soul

Chicken Soup for the Working Mom's Soul

Chicken Soup for the Soul: Celebrating Mothers and Daughters

Chicken Soup for the New Mom's Soul

Chicken Soup for the Soul: A Tribute to Moms

Chicken Soup for the Soul: Like Mother, Like Daughter

Stories about the Special Bond between Mothers and Daughters

978-1-935096-07-8

How often have you seen a teenage girl pretend to be perturbed, but secretly smile, when she is told that she acts or looks just like her mother? Fathers, brothers, and friends sometimes shake their head in wonder as girls "turn into their mothers." This new collection from Chicken Soup represents the best 101 stories from Chicken Soup's library on the special bond between mothers and daughters, and the magical, mysterious similarities between them. Mothers and daughters of all ages will laugh, cry, and find inspiration in these stories that remind them how much they appreciate each other.

Chicken Soup for the Soul: Moms & Sons

Stories by Mothers and Sons, in Appreciation of Each Other

978-1-935096-16-0

There is a special bond between mothers and their sons and it never goes away. This new book contains the 101 best stories and poems from Chicken Soup's library honoring that lifelong relationship between mothers and their male off-spring. These heartfelt and loving stories written by mothers, grandmothers, and sons, about each other, span generations and show how the mother-son bond transcends time. These stories will make readers laugh, and cry, and will warm their hearts and remind them of the things they love about each other.

Chicken Soup for the Soul: Grand and Great

Grandparents and Grandchildren Share Their Stories of Love and Wisdom

978-1-935096-09-2

The day the first grandchild is born, formerly serious and responsible adults go on shopping sprees for toys and baby clothing, smile incessantly, pull out photo albums that they "just happen to have" with them, and proudly display baby seats in their cars. And grandchildren love thse grandparents back with all their hearts. This new book includes the best stories on being a grandparent from 33 past Chicken soup books, representing a new reading experience for Chicken Soup fans.

About the Chicken Soup for the Soul Authors

Chicken Soup for the Soul®

Who Is
Jack Canfield?

J ack Canfield is the co-creator and editor of the Chicken Soup for the Soul series, which Time magazine has called "the publishing phenomenon of the decade." Jack is also the co-author of eight other bestselling books including *The Success Principles™: How to Get from Where You Are to Where You Want to Be, Dare to Win, The Aladdin Factor, You've Got to Read This Book,* and *The Power of Focus: How to Hit Your Business and Personal and Financial Targets with Absolute Certainty.*

Jack has recently developed a telephone coaching program and an online coaching program based on his most recent book *The Success Principles.* He also offers a seven-day Breakthrough to Success seminar every summer, which attracts 400 people from fifteen countries around the world.

Jack is the CEO of the Canfield Training Group in Santa Barbara, California, and founder of the Foundation for Self-Esteem in Culver City, California. He has conducted intensive personal and professional development seminars on the principles of success for over a million people in twenty-three countries. Jack is a dynamic keynote speaker and he has spoken to hundreds of thousands of others at more than 1,000 corporations, universities, professional conferences and conventions, and has been seen by millions more on national television shows such as The Today Show, Fox and Friends, Inside Edition, Hard Copy, CNN's Talk Back Live, 20/20, Eye to Eye, and the NBC Nightly News and the CBS Evening News.

Jack is the recipient of many awards and honors, including three honorary doctorates and a Guinness World Records Certificate for having seven books from the Chicken Soup for the Soul series appearing on the New York Times bestseller list on May 24, 1998.

To write to Jack or for inquiries about Jack as a speaker, his coaching programs, trainings or seminars, use the following contact information:

Jack Canfield
The Canfield Companies
P.O. Box 30880 • Santa Barbara, CA 93130
phone: 805-563-2935 • fax: 805-563-2945
E-mail: info@jackcanfield.com
www.jackcanfield.com

Who Is
Mark Victor Hansen?

Mark Victor Hansen is the co-founder of Chicken Soup for the Soul, along with Jack Canfield. He is also a sought-after keynote speaker, bestselling author, and marketing maven. For more than thirty years, Mark has focused solely on helping people from all walks of life reshape their personal vision of what's possible. His powerful messages of possibility, opportunity, and action have created powerful change in thousands of organizations and millions of individuals worldwide.

Mark's credentials include a lifetime of entrepreneurial success. He is a prolific writer with many bestselling books, such as *The One Minute Millionaire, Cracking the Millionaire Code, How to Make the Rest of Your Life the Best of Your Life, The Power of Focus, The Aladdin Factor*, and *Dare to Win*, in addition to the Chicken Soup for the Soul series. Mark has had a profound influence in the field of human potential through his library of audios, videos, and articles in the areas of big thinking, sales achievement, wealth building, publishing success, and personal and professional development.

Mark is the founder of the MEGA Seminar Series. MEGA Book Marketing University and Building Your MEGA Speaking Empire are annual conferences where Mark coaches and teaches new and aspiring authors, speakers, and experts on building lucrative publishing and speaking careers. Other MEGA events include MEGA Info-Marketing and My MEGA Life.

He has appeared on Oprah, CNN, and The Today Show. He

has been quoted in *Time*, *U.S. News & World Report*, *USA Today*, *New York Times*, and *Entrepreneur* and has had countless radio interviews, assuring our planet's people that "You can easily create the life you deserve."

As a philanthropist and humanitarian, Mark works tirelessly for organizations such as Habitat for Humanity, American Red Cross, March of Dimes, Childhelp USA, and many others. He is the recipient of numerous awards that honor his entrepreneurial spirit, philanthropic heart, and business acumen. He is a lifetime member of the Horatio Alger Association of Distinguished Americans, an organization that honored Mark with the prestigious Horatio Alger Award for his extraordinary life achievements.

Mark Victor Hansen is an enthusiastic crusader of what's possible and is driven to make the world a better place.

Mark Victor Hansen & Associates, Inc.
P.O. Box 7665 • Newport Beach, CA 92658
phone: 949-764-2640 • fax: 949-722-6912
www.markvictorhansen.com

Who Is
Amy Newmark?

A my Newmark was recently named publisher of Chicken Soup for the Soul, after a thirty-year career as a writer, speaker, financial analyst, and business executive in the worlds of finance and telecommunications.

Amy is a graduate of Harvard College, where she majored in Portuguese, minored in French, and traveled extensively. She is also the mother of two children in college and has two grown stepchildren.

After a long career writing books on telecommunications, voluminous financial reports, business plans, and corporate press releases, Chicken Soup for the Soul is a breath of fresh air for Amy. She has fallen in love with Chicken Soup for the Soul and its life-changing books, and found it a true pleasure to conceptualize, compile, and edit the "101 Best Stories" books for our readers.

The best way to contact Chicken Soup for the Soul is through our web site, at www.chickensoup.com. This will always get the fastest attention.

If you do not have access to the Internet, please contact us by mail or by facsimile.

Chicken Soup for the Soul
P.O. Box 700
Cos Cob, CT 06807-0700
Fax 1-203-861-7194

Acknowledgments

Chicken Soup for the Soul

Thank You!

Our first thanks go to our loyal readers who have inspired the entire Chicken Soup team for the past fifteen years. Your appreciative letters and emails have reminded us why we work so hard on these books.

We owe huge thanks to all of our contributors as well. We know that you pour your hearts and souls into the stories and poems that you share with us, and ultimately with each other. We appreciate your willingness to open up your lives to other Chicken Soup readers.

We can only publish a small percentage of the stories that are submitted, but we read every single one and even the ones that do not appear in a book have an influence on us and on the final manuscripts.

As always, we would like to thank the entire staff of Chicken Soup for the Soul for their help on this project and the 101 Best series in general.

Among our California staff, we would especially like to single out the following people:

- D'ette Corona, who is the heart and soul of the Chicken Soup publishing operation, and who put together the first draft of this manuscript

- Barbara LoMonaco for invaluable assistance in obtaining the fabulous quotations that add depth and meaning to this book
- Patty Hansen for her extra special help with the permissions for these fabulous stories and for her amazing knowledge of the Chicken Soup library
- and Patti Clement for her help with permissions and other organizational matters.

In our Connecticut office, we would like to thank our able editorial assistant, Valerie Howlett, for her assistance in setting up our new offices, editing, and helping us put together the best possible books for teenagers.

We would also like to thank our master of design, book producer and Creative Director, Brian Taylor, at Pneuma Books LLC, for his brilliant vision for our covers and interiors.

Finally, none of this would be possible without the business and creative leadership of our CEO, Bill Rouhana, and our president, Bob Jacobs.